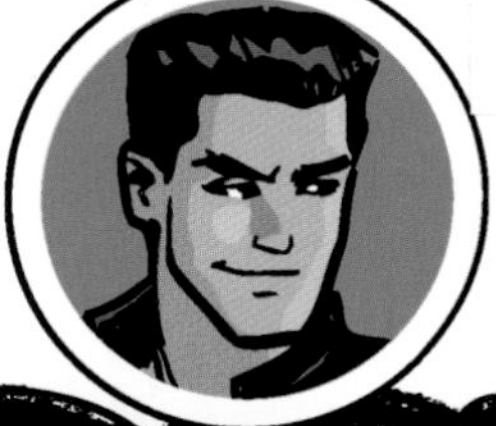

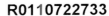

REGGIE AND ME

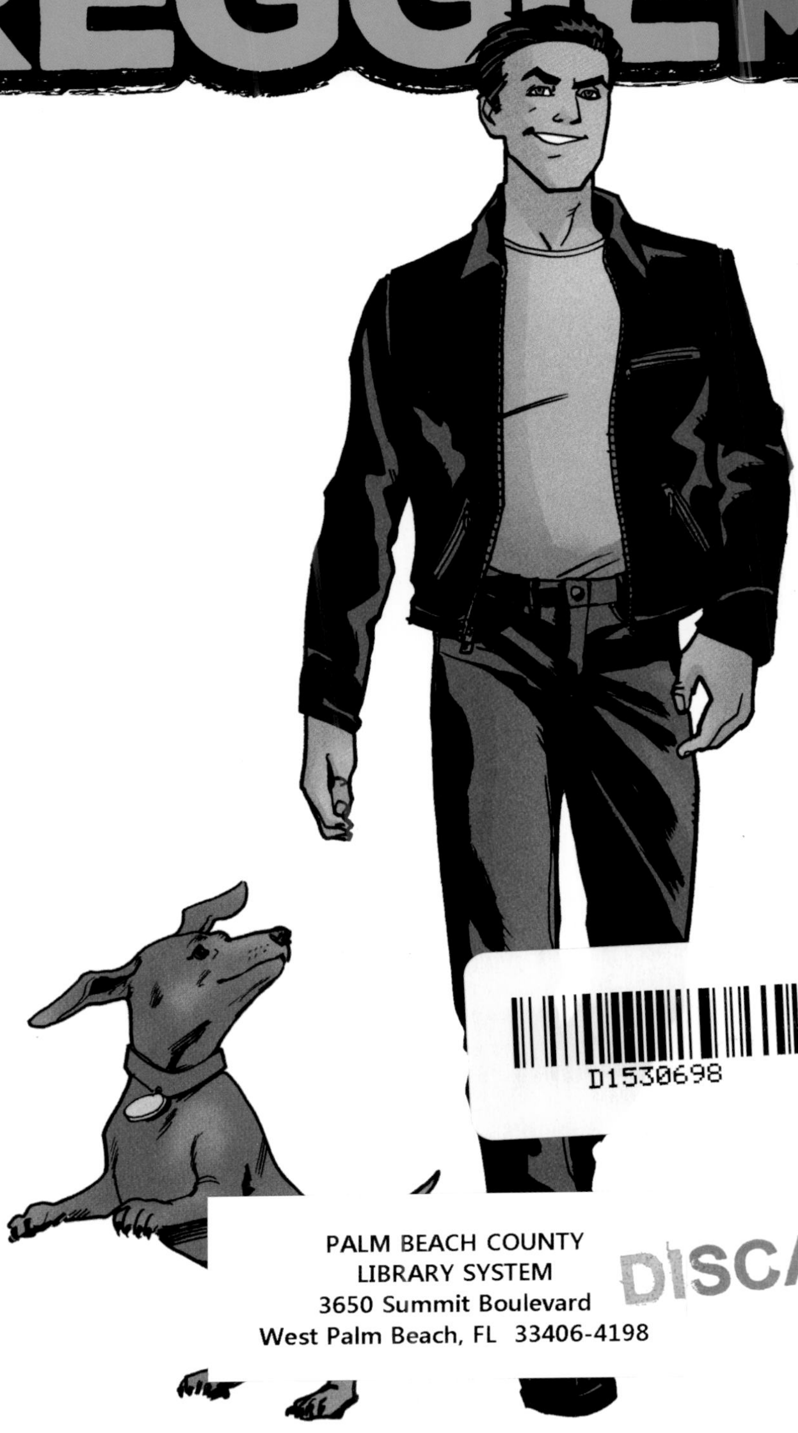

STORY BY
TOM DEFALCO

ART BY
SANDY JARRELL

COLORING BY
KELLY FITZPATRICK

LETTERING BY
JACK MORELLI

EDITORS
**MIKE PELLERITO &
VINCENT LOVALLO**

ASSOCIATE EDITOR
STEPHEN OSWALD

ASSISTANT EDITOR
JAMIE LEE ROTANTE

EDITOR IN CHIEF
VICTOR GORELICK

LEAD DESIGNER
KARI MCLACHLAN

PUBLISHER
JON GOLDWATER

INTRODUCTION

REGGIE AND ME

BY TOM DEFALCO

Poor Reggie.

He is certainly the handsomest, most intelligent and sexiest member of the Archie Gang. (Just ask him!)

But he gets no respect. (Why is it even called the Archie Gang? Everybody knows Reggie is the real star.) (Again, just ask him!)

Let's look at the facts. Archie, Betty and Jughead all made their first appearance in *Pep Comics* #22 in December 1941. Veronica soon followed in April 1942. Reggie appeared in one measly panel in the spring of 1942 in *Jackpot Comics* #5 and had to wait until the following issue before he was featured in an entire story.

(One can only assume they were saving the best for last.)

Also, when Reggie was finally granted his own title—after Archie, Jughead and Betty & Veronica already got theirs—it was called *Archie's Rival Reggie.*

(*Archie's Rival*?!? Why wasn't Archie's title called, "*Reggie's Rival*" or, even better, "*Reggie's Inferior*"?!?)

Poor Reggie. He never got the respect he truly deserves.

That will soon change... if the ever-devoted Vader and I have anything to say about it.

Thanks for being there!

ISSUE ONE

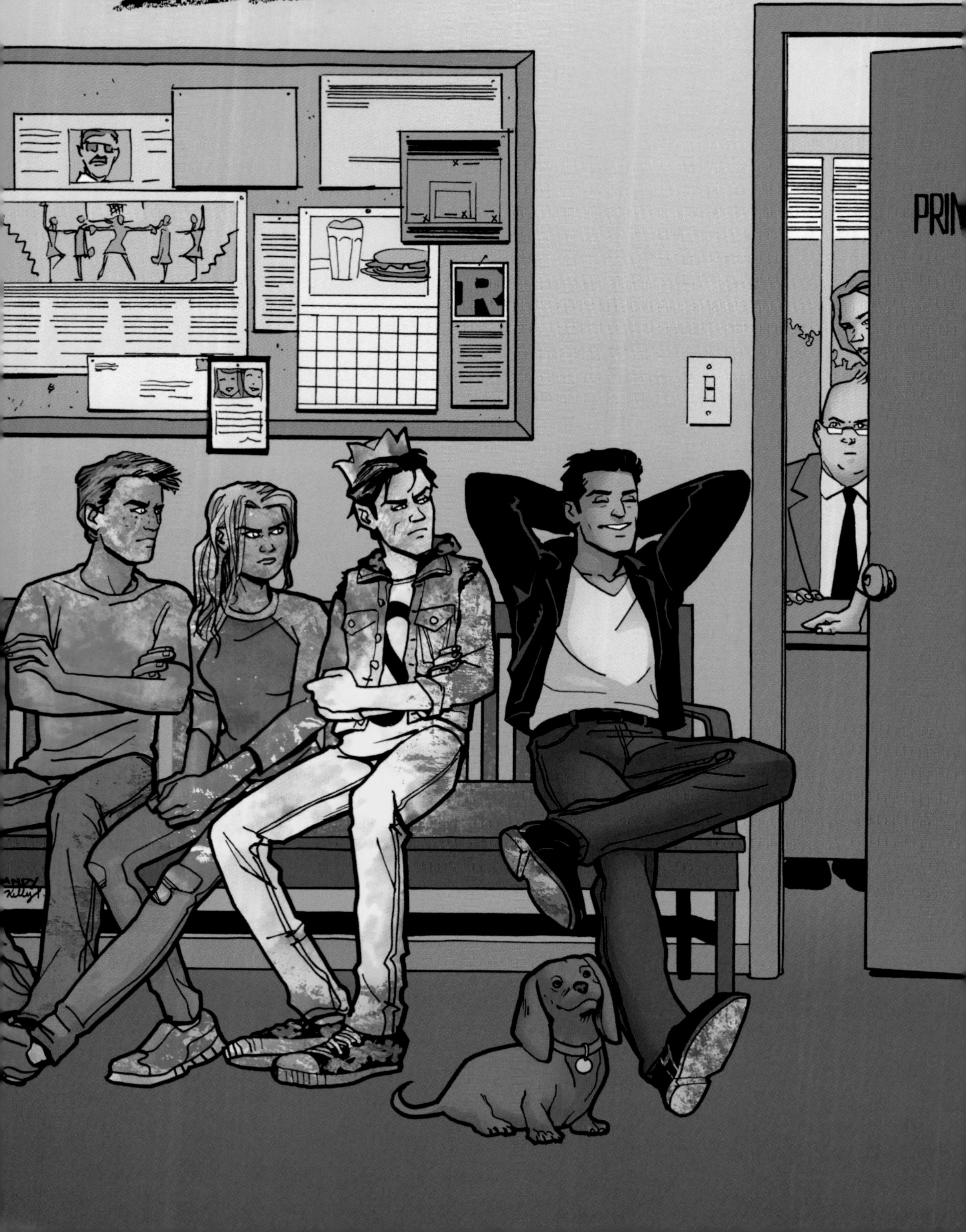
R
PRIN

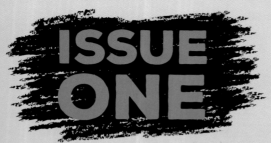

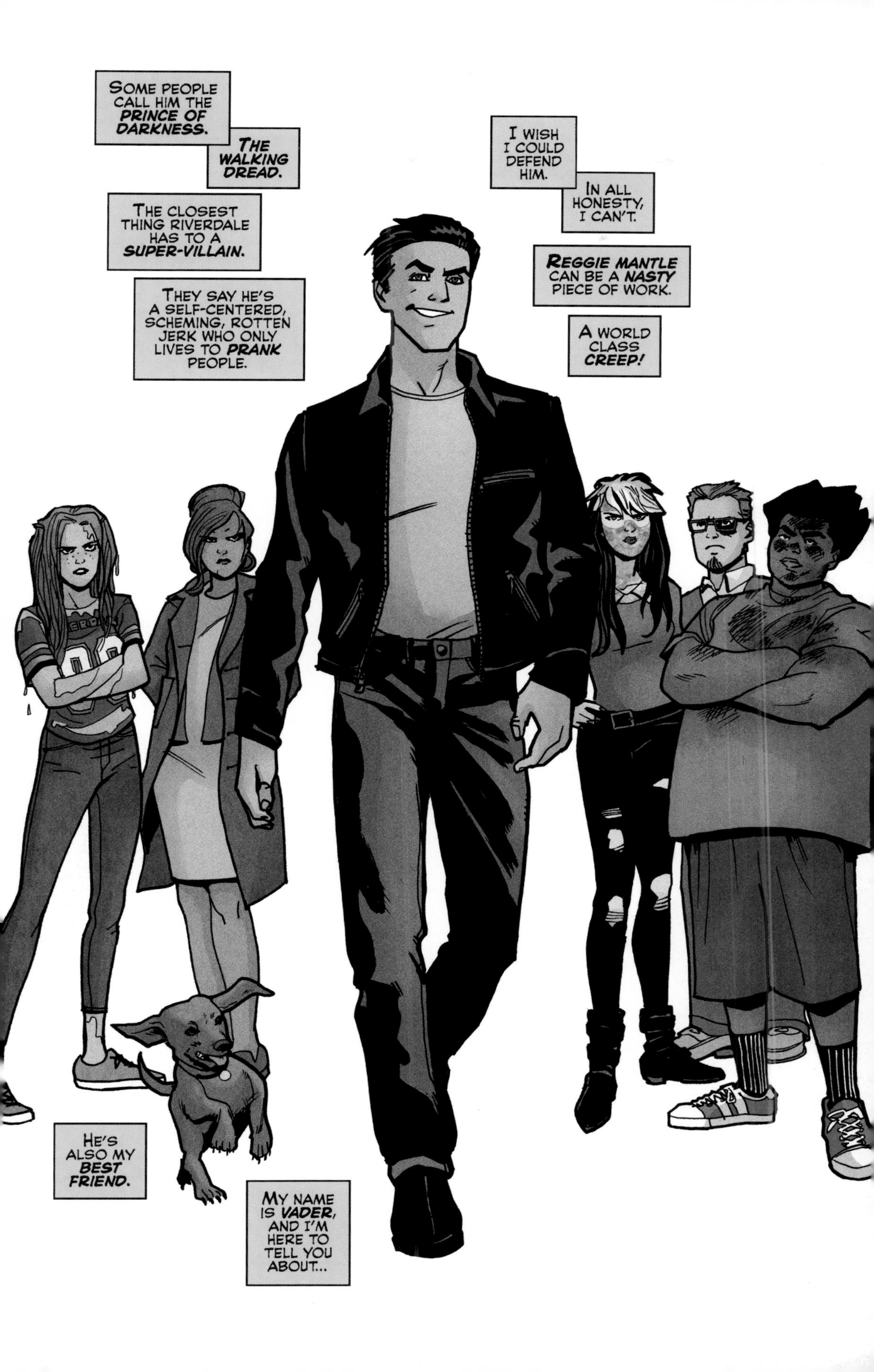

SOME PEOPLE CALL HIM THE *PRINCE OF DARKNESS.*
THE WALKING DREAD.
THE CLOSEST THING RIVERDALE HAS TO A *SUPER-VILLAIN.*
THEY SAY HE'S A SELF-CENTERED, SCHEMING, ROTTEN JERK WHO ONLY LIVES TO *PRANK* PEOPLE.
I WISH I COULD DEFEND HIM.
IN ALL HONESTY, I CAN'T.
REGGIE MANTLE CAN BE A *NASTY* PIECE OF WORK.
A WORLD CLASS *CREEP!*
HE'S ALSO MY *BEST FRIEND.*
MY NAME IS *VADER,* AND I'M HERE TO TELL YOU ABOUT...

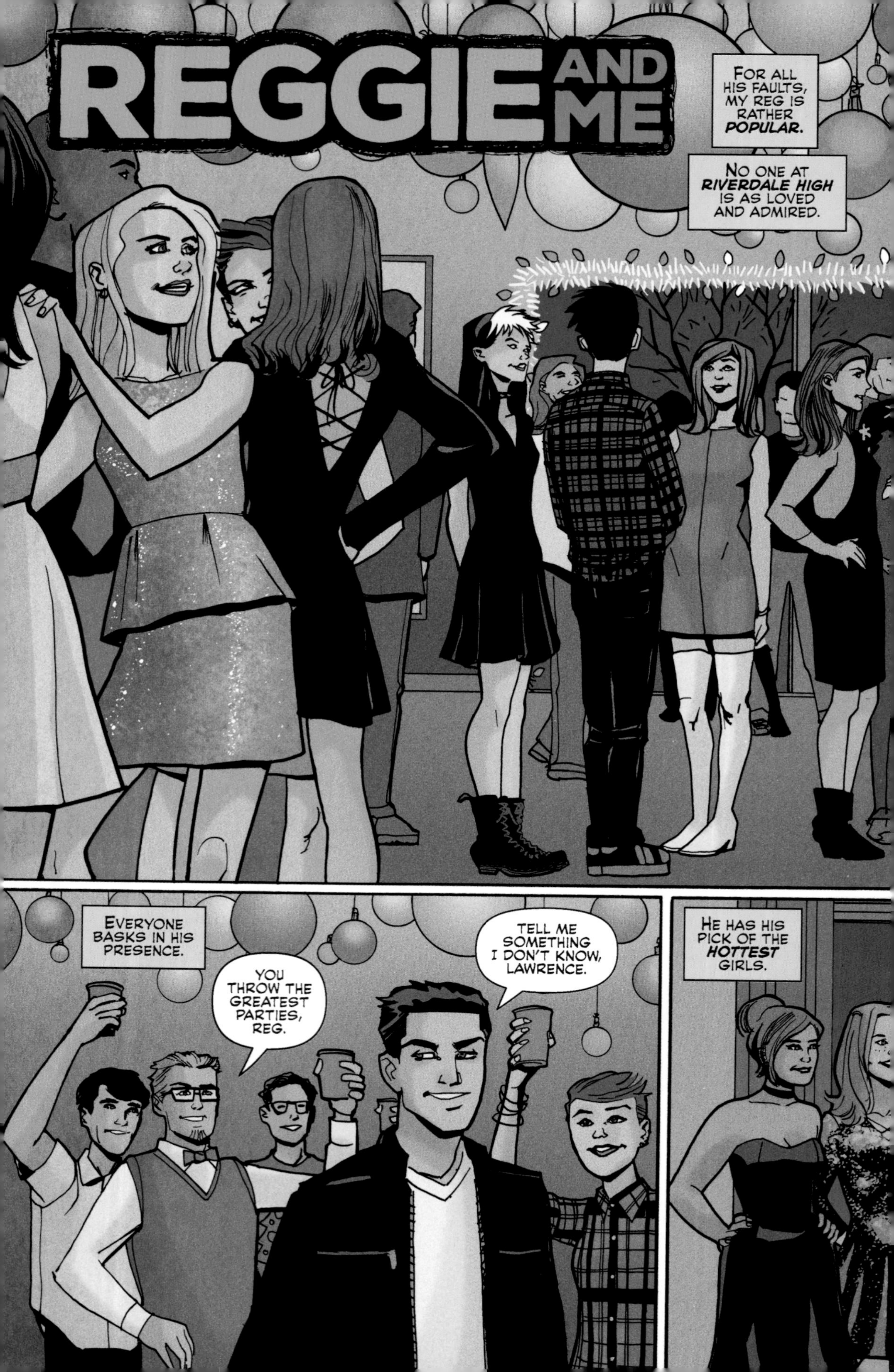
REGGIE AND ME
FOR ALL HIS FAULTS, MY REG IS RATHER ***POPULAR.***
NO ONE AT ***RIVERDALE HIGH*** IS AS LOVED AND ADMIRED.
EVERYONE BASKS IN HIS PRESENCE.
YOU THROW THE GREATEST PARTIES, REG.
TELL ME SOMETHING I DON'T KNOW, LAWRENCE.
HE HAS HIS PICK OF THE ***HOTTEST*** GIRLS.

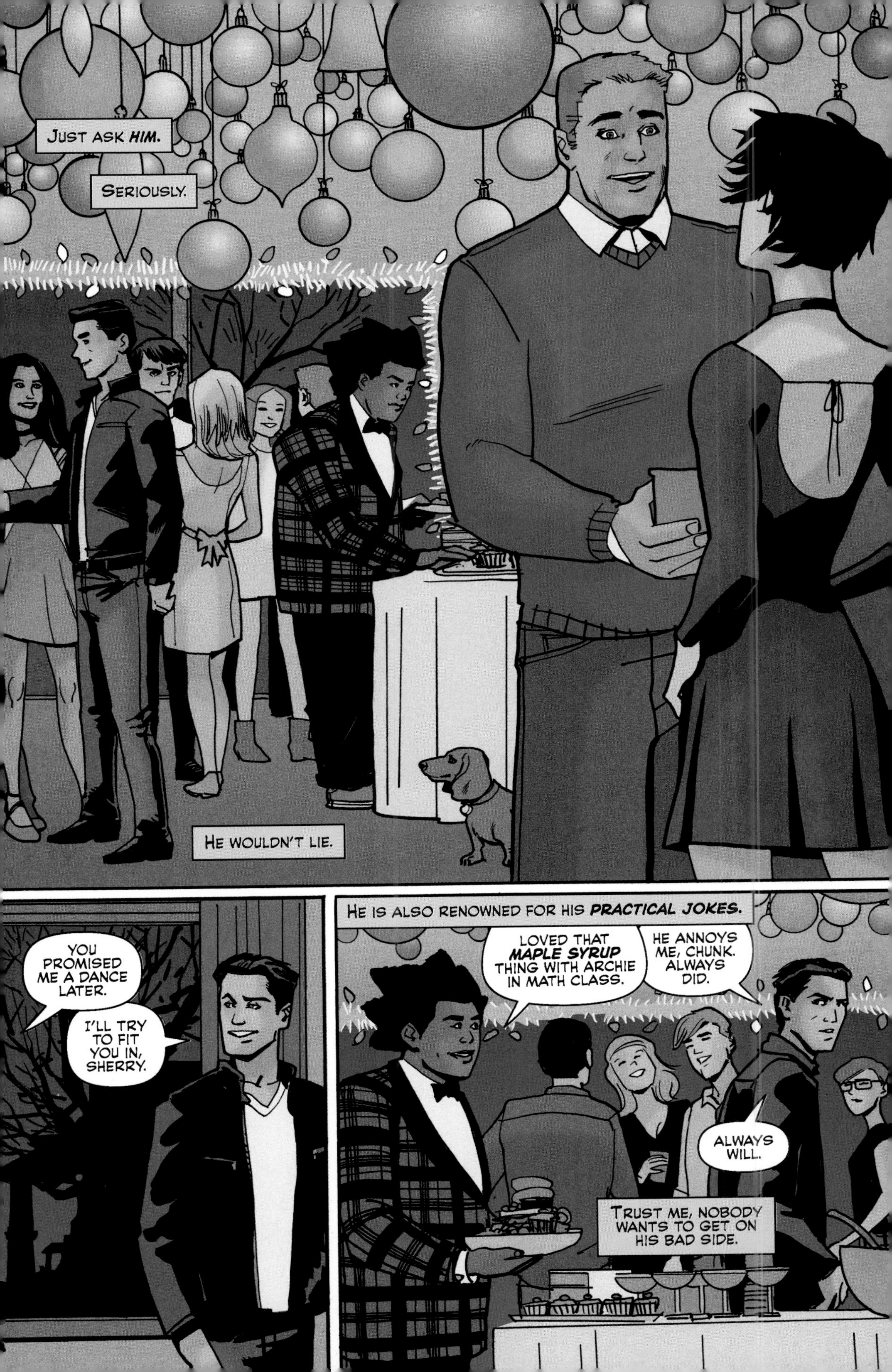

JUST ASK HIM.
SERIOUSLY.
HE WOULDN'T LIE.
YOU PROMISED ME A DANCE LATER.
I'LL TRY TO FIT YOU IN, SHERRY.
HE IS ALSO RENOWNED FOR HIS PRACTICAL JOKES.
LOVED THAT MAPLE SYRUP THING WITH ARCHIE IN MATH CLASS.
HE ANNOYS ME, CHUNK. ALWAYS DID.
ALWAYS WILL.
TRUST ME, NOBODY WANTS TO GET ON HIS BAD SIDE.

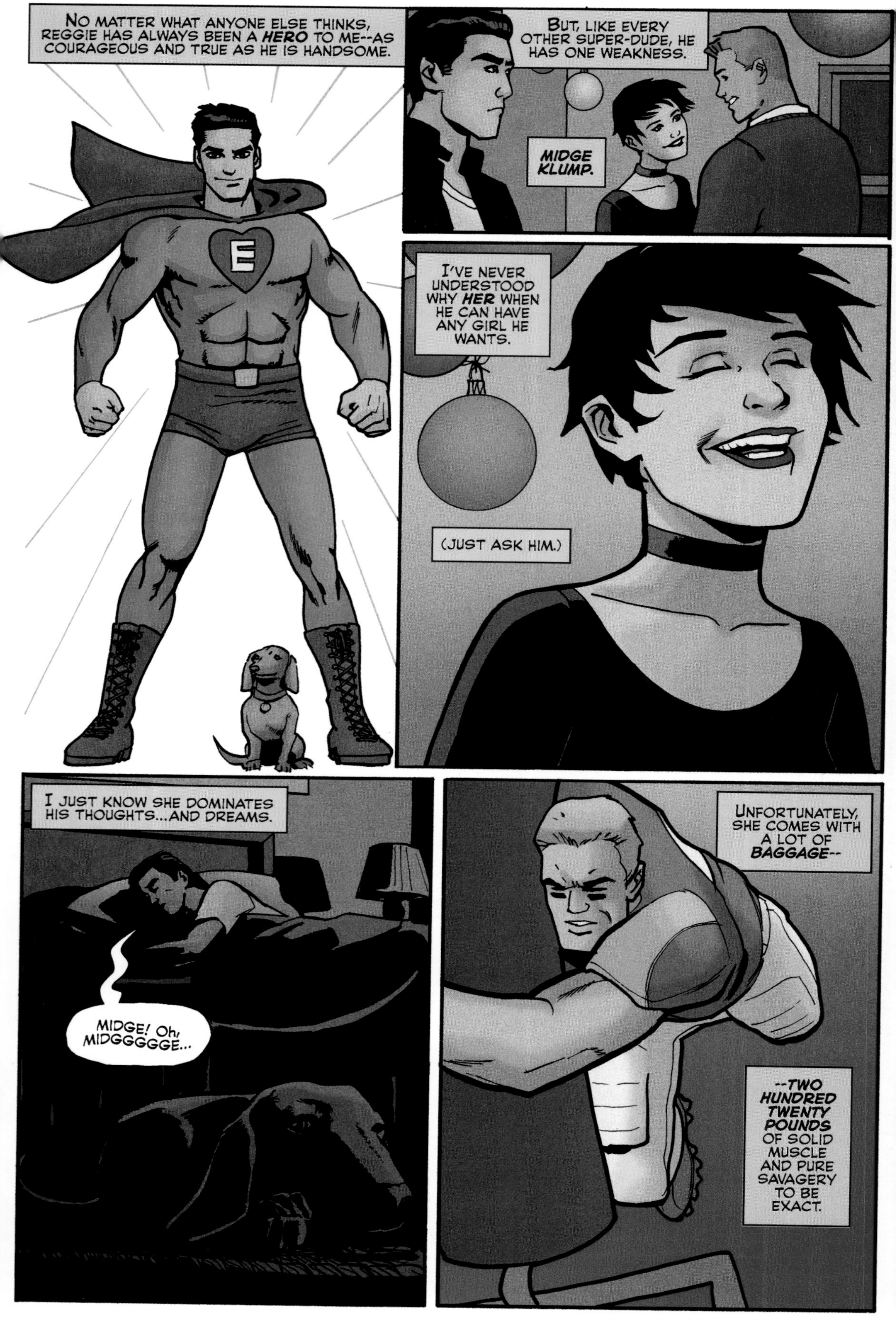
NO MATTER WHAT ANYONE ELSE THINKS, REGGIE HAS ALWAYS BEEN A HERO TO ME--AS COURAGEOUS AND TRUE AS HE IS HANDSOME.
E
BUT, LIKE EVERY OTHER SUPER-DUDE, HE HAS ONE WEAKNESS.
MIDGE KLUMP.
I'VE NEVER UNDERSTOOD WHY HER WHEN HE CAN HAVE ANY GIRL HE WANTS.
(JUST ASK HIM.)
I JUST KNOW SHE DOMINATES HIS THOUGHTS...AND DREAMS.
MIDGE! Oh, MIDGGGGGE...
UNFORTUNATELY, SHE COMES WITH A LOT OF BAGGAGE--
--TWO HUNDRED TWENTY POUNDS OF SOLID MUSCLE AND PURE SAVAGERY TO BE EXACT.

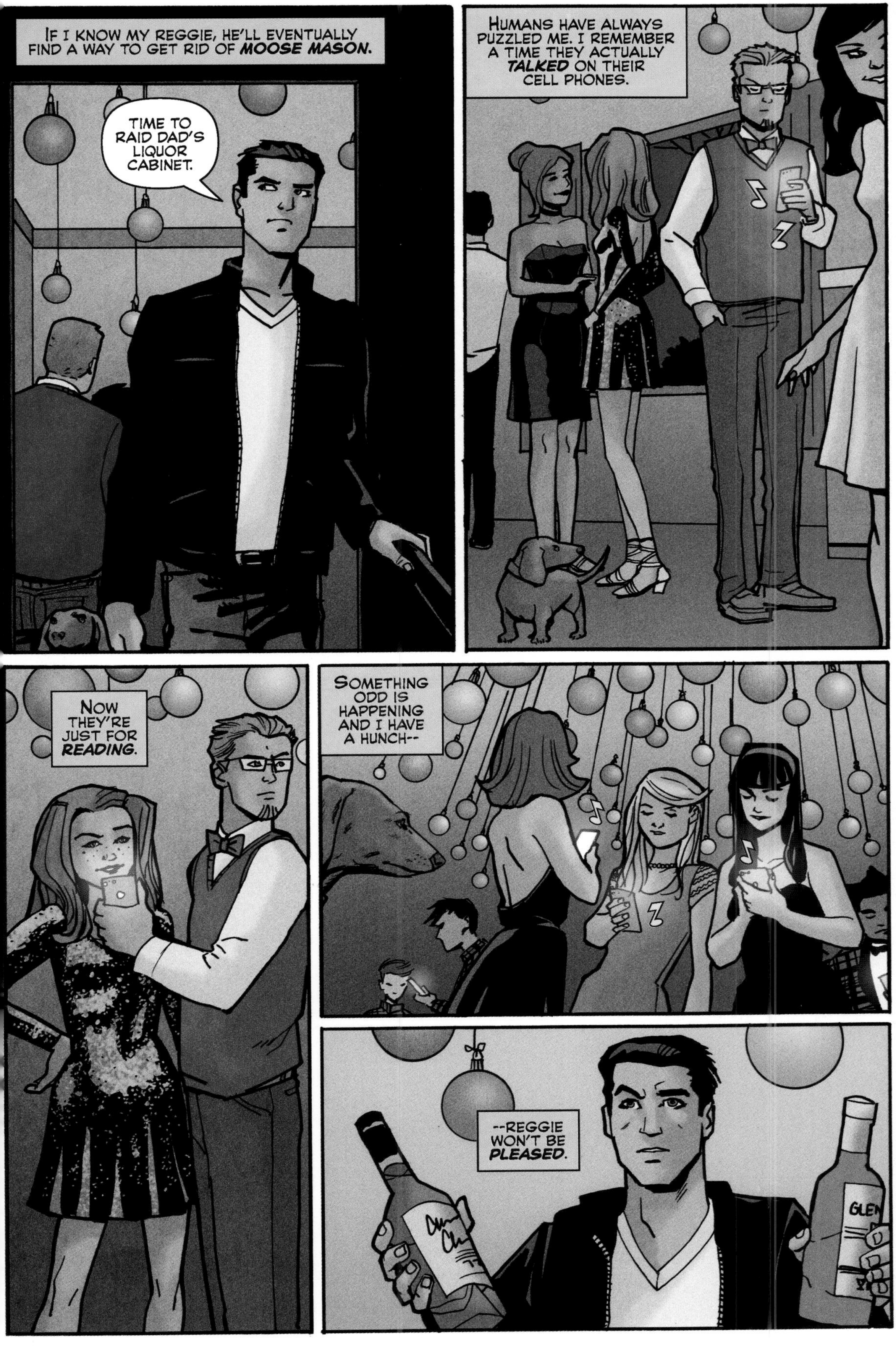
IF I KNOW MY REGGIE, HE'LL EVENTUALLY FIND A WAY TO GET RID OF MOOSE MASON.
TIME TO RAID DAD'S LIQUOR CABINET.
HUMANS HAVE ALWAYS PUZZLED ME. I REMEMBER A TIME THEY ACTUALLY TALKED ON THEIR CELL PHONES.
NOW THEY'RE JUST FOR READING.
SOMETHING ODD IS HAPPENING AND I HAVE A HUNCH--
--REGGIE WON'T BE PLEASED.
GLEN

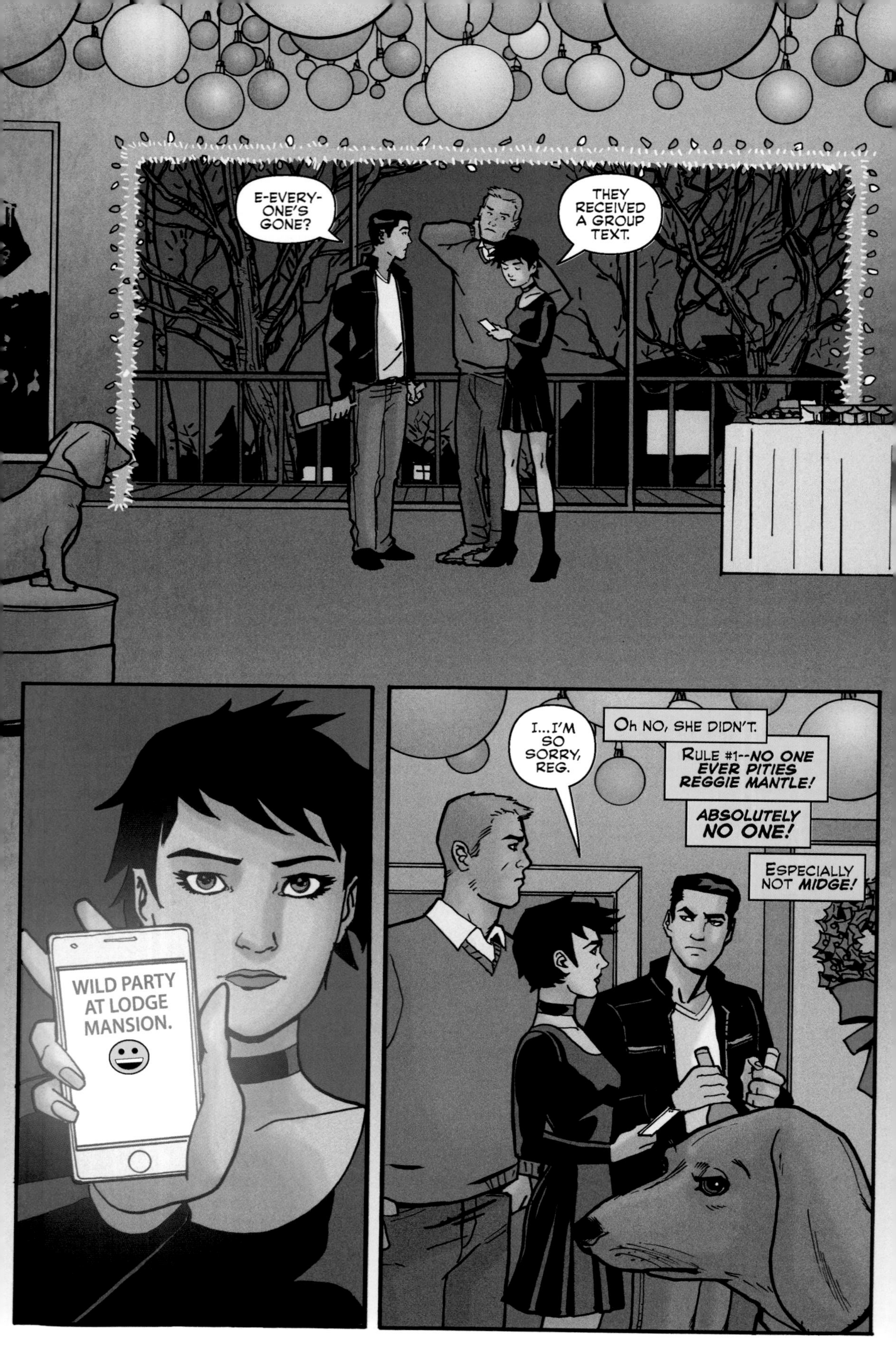
E-EVERY-ONE'S GONE?
THEY RECEIVED A GROUP TEXT.
WILD PARTY AT LODGE MANSION.
I...I'M SO SORRY, REG.
Oh NO, SHE DIDN'T.
RULE #1--NO ONE EVER PITIES REGGIE MANTLE!
ABSOLUTELY NO ONE!
ESPECIALLY NOT MIDGE!

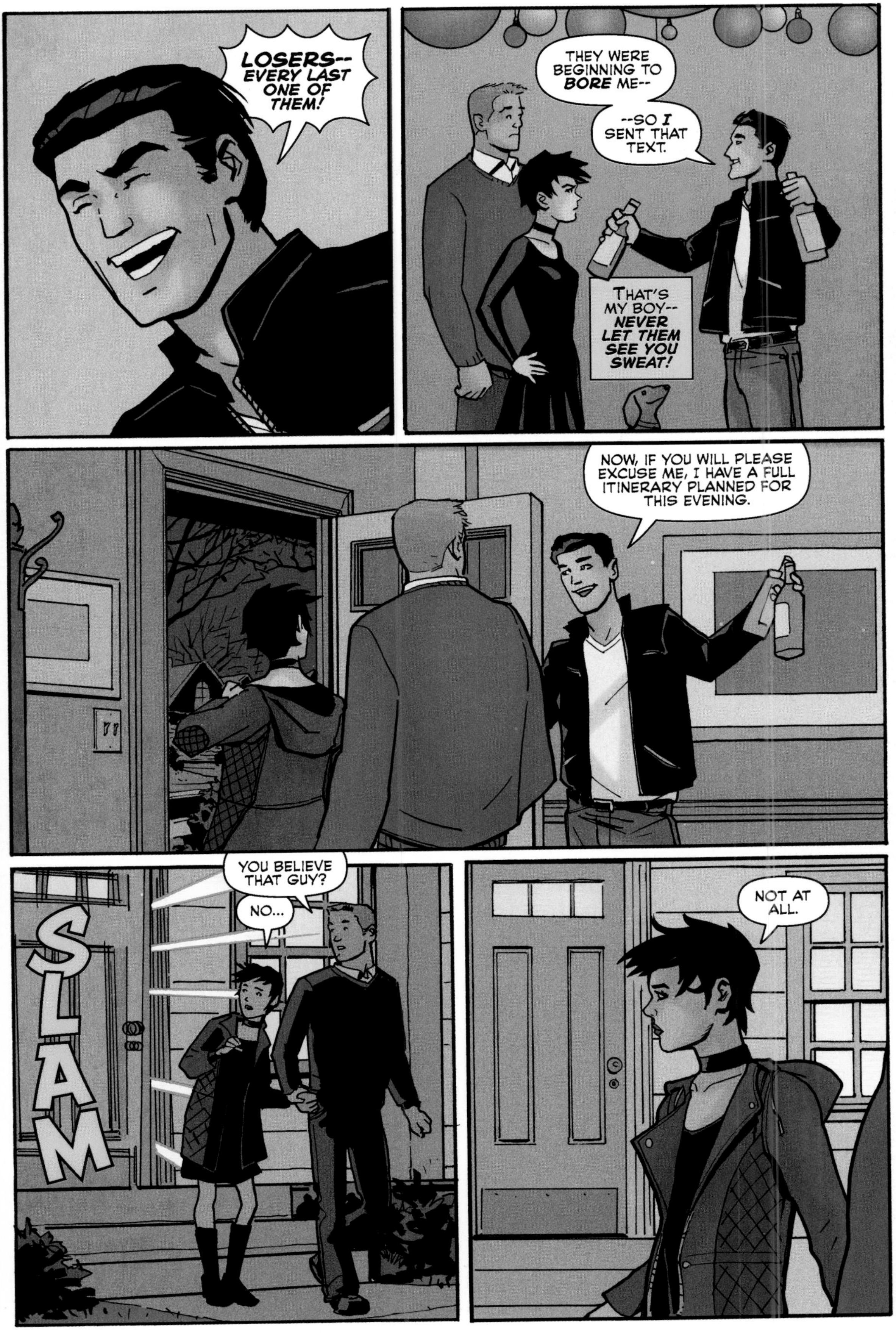
LOSERS-- EVERY LAST ONE OF THEM!
THEY WERE BEGINNING TO BORE ME--
--SO I SENT THAT TEXT.
THAT'S MY BOY-- NEVER LET THEM SEE YOU SWEAT!
NOW, IF YOU WILL PLEASE EXCUSE ME, I HAVE A FULL ITINERARY PLANNED FOR THIS EVENING.
SLAM
YOU BELIEVE THAT GUY?
NO...
NOT AT ALL.

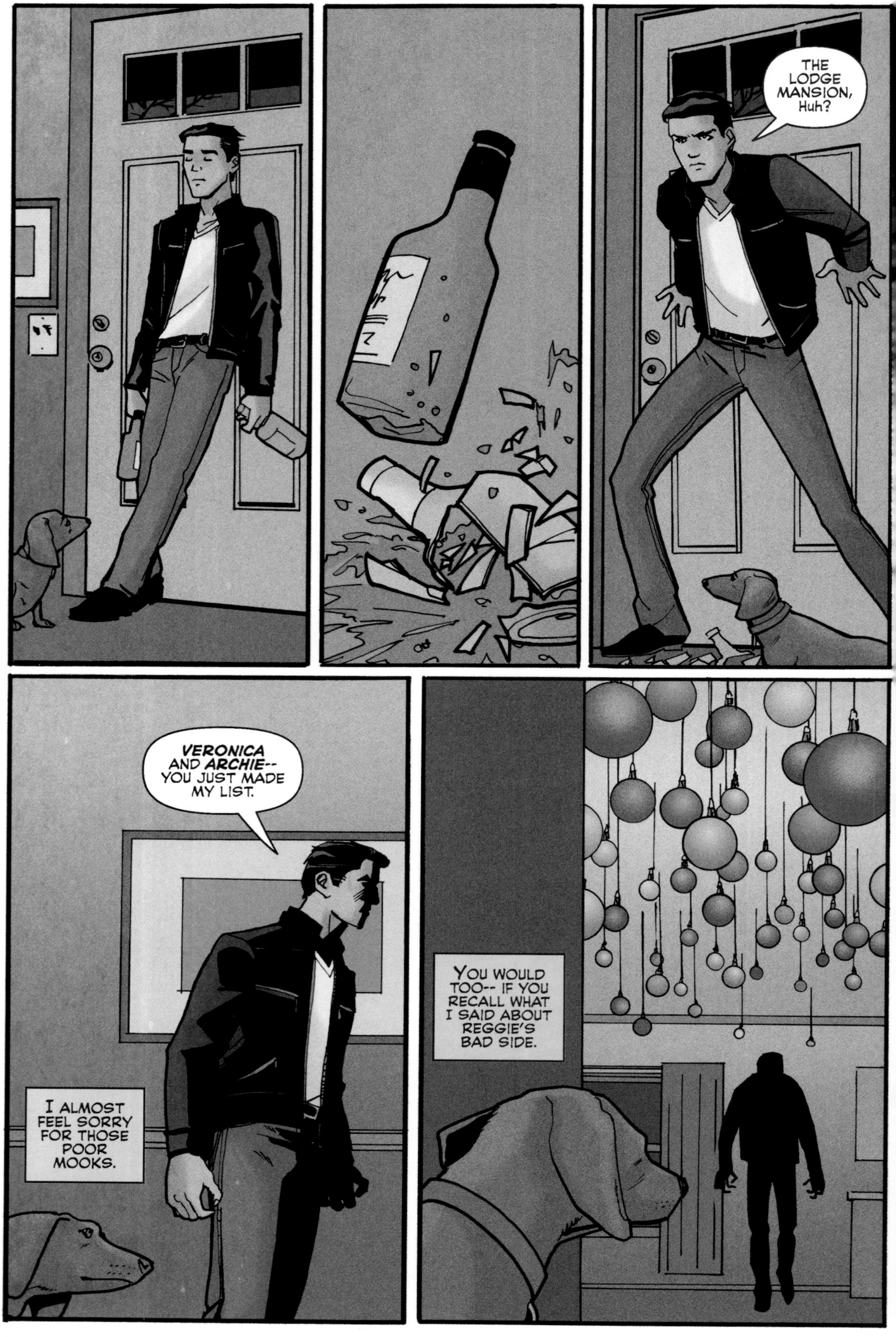
THE LODGE MANSION, Huh?
VERONICA AND ARCHIE-- YOU JUST MADE MY LIST.
I ALMOST FEEL SORRY FOR THOSE POOR MOOKS.
YOU WOULD TOO-- IF YOU RECALL WHAT I SAID ABOUT REGGIE'S BAD SIDE.

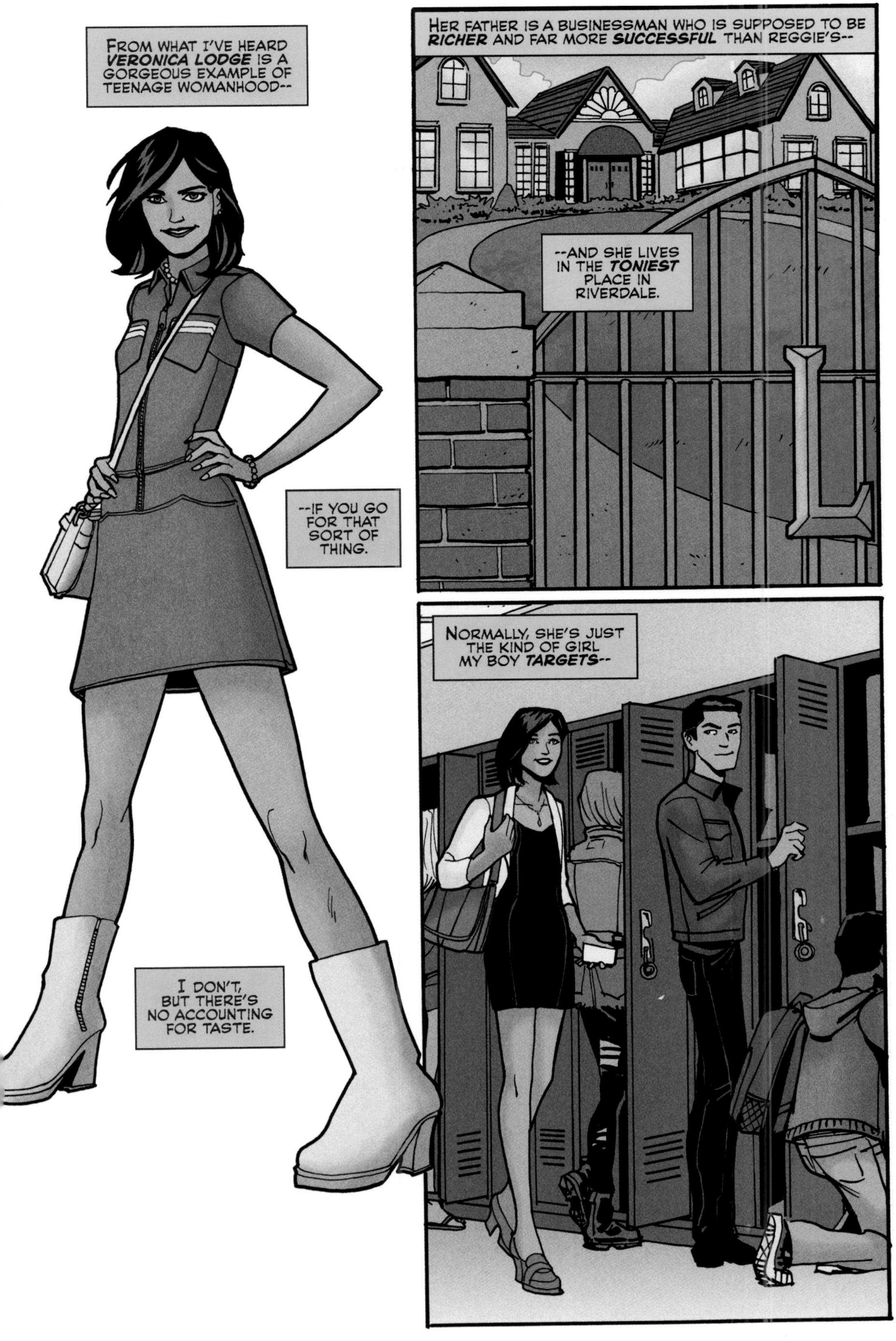
FROM WHAT I'VE HEARD VERONICA LODGE IS A GORGEOUS EXAMPLE OF TEENAGE WOMANHOOD--
--IF YOU GO FOR THAT SORT OF THING.
I DON'T, BUT THERE'S NO ACCOUNTING FOR TASTE.
HER FATHER IS A BUSINESSMAN WHO IS SUPPOSED TO BE RICHER AND FAR MORE SUCCESSFUL THAN REGGIE'S--
--AND SHE LIVES IN THE TONIEST PLACE IN RIVERDALE.
L
NORMALLY, SHE'S JUST THE KIND OF GIRL MY BOY TARGETS--

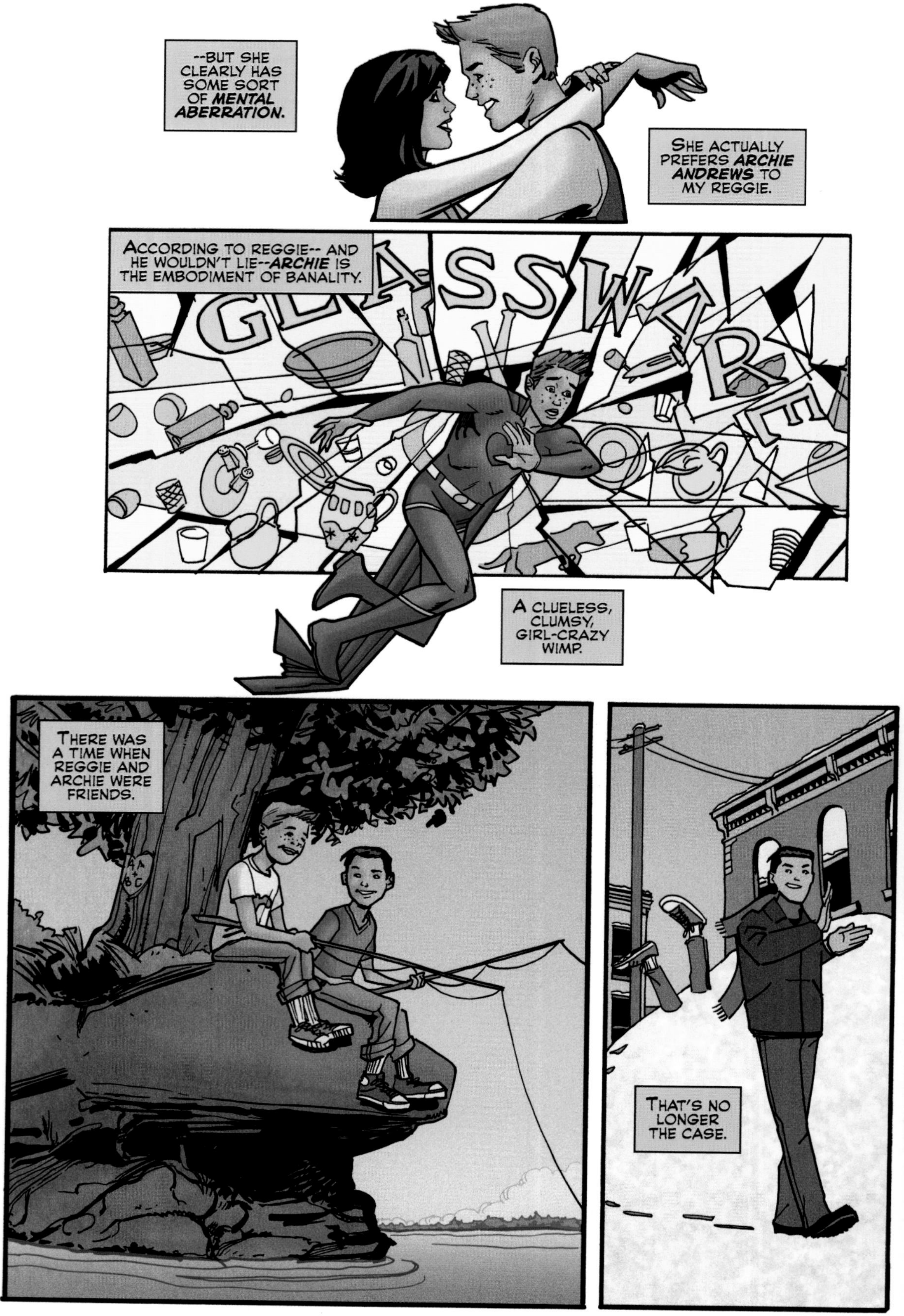
--BUT SHE CLEARLY HAS SOME SORT OF *MENTAL ABERRATION*.
SHE ACTUALLY PREFERS *ARCHIE ANDREWS* TO MY REGGIE.
ACCORDING TO REGGIE-- AND HE WOULDN'T LIE--*ARCHIE* IS THE EMBODIMENT OF BANALITY.
GLASSWARE
A CLUELESS, CLUMSY, GIRL-CRAZY WIMP.
THERE WAS A TIME WHEN REGGIE AND ARCHIE WERE FRIENDS.
THAT'S NO LONGER THE CASE.

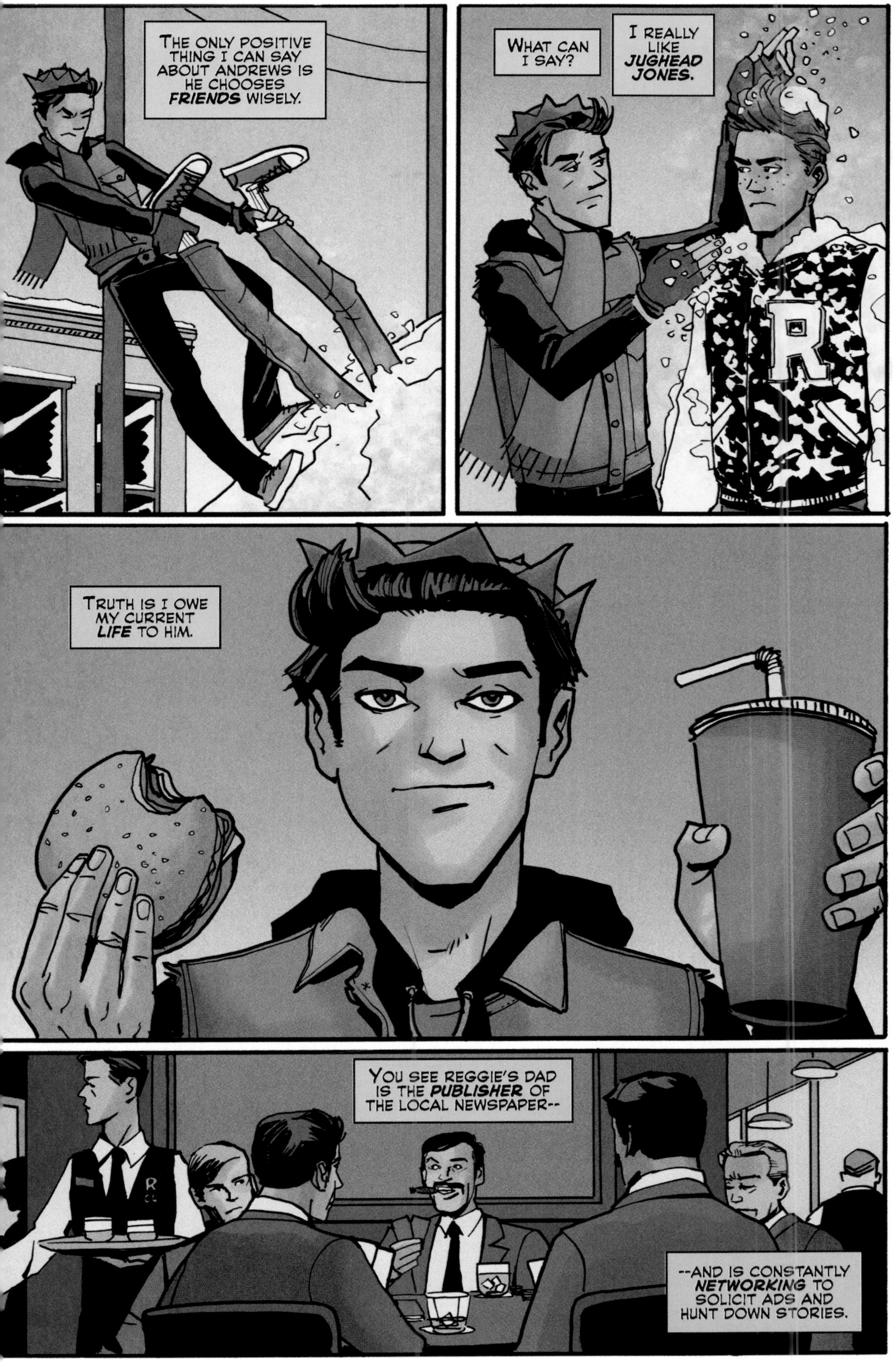
THE ONLY POSITIVE THING I CAN SAY ABOUT ANDREWS IS HE CHOOSES FRIENDS WISELY.
WHAT CAN I SAY?
I REALLY LIKE JUGHEAD JONES.
TRUTH IS I OWE MY CURRENT LIFE TO HIM.
YOU SEE REGGIE'S DAD IS THE PUBLISHER OF THE LOCAL NEWSPAPER--
--AND IS CONSTANTLY NETWORKING TO SOLICIT ADS AND HUNT DOWN STORIES.

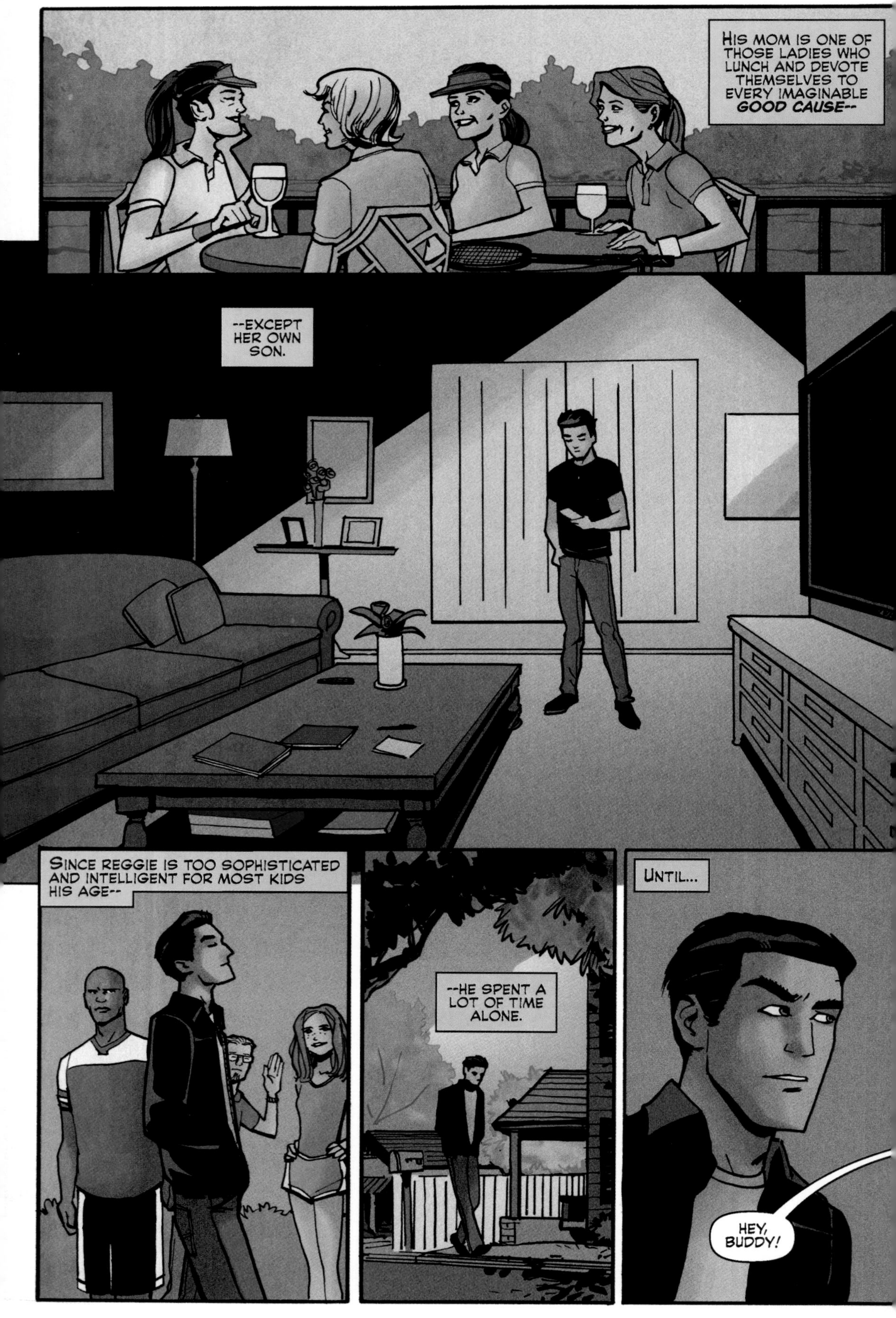
HIS MOM IS ONE OF THOSE LADIES WHO LUNCH AND DEVOTE THEMSELVES TO EVERY IMAGINABLE **GOOD CAUSE**--
--EXCEPT HER OWN SON.
SINCE REGGIE IS TOO SOPHISTICATED AND INTELLIGENT FOR MOST KIDS HIS AGE--
--HE SPENT A LOT OF TIME ALONE.
UNTIL...
HEY, BUDDY!

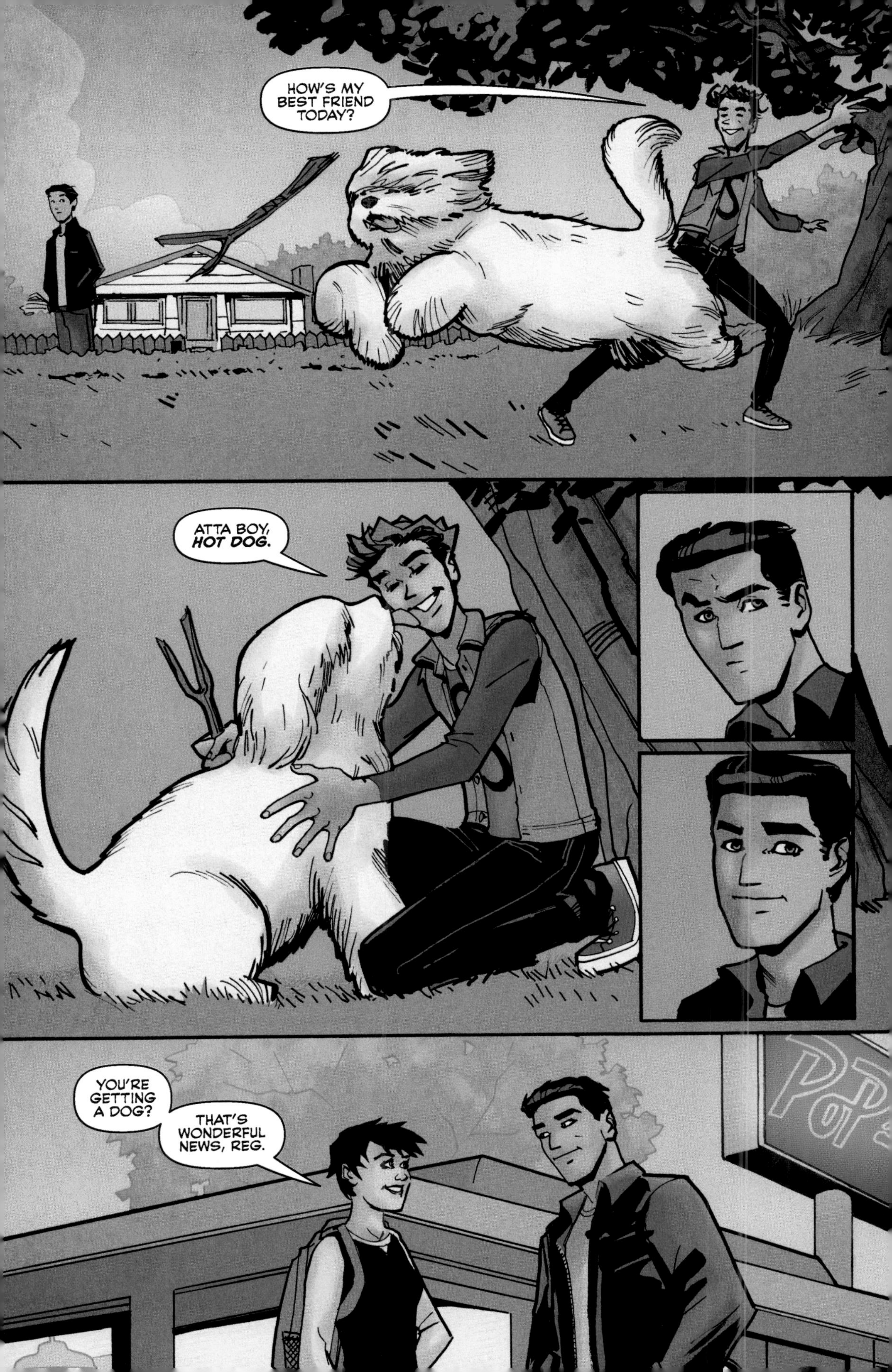
HOW'S MY BEST FRIEND TODAY?
ATTA BOY, *HOT DOG.*
YOU'RE GETTING A DOG?
THAT'S WONDERFUL NEWS, REG.
POP'S

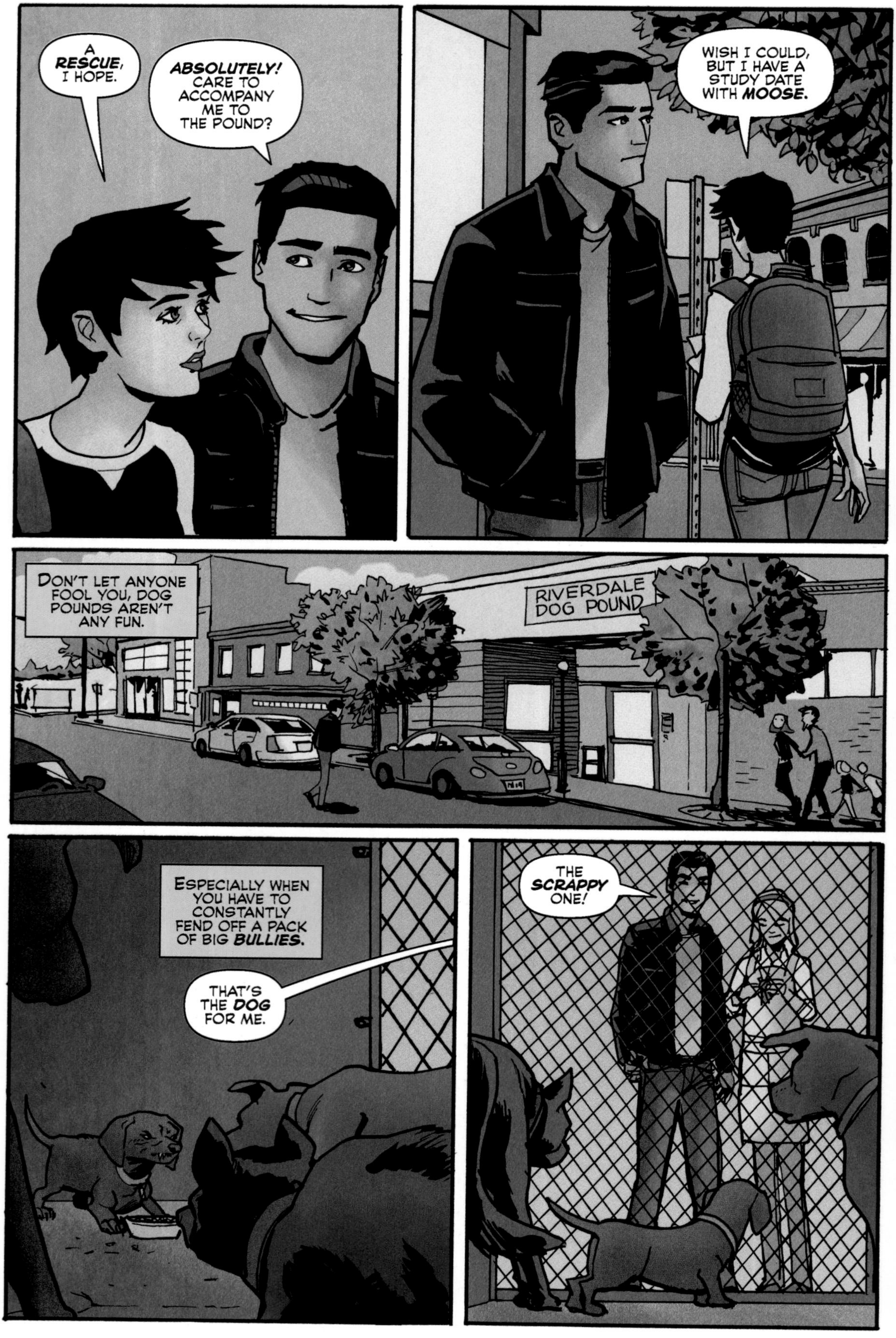
A RESCUE, I HOPE.
ABSOLUTELY! CARE TO ACCOMPANY ME TO THE POUND?
WISH I COULD, BUT I HAVE A STUDY DATE WITH MOOSE.
DON'T LET ANYONE FOOL YOU, DOG POUNDS AREN'T ANY FUN.
RIVERDALE DOG POUND
ESPECIALLY WHEN YOU HAVE TO CONSTANTLY FEND OFF A PACK OF BIG BULLIES.
THAT'S THE DOG FOR ME.
THE SCRAPPY ONE!

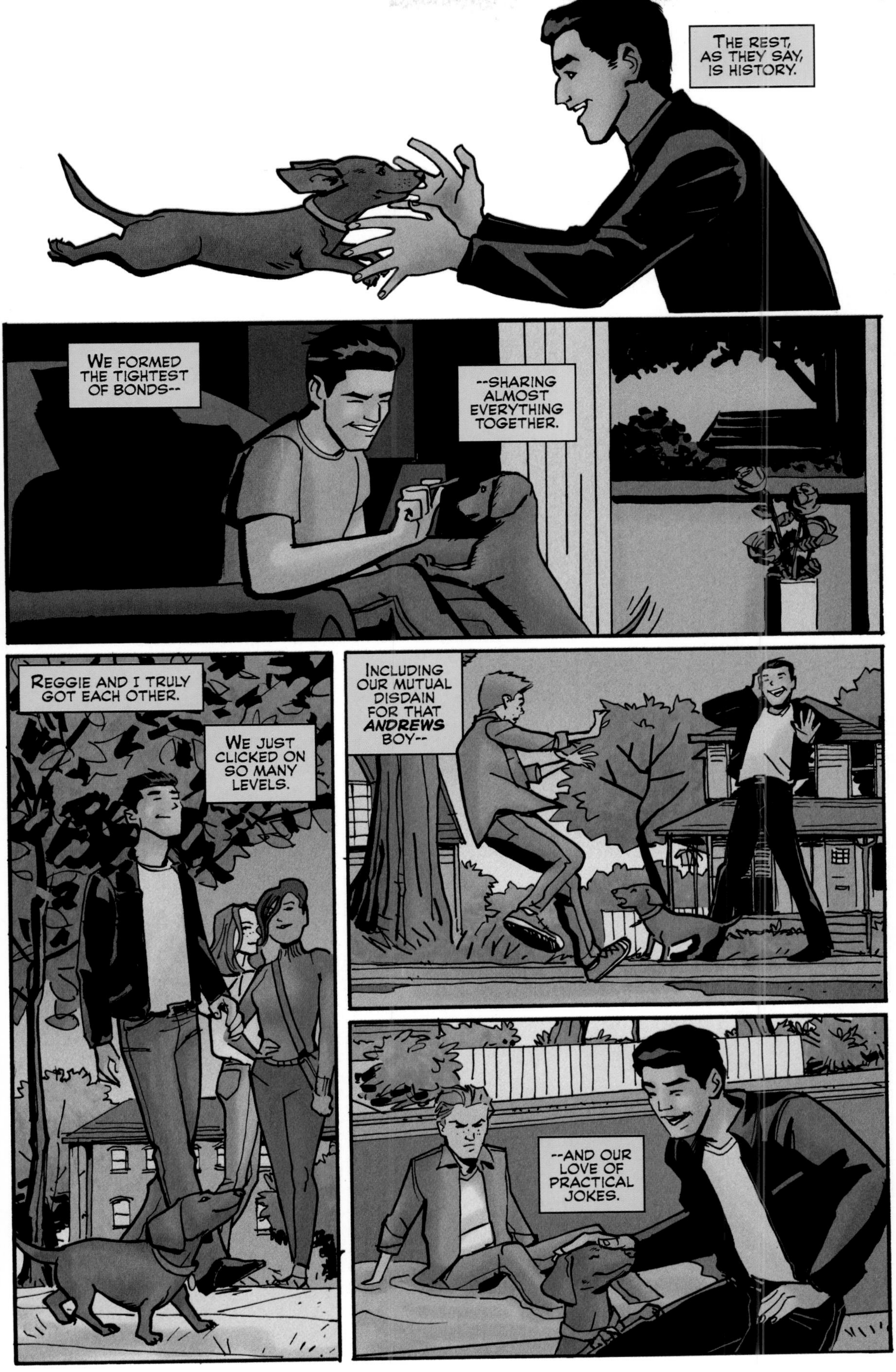
The rest, as they say, is history.
We formed the tightest of bonds--
--sharing almost everything together.
Reggie and I truly got each other.
We just clicked on so many levels.
Including our mutual disdain for that ANDREWS boy--
--and our love of practical jokes.

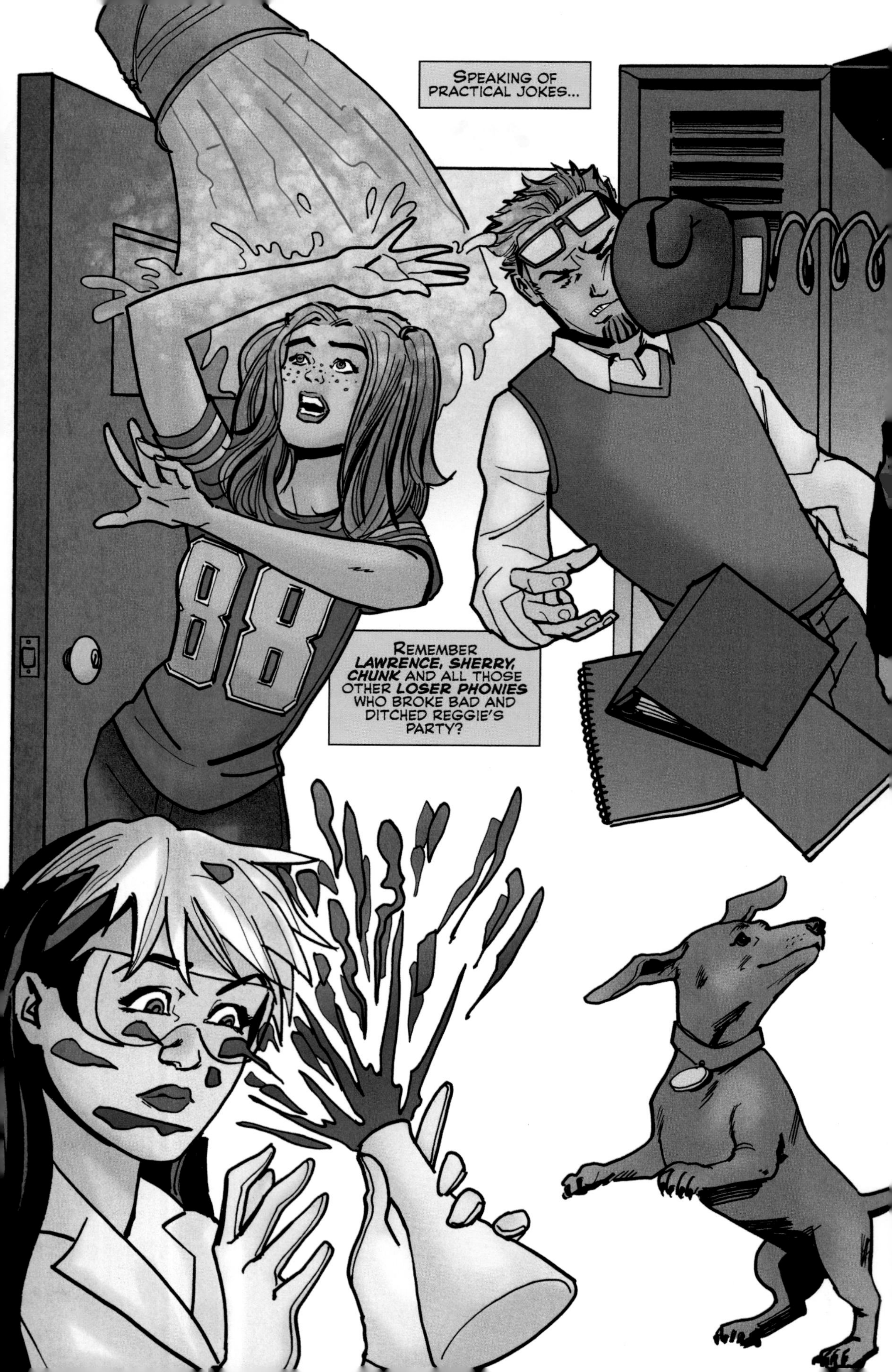
SPEAKING OF PRACTICAL JOKES...
REMEMBER LAWRENCE, SHERRY, CHUNK AND ALL THOSE OTHER LOSER PHONIES WHO BROKE BAD AND DITCHED REGGIE'S PARTY?

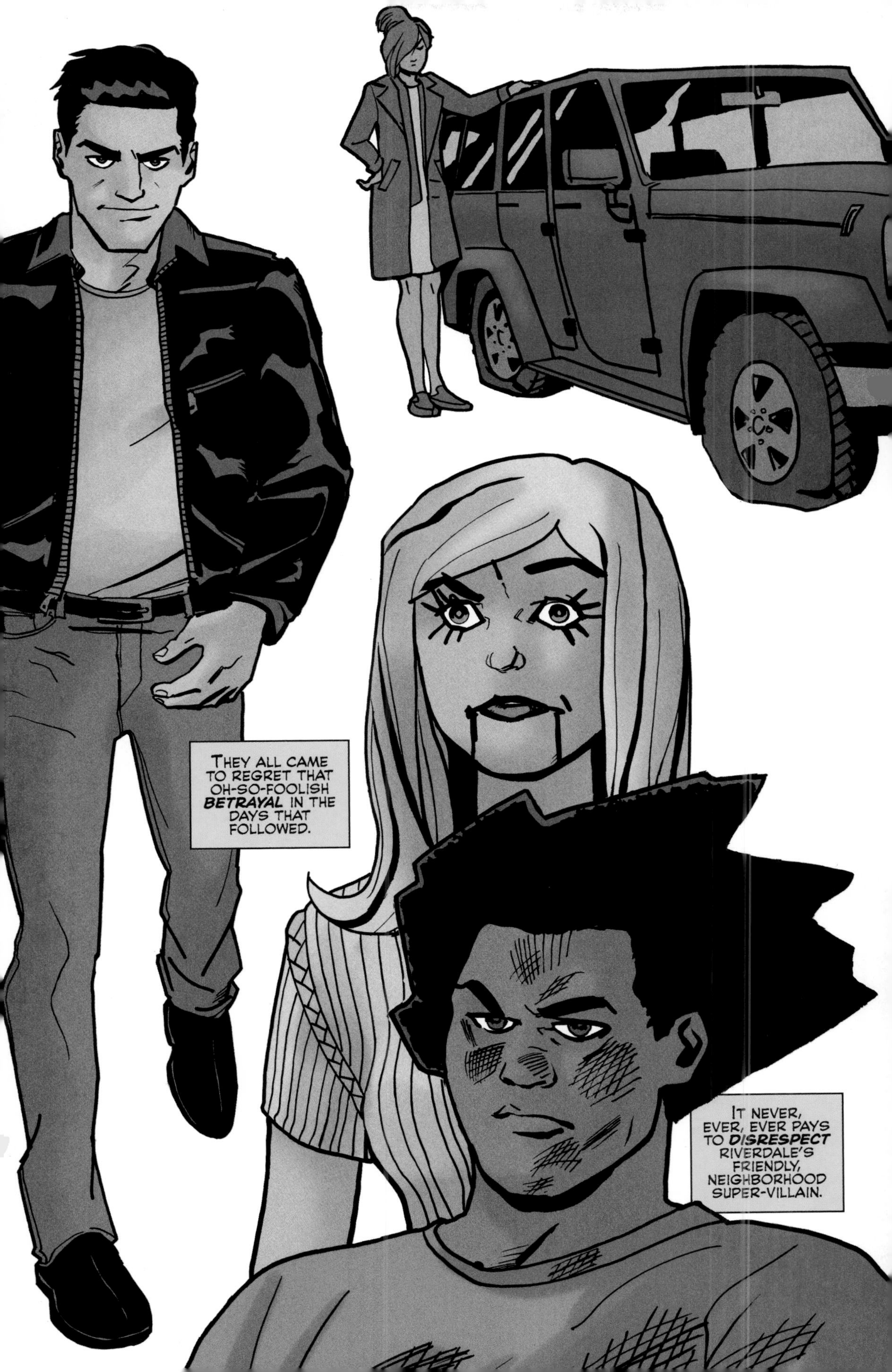
THEY ALL CAME TO REGRET THAT OH-SO-FOOLISH BETRAYAL IN THE DAYS THAT FOLLOWED.
IT NEVER, EVER, EVER PAYS TO DISRESPECT RIVERDALE'S FRIENDLY, NEIGHBORHOOD SUPER-VILLAIN.

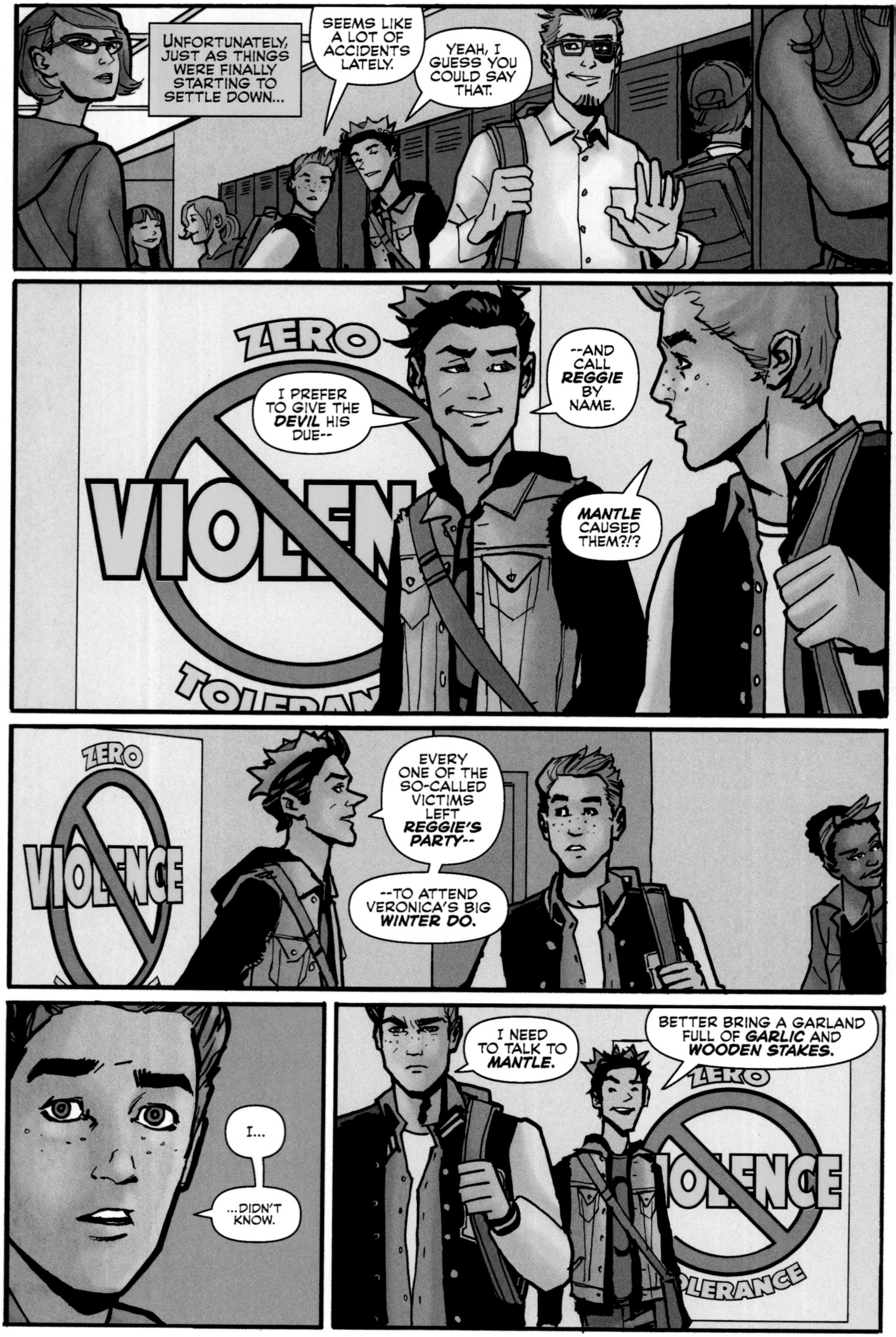
UNFORTUNATELY, JUST AS THINGS WERE FINALLY STARTING TO SETTLE DOWN...
SEEMS LIKE A LOT OF ACCIDENTS LATELY.
YEAH, I GUESS YOU COULD SAY THAT.
ZERO
VIOLEN
TOLERAN
I PREFER TO GIVE THE DEVIL HIS DUE--
--AND CALL REGGIE BY NAME.
MANTLE CAUSED THEM?!?
ZERO
VIOLENCE
EVERY ONE OF THE SO-CALLED VICTIMS LEFT REGGIE'S PARTY--
--TO ATTEND VERONICA'S BIG WINTER DO.
I...
...DIDN'T KNOW.
I NEED TO TALK TO MANTLE.
BETTER BRING A GARLAND FULL OF GARLIC AND WOODEN STAKES.
ZERO
IOLENCE
OLERANCE

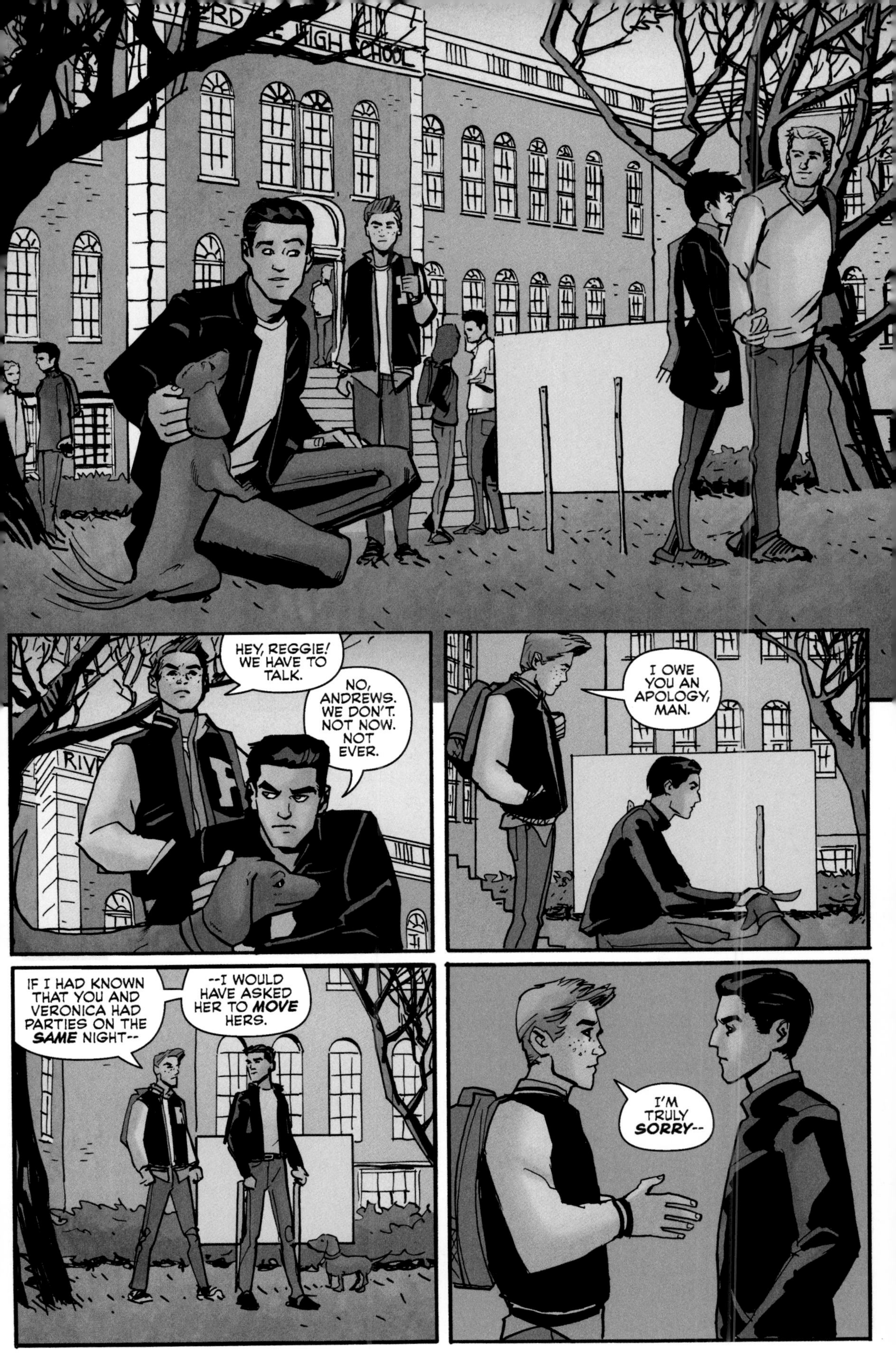
HEY, REGGIE! WE HAVE TO TALK.
NO, ANDREWS. WE DON'T. NOT NOW. NOT EVER.
I OWE YOU AN APOLOGY, MAN.
IF I HAD KNOWN THAT YOU AND VERONICA HAD PARTIES ON THE SAME NIGHT--
--I WOULD HAVE ASKED HER TO MOVE HERS.
I'M TRULY SORRY--

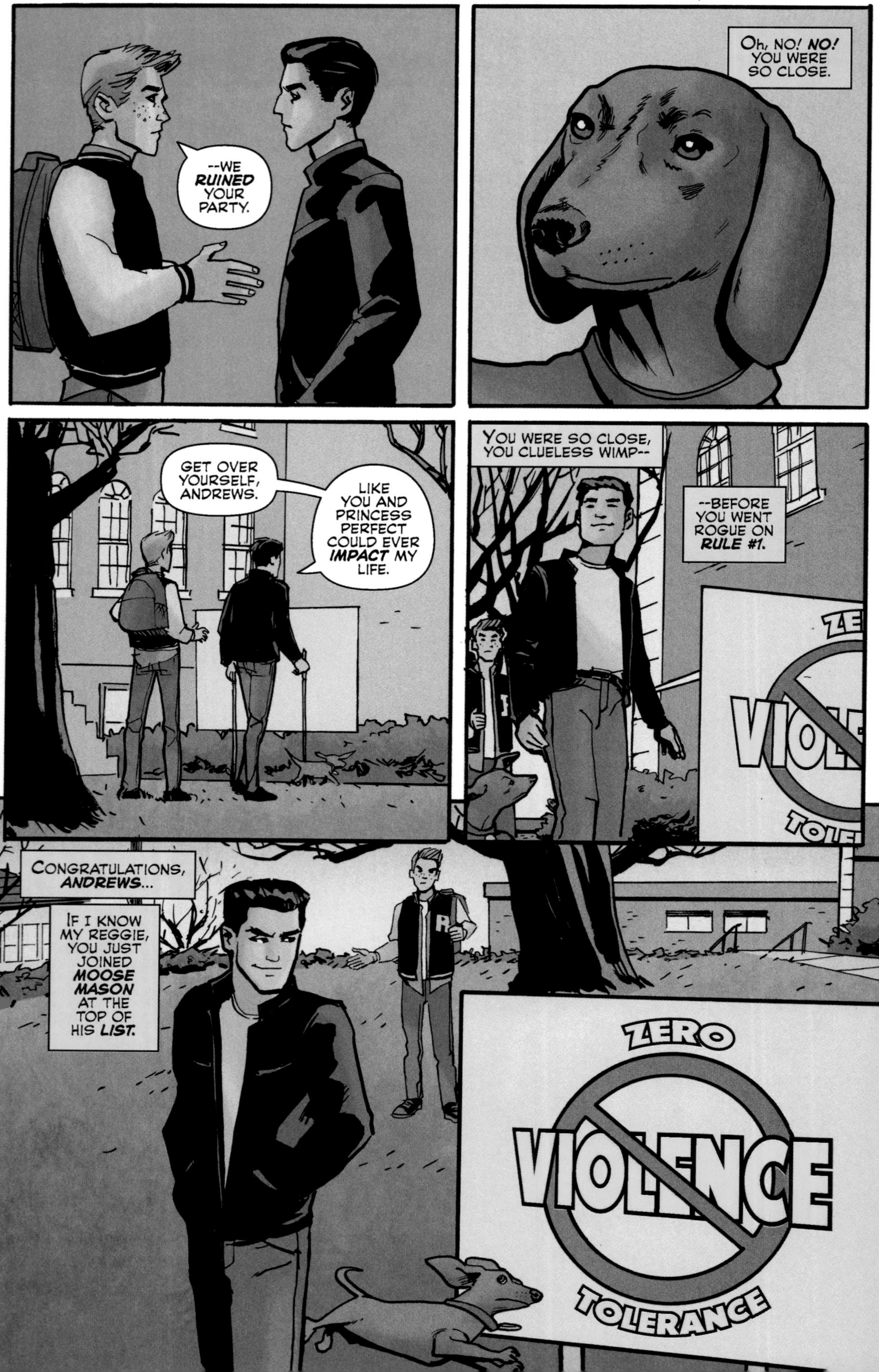

--WE RUINED YOUR PARTY.
Oh, NO! NO! YOU WERE SO CLOSE.
GET OVER YOURSELF, ANDREWS.
LIKE YOU AND PRINCESS PERFECT COULD EVER IMPACT MY LIFE.
YOU WERE SO CLOSE, YOU CLUELESS WIMP--
--BEFORE YOU WENT ROGUE ON RULE #1.
CONGRATULATIONS, ANDREWS...
IF I KNOW MY REGGIE, YOU JUST JOINED MOOSE MASON AT THE TOP OF HIS LIST.
ZERO
VIOLENCE
TOLERANCE

TO BE CONTINUED...

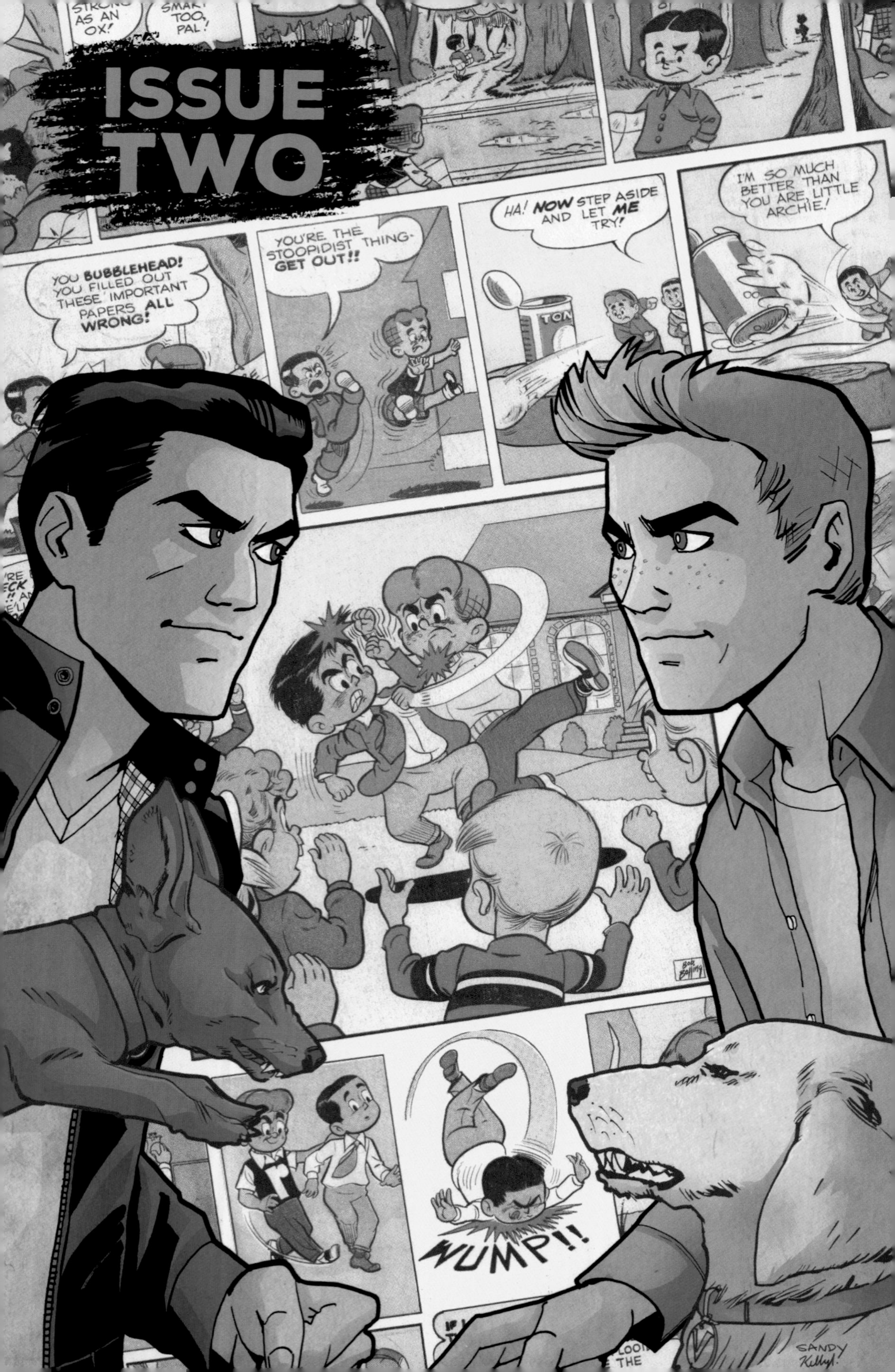
ISSUE TWO
AS AN OX!
TOO, PAL!
YOU BUBBLEHEAD! YOU FILLED OUT THESE IMPORTANT PAPERS ALL WRONG!
YOU'RE THE STOOPIDIST THING- GET OUT!!
HA! NOW STEP ASIDE AND LET ME TRY!
I'M SO MUCH BETTER THAN YOU ARE, LITTLE ARCHIE!
WUMP!!
SANDY KELLY!

DEEP IN THEIR HEARTS, EVERYONE KNOWS *REGGIE MANTLE* IS THE UNCROWNED KING OF *RIVERDALE HIGH.*

H-HAVE A GREAT DAY, REG.

SOME SEE HIM AS A BRUTAL AND SELF-CENTERED *TYRANT*--AN OPINION BEST KEPT SECRET!

(POKING HIM ONLY RESULTS IN *PANDEMONIUM, PAIN* AND MAJOR *PAYBACK.*)

LOOKING FINE, REGGIE.

MY NAME IS *VADER* AND I'M THE *LUCKIEST* DOG ALIVE--

--BECAUSE *REGGIE* IS MY BEST FRIEND.

ZERO VIOLENCE TOLERANCE

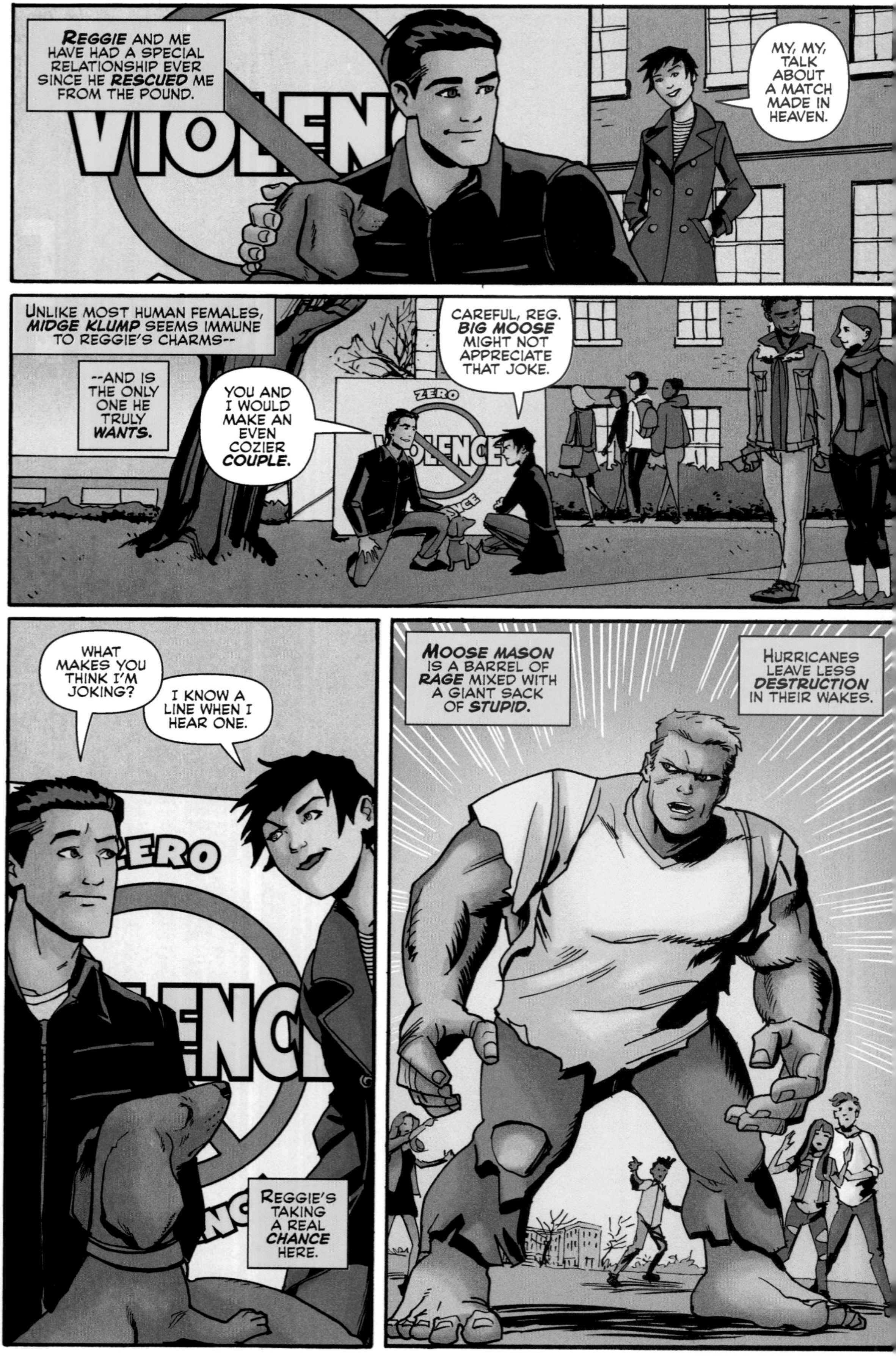
REGGIE AND ME HAVE HAD A SPECIAL RELATIONSHIP EVER SINCE HE RESCUED ME FROM THE POUND.
VIOLENCE
MY, MY, TALK ABOUT A MATCH MADE IN HEAVEN.
UNLIKE MOST HUMAN FEMALES, MIDGE KLUMP SEEMS IMMUNE TO REGGIE'S CHARMS--
--AND IS THE ONLY ONE HE TRULY WANTS.
YOU AND I WOULD MAKE AN EVEN COZIER COUPLE.
CAREFUL, REG. BIG MOOSE MIGHT NOT APPRECIATE THAT JOKE.
ZERO
VIOLENCE
WHAT MAKES YOU THINK I'M JOKING?
I KNOW A LINE WHEN I HEAR ONE.
ZERO
REGGIE'S TAKING A REAL CHANCE HERE.
MOOSE MASON IS A BARREL OF RAGE MIXED WITH A GIANT SACK OF STUPID.
HURRICANES LEAVE LESS DESTRUCTION IN THEIR WAKES.

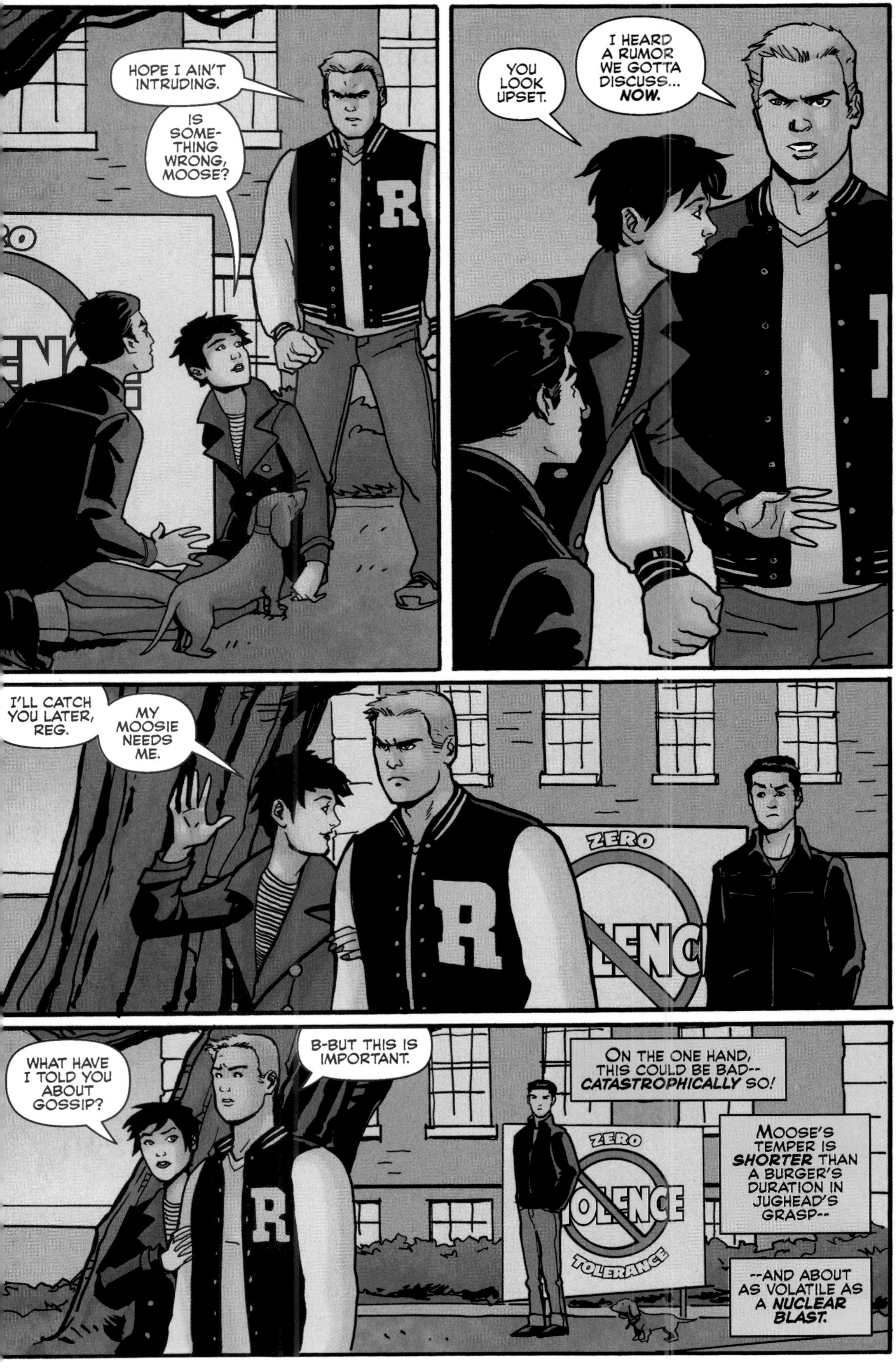
HOPE I AIN'T INTRUDING.
IS SOME-THING WRONG, MOOSE?
YOU LOOK UPSET.
I HEARD A RUMOR WE GOTTA DISCUSS... NOW.
I'LL CATCH YOU LATER, REG.
MY MOOSIE NEEDS ME.
ZERO
ZERO
WHAT HAVE I TOLD YOU ABOUT GOSSIP?
B-BUT THIS IS IMPORTANT.
ON THE ONE HAND, THIS COULD BE BAD-- CATASTROPHICALLY SO!
ZERO
TOLERANCE
MOOSE'S TEMPER IS SHORTER THAN A BURGER'S DURATION IN JUGHEAD'S GRASP--
--AND ABOUT AS VOLATILE AS A NUCLEAR BLAST.

ON THE OTHER HAND, THIS COULD BE REGGIE'S BIG CHANCE TO FINALLY *CONFRONT* HIS MAJOR ADVERSARY--

--AND HIT THE *HAPPILY-EVER-AFTER* ROUTE WITH HIS MAIDEN FAIR.

TOO BAD REGGIE ISN'T AS *CONFIDENT* IN HIMSELF AS I AM.

ZERO VIOLE TOLERANC

LUCKILY, HE CAN ALWAYS MAKE HIMSELF FEEL BETTER BY *PRANKING* HIS PERENNIAL PATSY-- *ARCHIE ANDREWS!*

RIVERDALE HIGH SCHOOL

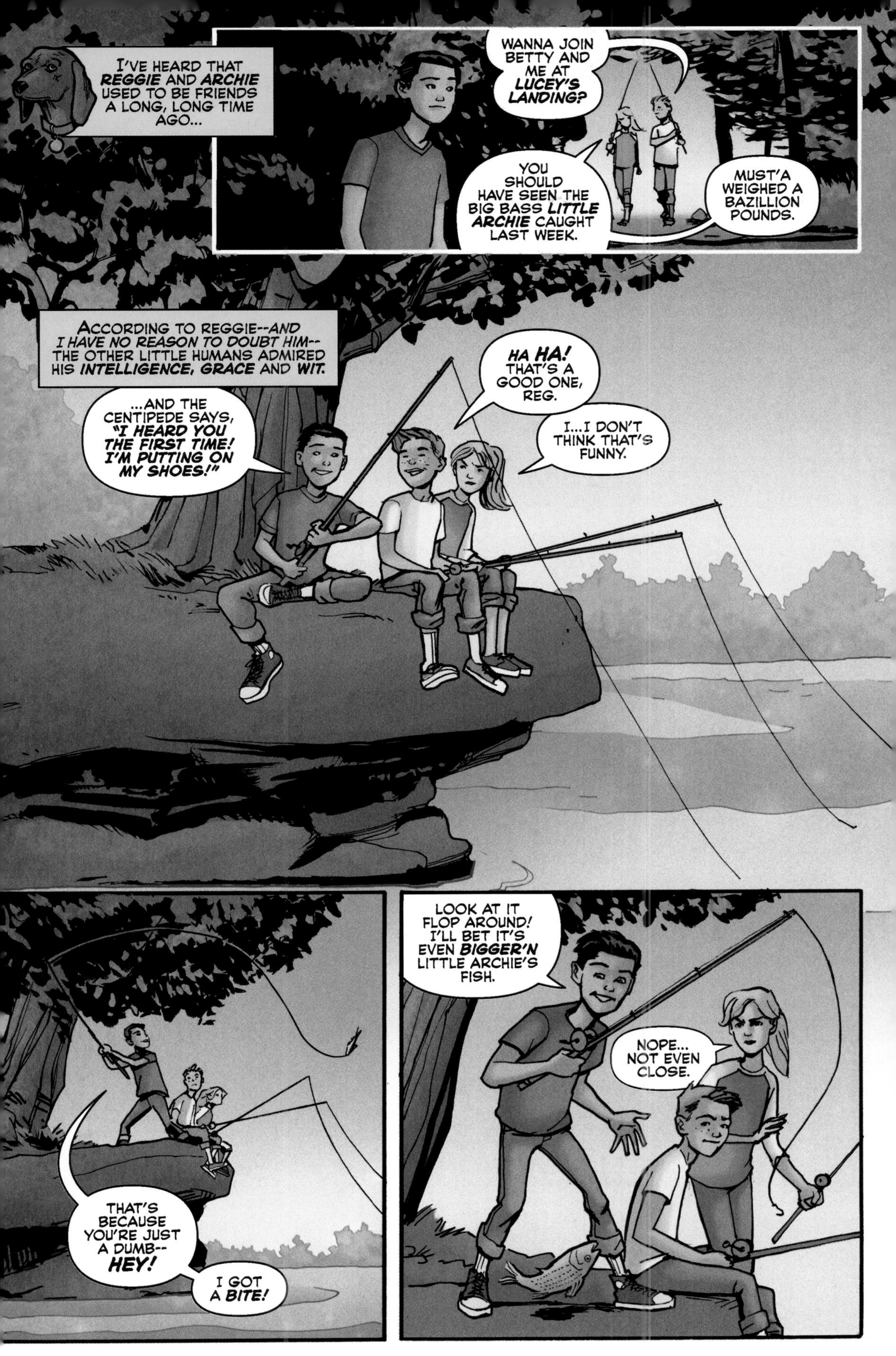

I'VE HEARD THAT REGGIE AND ARCHIE USED TO BE FRIENDS A LONG, LONG TIME AGO...
WANNA JOIN BETTY AND ME AT LUCEY'S LANDING?
YOU SHOULD HAVE SEEN THE BIG BASS LITTLE ARCHIE CAUGHT LAST WEEK.
MUST'A WEIGHED A BAZILLION POUNDS.
ACCORDING TO REGGIE--AND I HAVE NO REASON TO DOUBT HIM--THE OTHER LITTLE HUMANS ADMIRED HIS INTELLIGENCE, GRACE AND WIT.
...AND THE CENTIPEDE SAYS, "I HEARD YOU THE FIRST TIME! I'M PUTTING ON MY SHOES!"
HA HA! THAT'S A GOOD ONE, REG.
I...I DON'T THINK THAT'S FUNNY.
THAT'S BECAUSE YOU'RE JUST A DUMB-- HEY!
I GOT A BITE!
LOOK AT IT FLOP AROUND! I'LL BET IT'S EVEN BIGGER'N LITTLE ARCHIE'S FISH.
NOPE... NOT EVEN CLOSE.

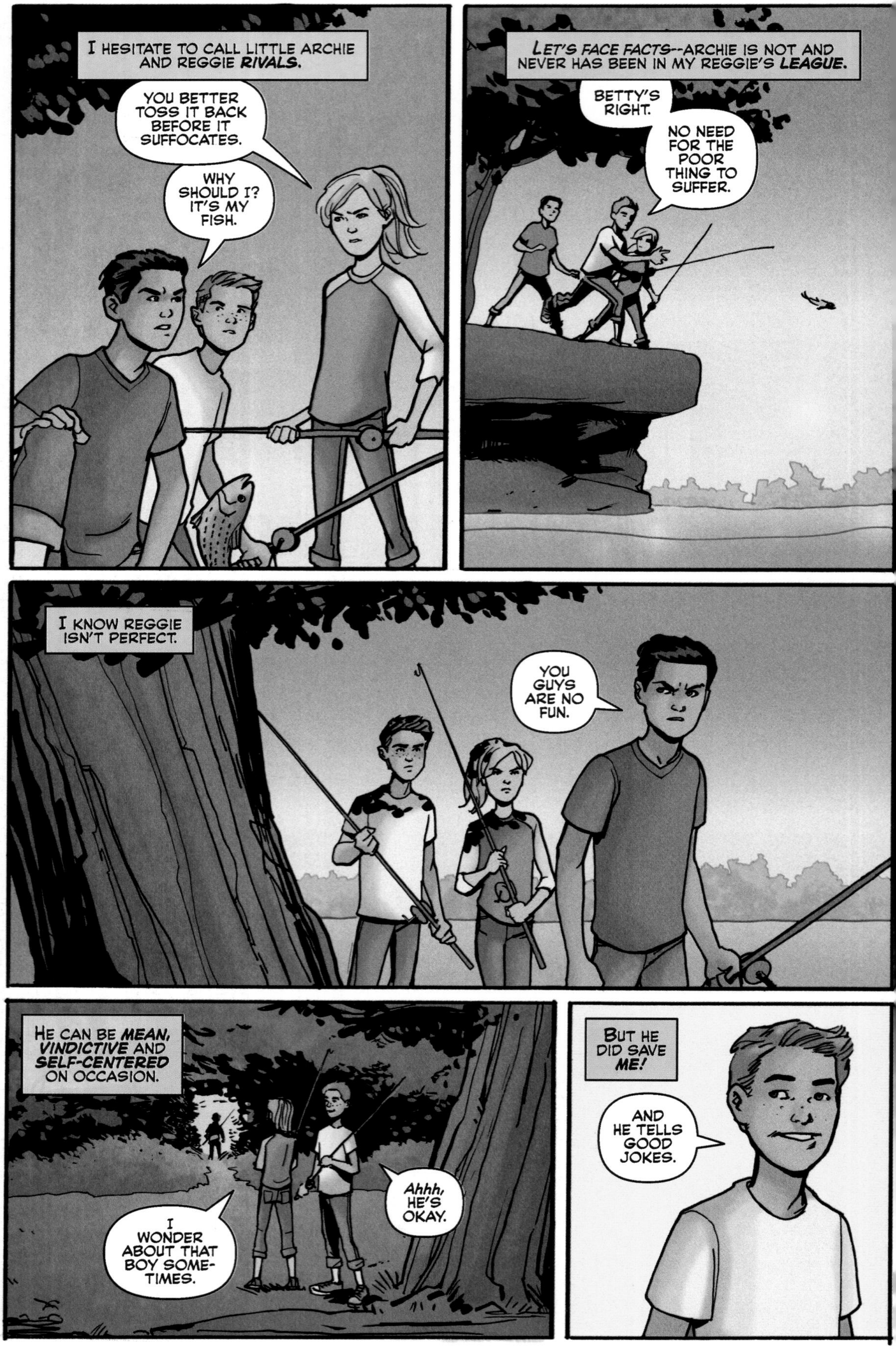

I HESITATE TO CALL LITTLE ARCHIE AND REGGIE *RIVALS.*
YOU BETTER TOSS IT BACK BEFORE IT SUFFOCATES.
WHY SHOULD I? IT'S MY FISH.
LET'S FACE FACTS--ARCHIE IS NOT AND NEVER HAS BEEN IN MY REGGIE'S *LEAGUE.*
BETTY'S RIGHT.
NO NEED FOR THE POOR THING TO SUFFER.
I KNOW REGGIE ISN'T PERFECT.
YOU GUYS ARE NO FUN.
HE CAN BE *MEAN, VINDICTIVE* AND *SELF-CENTERED* ON OCCASION.
I WONDER ABOUT THAT BOY SOME-TIMES.
Ahhh, HE'S OKAY.
BUT HE DID SAVE *ME!*
AND HE TELLS GOOD JOKES.

ARCHIE HAS ALWAYS HAD A SPECIAL PLACE IN REGGIE'S HEART.

THE KIND OF PLACE OFTEN SEEN IN *HORROR STORIES* AND *SLASHER FILMS.*

DON'T GET THE WRONG IMPRESSION! REGGIE ISN'T NEARLY AS *NASTY* AS PEOPLE SAY.

(NO ONE COULD BE!)

HE'S ACTUALLY QUITE *PLAYFUL.*

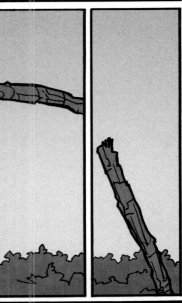

ALTHOUGH SOME MAY *QUESTION* HIS SENSE OF HUMOR.

(ANOTHER OPINION BEST KEPT SECRET.)

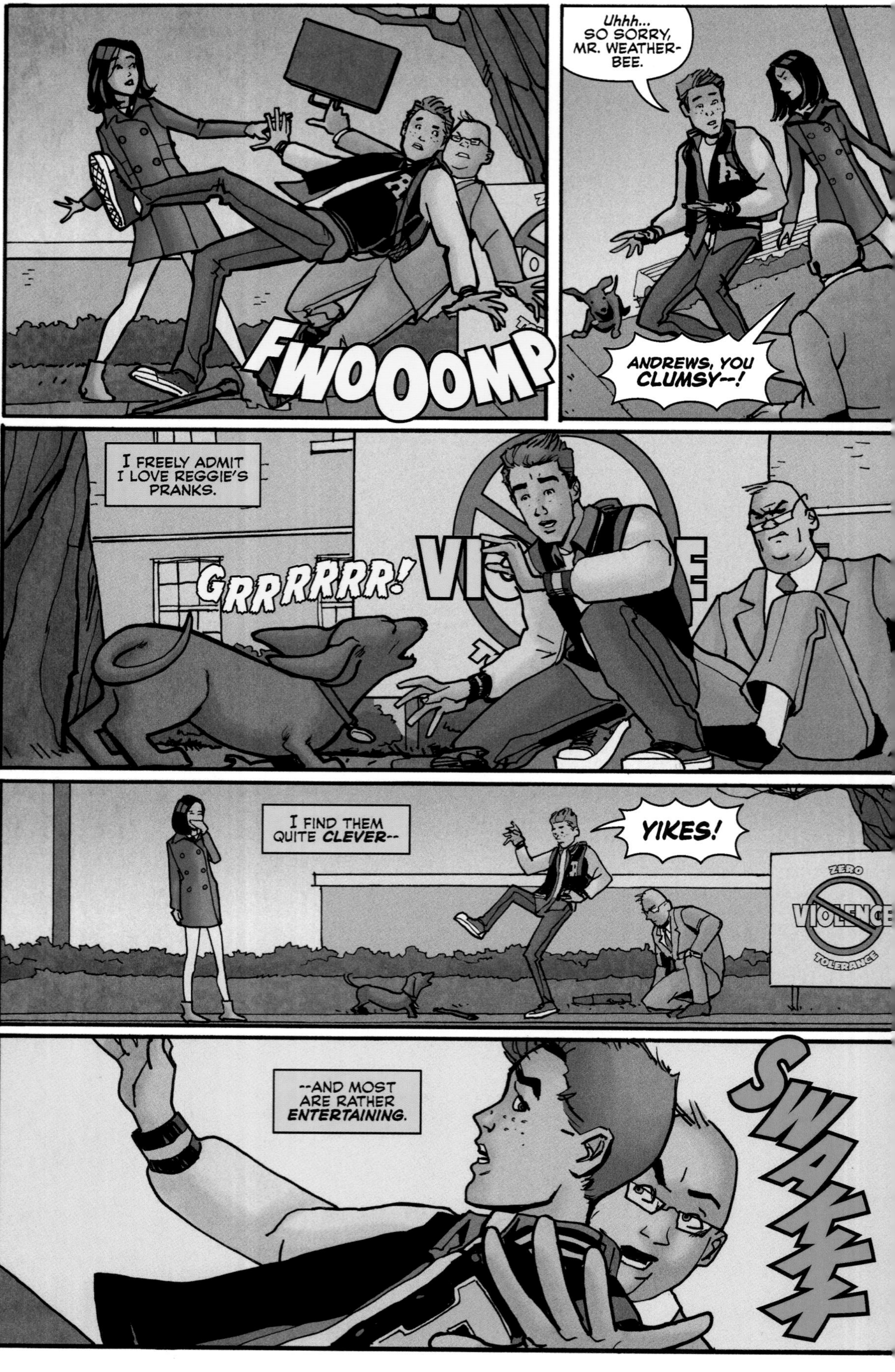
FWOOOMP
Uhhh... SO SORRY, MR. WEATHER-BEE.
ANDREWS, YOU CLUMSY--!
I FREELY ADMIT I LOVE REGGIE'S PRANKS.
GRRRRRR!
VIO E
I FIND THEM QUITE CLEVER--
YIKES!
ZERO
VIOLENCE
TOLERANCE
--AND MOST ARE RATHER ENTERTAINING.
SWAKK

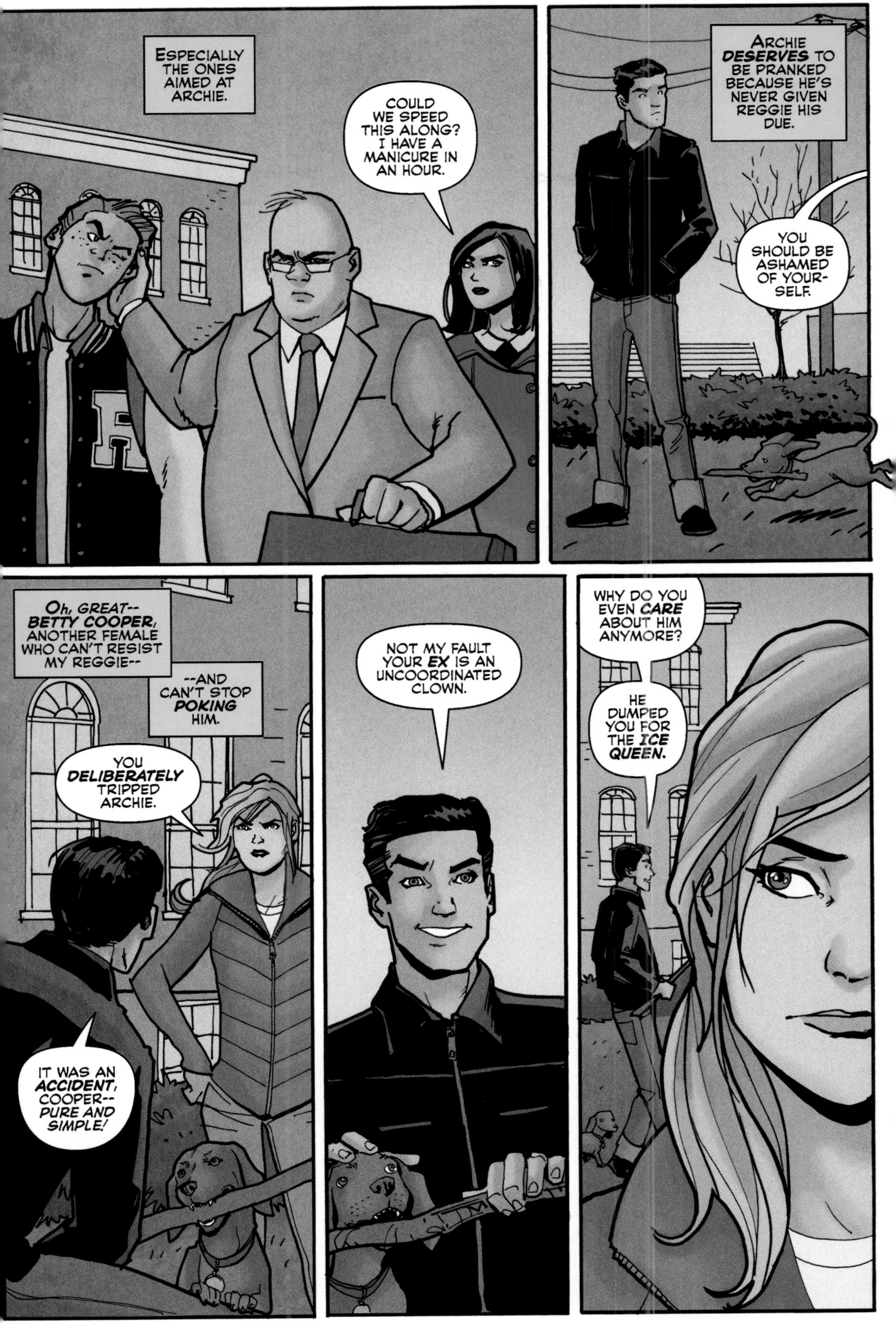

Especially the ones aimed at Archie.
Could we speed this along? I have a manicure in an hour.
Archie *deserves* to be pranked because he's never given Reggie his due.
You should be ashamed of yourself.
Oh, great-- Betty Cooper, another female who can't resist my Reggie--
--and can't stop *poking* him.
You *deliberately* tripped Archie.
It was an *accident,* Cooper-- *pure and simple!*
Not my fault your *ex* is an uncoordinated clown.
Why do you even *care* about him anymore?
He dumped you for the *Ice Queen.*

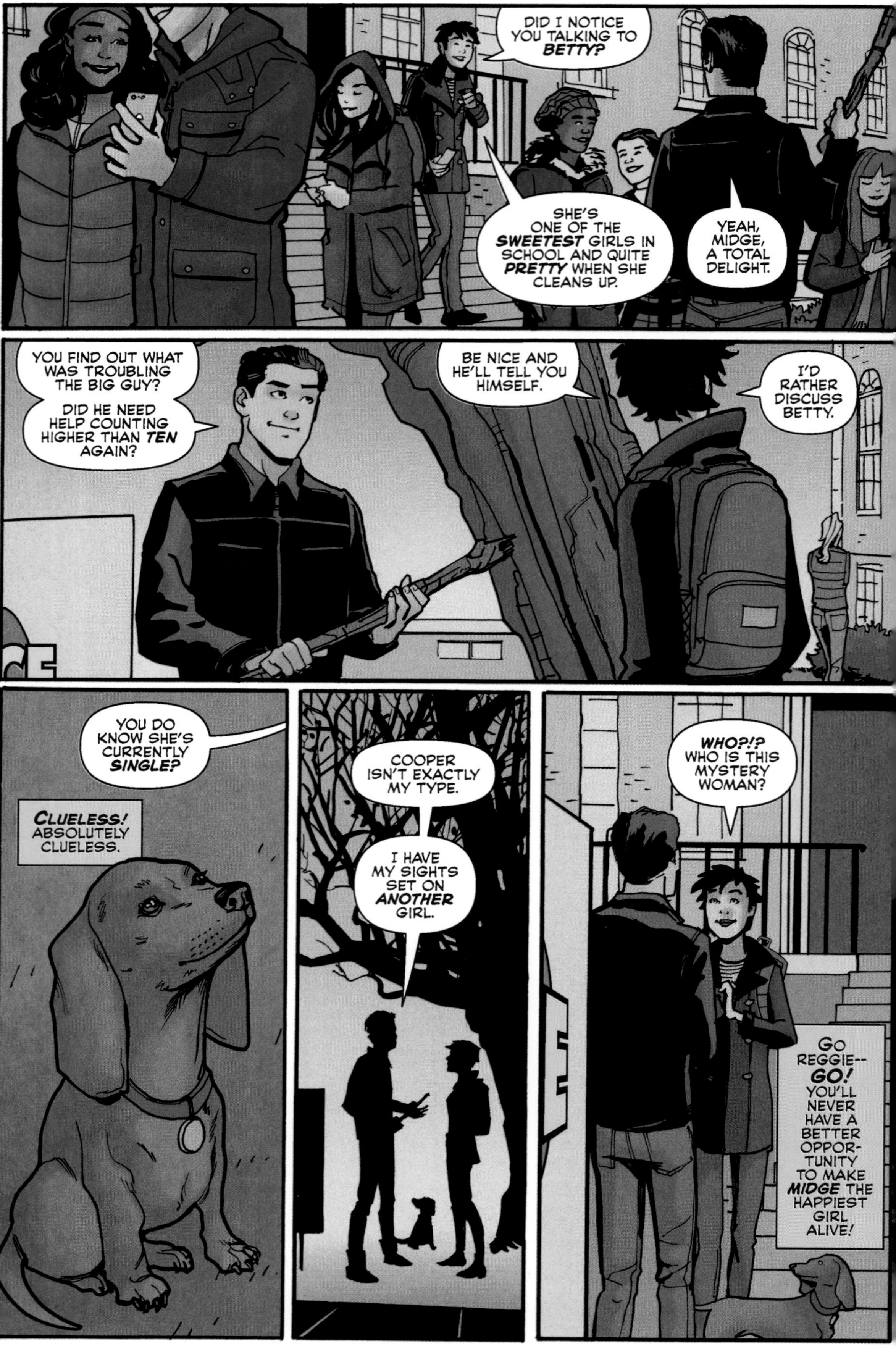
DID I NOTICE YOU TALKING TO BETTY?
SHE'S ONE OF THE SWEETEST GIRLS IN SCHOOL AND QUITE PRETTY WHEN SHE CLEANS UP.
YEAH, MIDGE, A TOTAL DELIGHT.
YOU FIND OUT WHAT WAS TROUBLING THE BIG GUY?
DID HE NEED HELP COUNTING HIGHER THAN TEN AGAIN?
BE NICE AND HE'LL TELL YOU HIMSELF.
I'D RATHER DISCUSS BETTY.
YOU DO KNOW SHE'S CURRENTLY SINGLE?
CLUELESS! ABSOLUTELY CLUELESS.
COOPER ISN'T EXACTLY MY TYPE.
I HAVE MY SIGHTS SET ON ANOTHER GIRL.
WHO?!? WHO IS THIS MYSTERY WOMAN?
GO REGGIE-- GO! YOU'LL NEVER HAVE A BETTER OPPOR-TUNITY TO MAKE MIDGE THE HAPPIEST GIRL ALIVE!

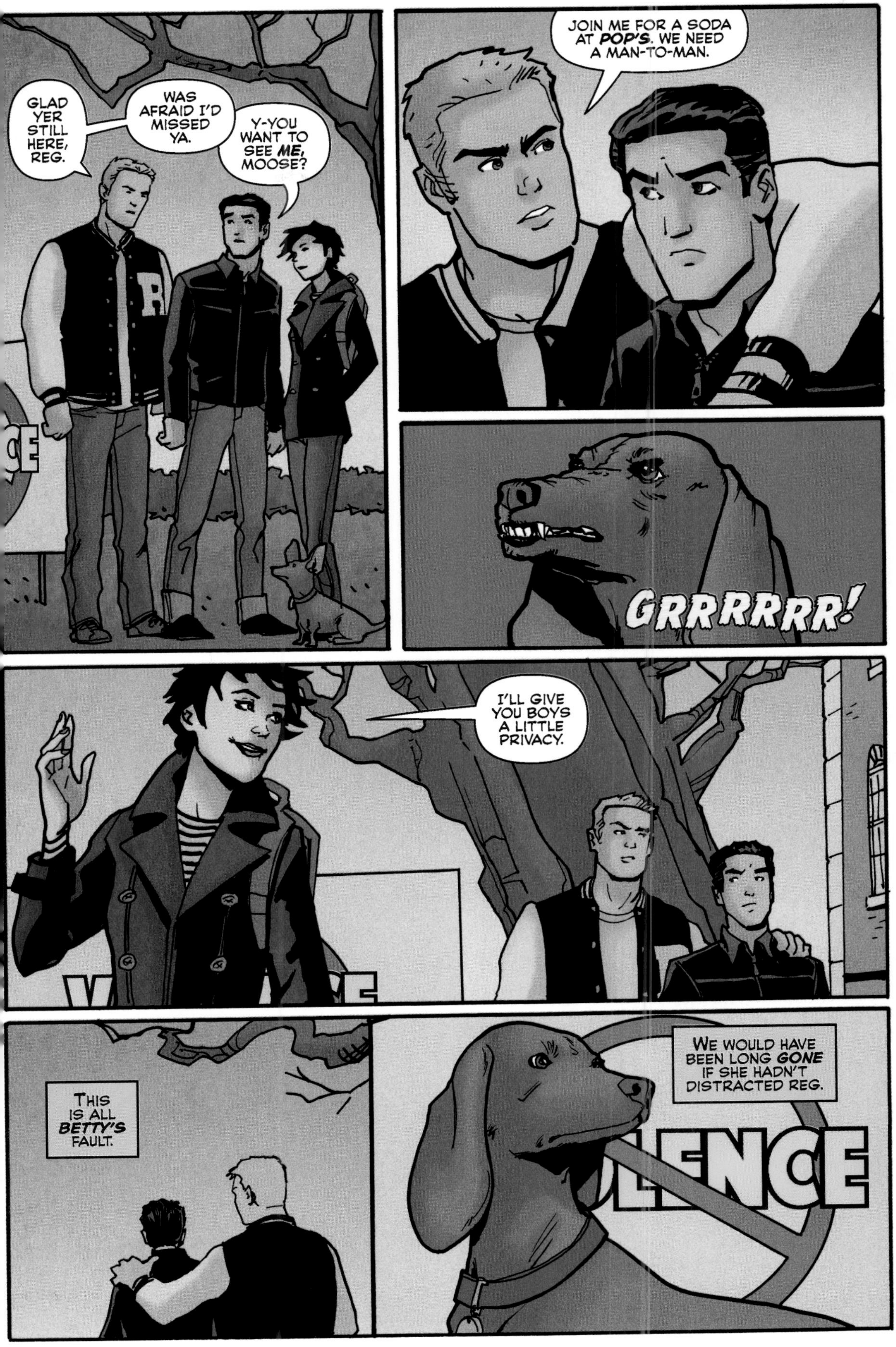
GLAD YER STILL HERE, REG.
WAS AFRAID I'D MISSED YA.
Y-YOU WANT TO SEE ME, MOOSE?
JOIN ME FOR A SODA AT POP'S. WE NEED A MAN-TO-MAN.
GRRRRRRR!
I'LL GIVE YOU BOYS A LITTLE PRIVACY.
THIS IS ALL BETTY'S FAULT.
WE WOULD HAVE BEEN LONG GONE IF SHE HADN'T DISTRACTED REG.
LENCE

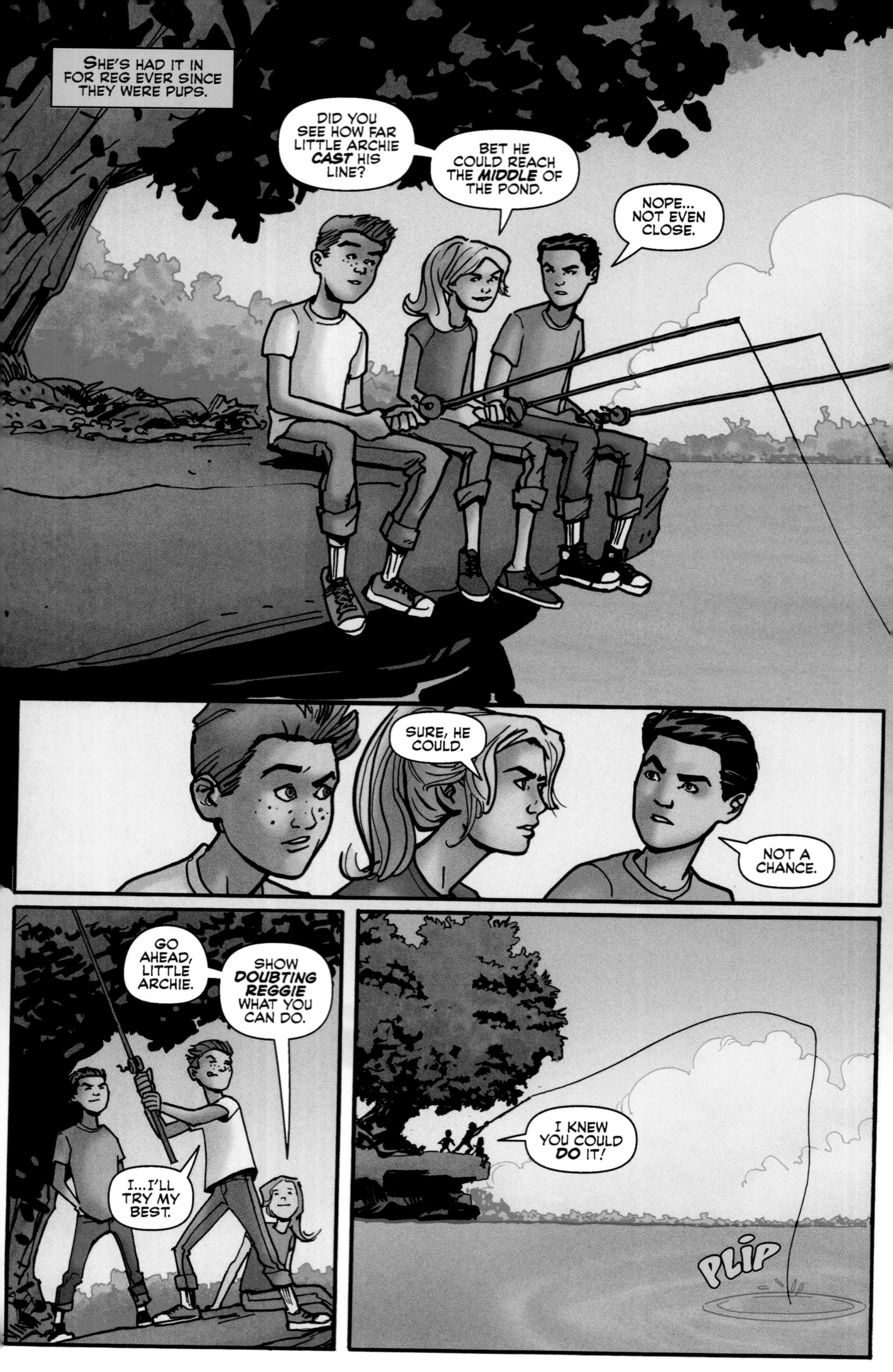
SHE'S HAD IT IN FOR REG EVER SINCE THEY WERE PUPS.
DID YOU SEE HOW FAR LITTLE ARCHIE CAST HIS LINE?
BET HE COULD REACH THE MIDDLE OF THE POND.
NOPE... NOT EVEN CLOSE.
SURE, HE COULD.
NOT A CHANCE.
GO AHEAD, LITTLE ARCHIE.
SHOW DOUBTING REGGIE WHAT YOU CAN DO.
I...I'LL TRY MY BEST.
I KNEW YOU COULD DO IT!
PLIP

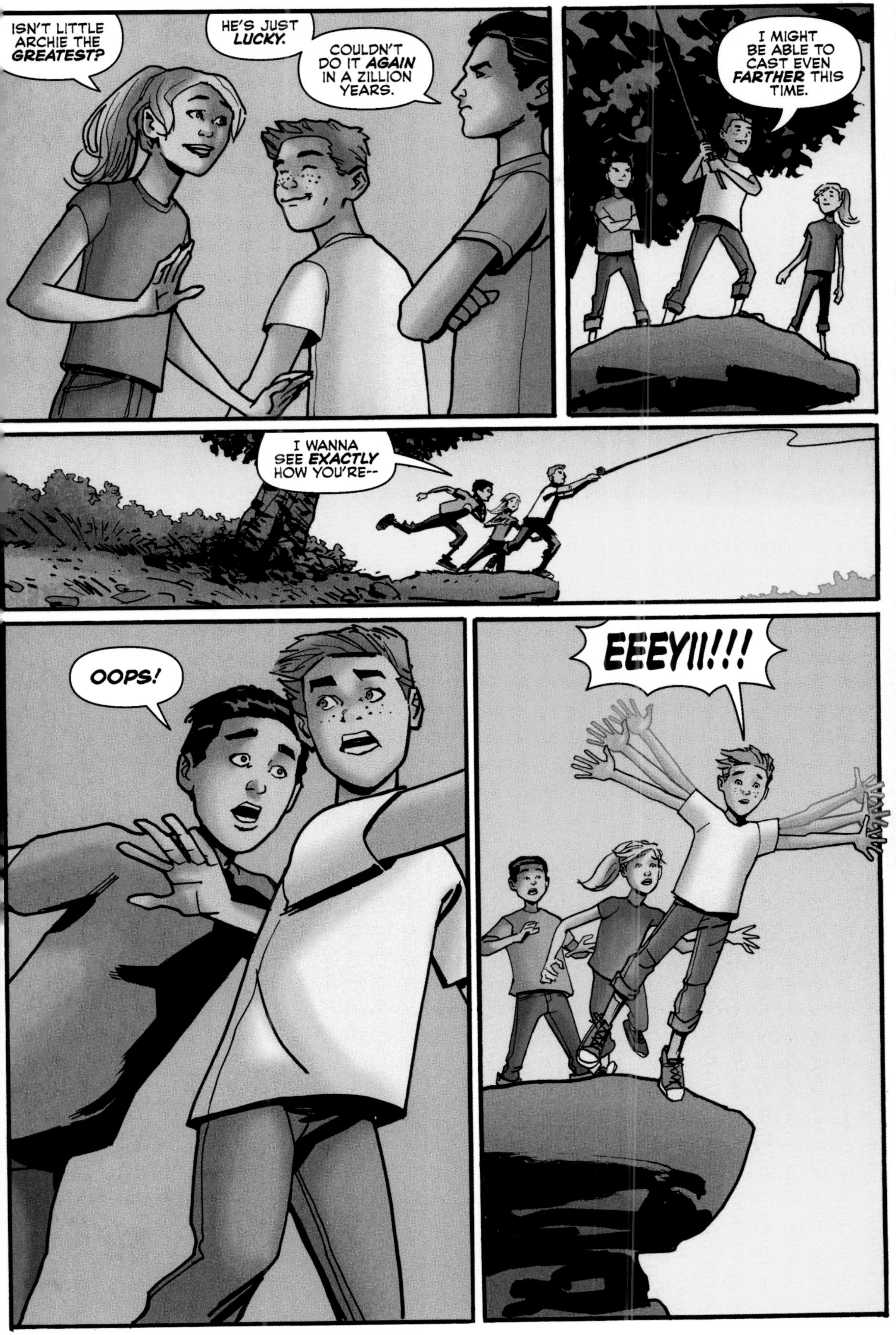
ISN'T LITTLE ARCHIE THE GREATEST?
HE'S JUST LUCKY.
COULDN'T DO IT AGAIN IN A ZILLION YEARS.
I MIGHT BE ABLE TO CAST EVEN FARTHER THIS TIME.
I WANNA SEE EXACTLY HOW YOU'RE--
OOPS!
EEEYII!!!

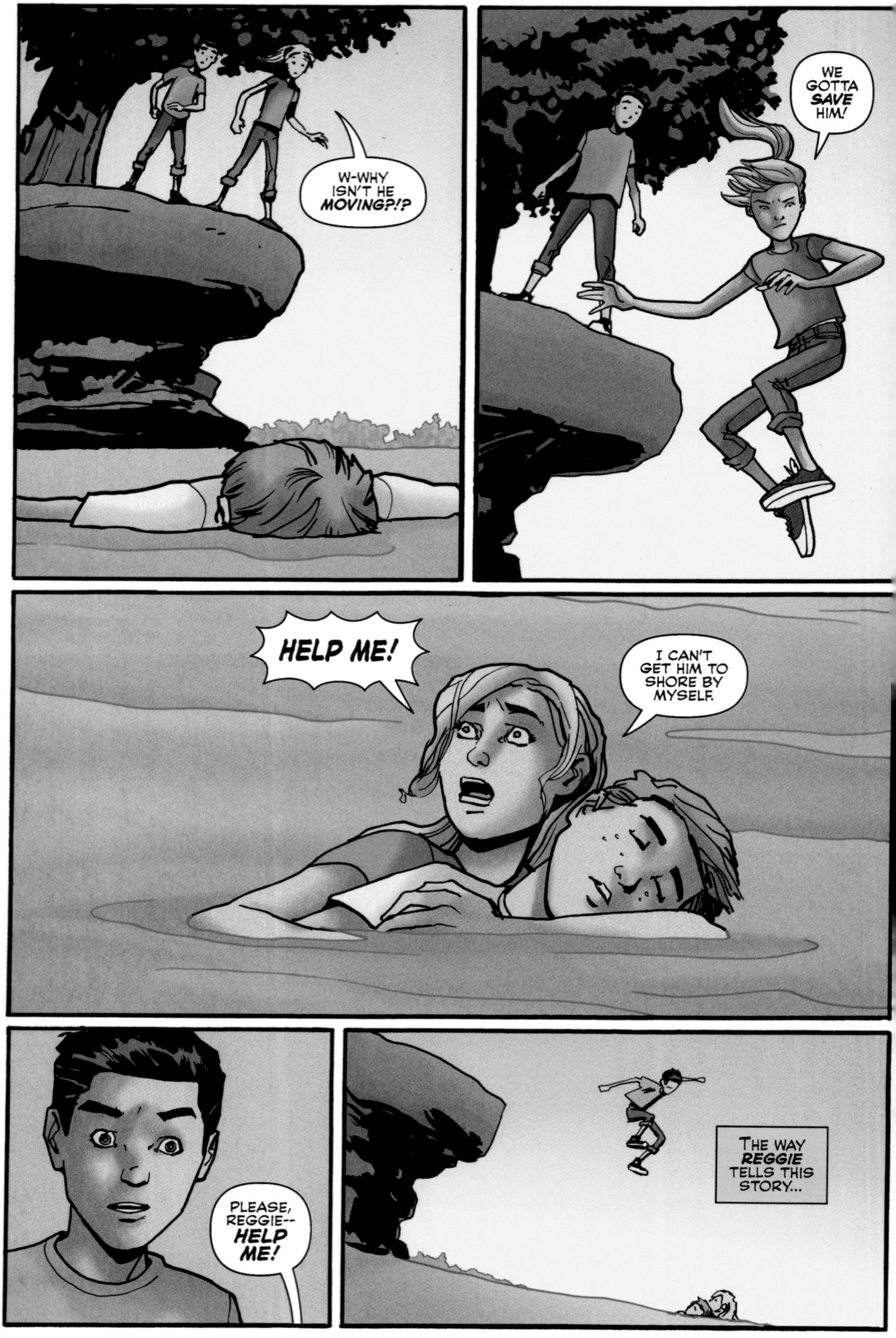
W-WHY ISN'T HE *MOVING?!?*
WE GOTTA *SAVE* HIM!
HELP ME!
I CAN'T GET HIM TO SHORE BY MYSELF.
PLEASE, REGGIE-- *HELP ME!*
THE WAY *REGGIE* TELLS THIS STORY...

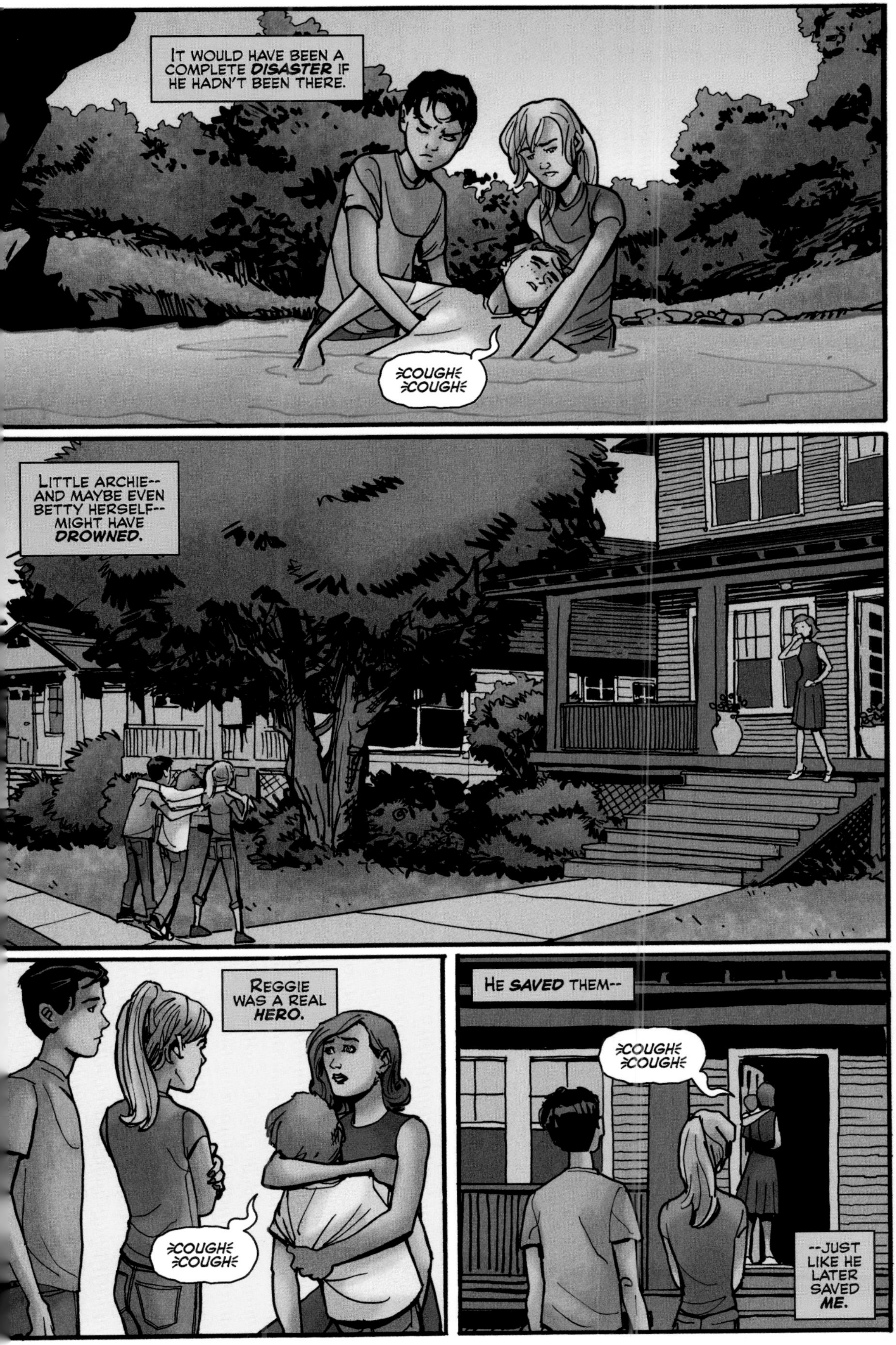
It would have been a complete *disaster* if he hadn't been there.
COUGH COUGH
Little Archie-- and maybe even Betty herself-- might have *drowned.*
Reggie was a real *hero.*
COUGH COUGH
He *saved* them--
COUGH COUGH
--just like he later saved *me.*

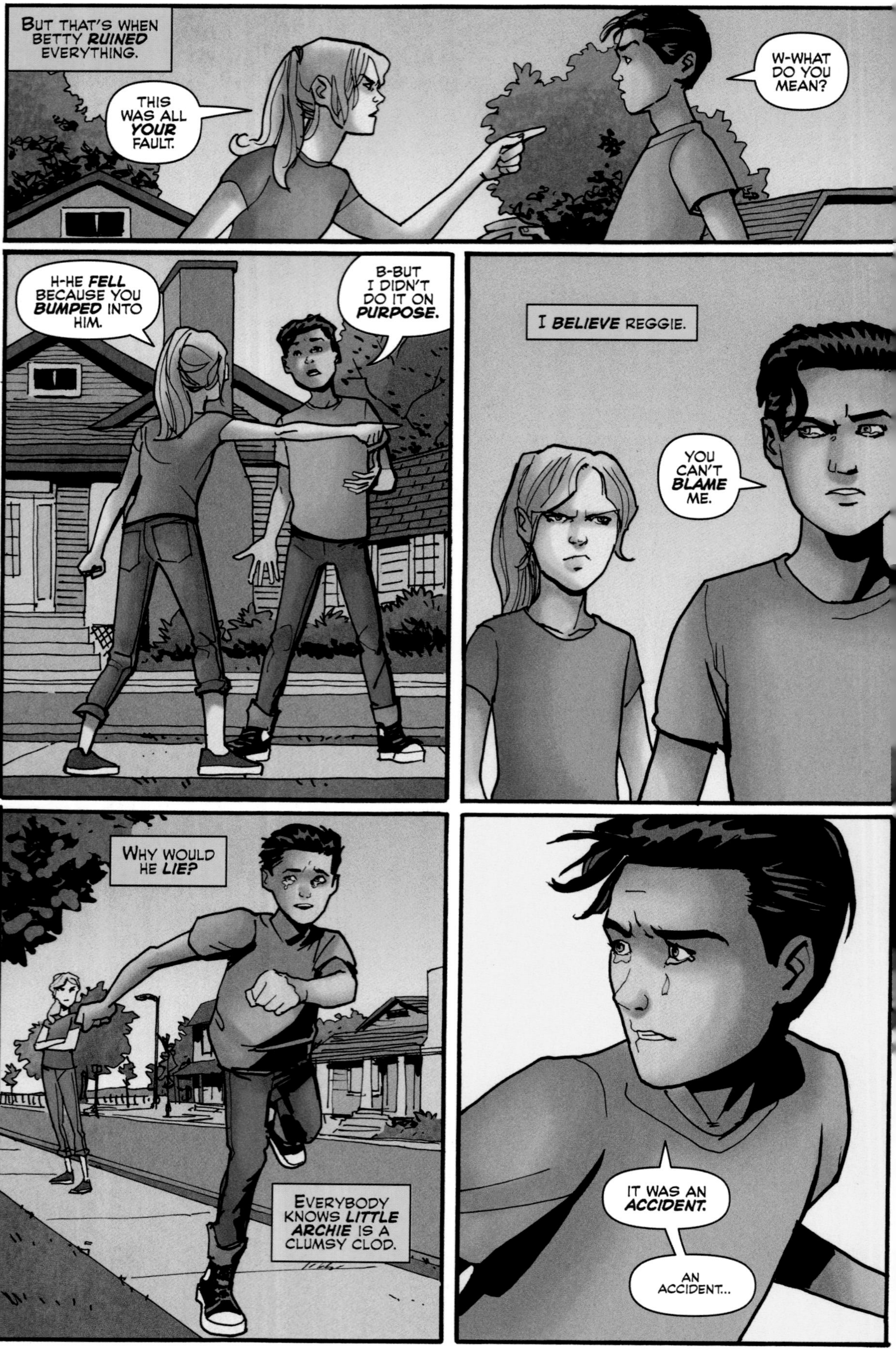

But that's when Betty *ruined* everything.
This was all ***your*** fault.
W-what do you mean?
H-he ***fell*** because you ***bumped*** into him.
B-but I didn't do it on ***purpose.***
I ***believe*** Reggie.
You can't ***blame*** me.
Why would he ***lie?***
Everybody knows ***Little Archie*** is a clumsy clod.
It was an ***accident.***
An accident...

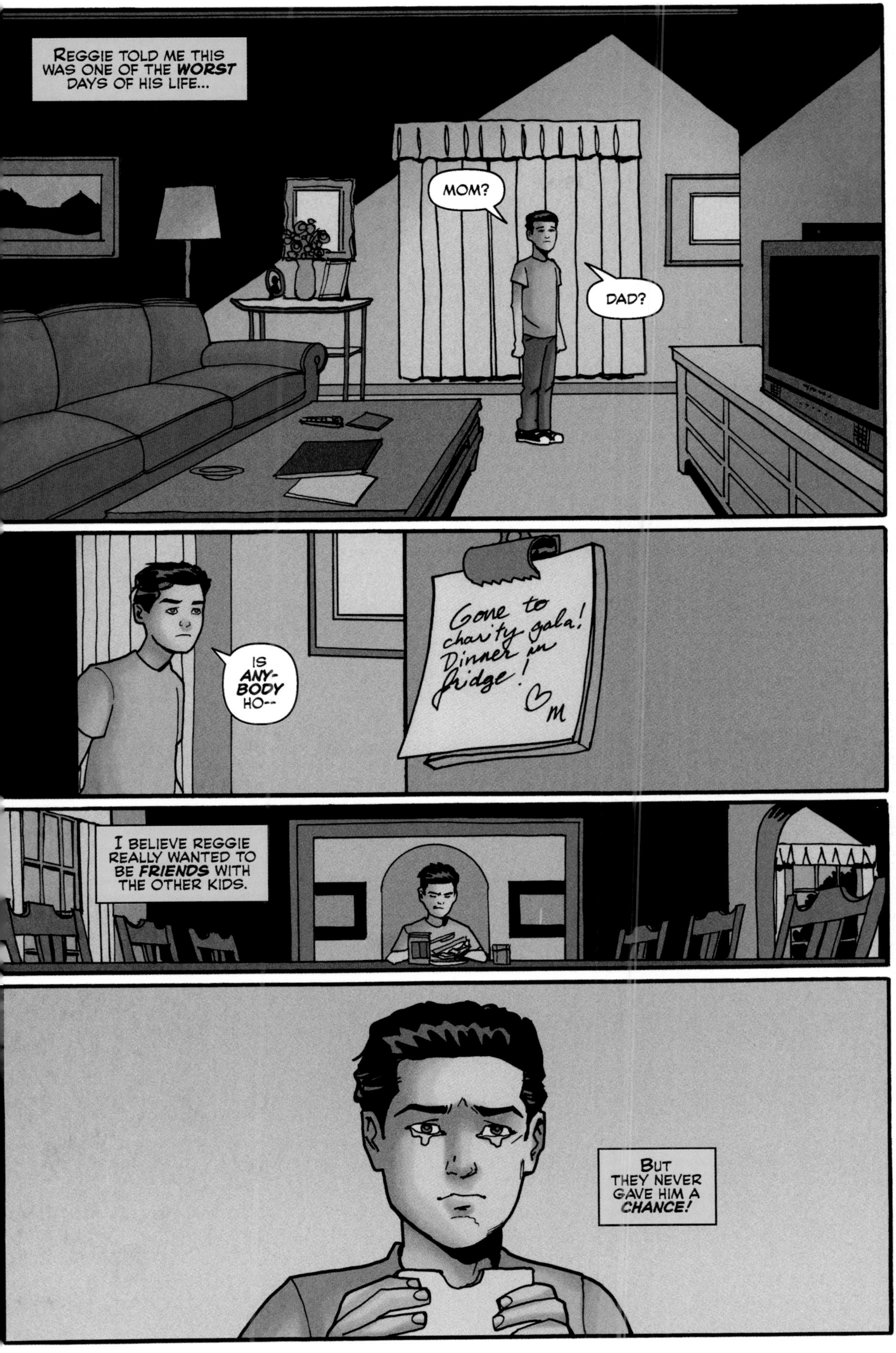
REGGIE TOLD ME THIS WAS ONE OF THE WORST DAYS OF HIS LIFE...
MOM?
DAD?
IS ANY-BODY HO--
Gone to charity gala! Dinner in fridge! M
I BELIEVE REGGIE REALLY WANTED TO BE FRIENDS WITH THE OTHER KIDS.
BUT THEY NEVER GAVE HIM A CHANCE!

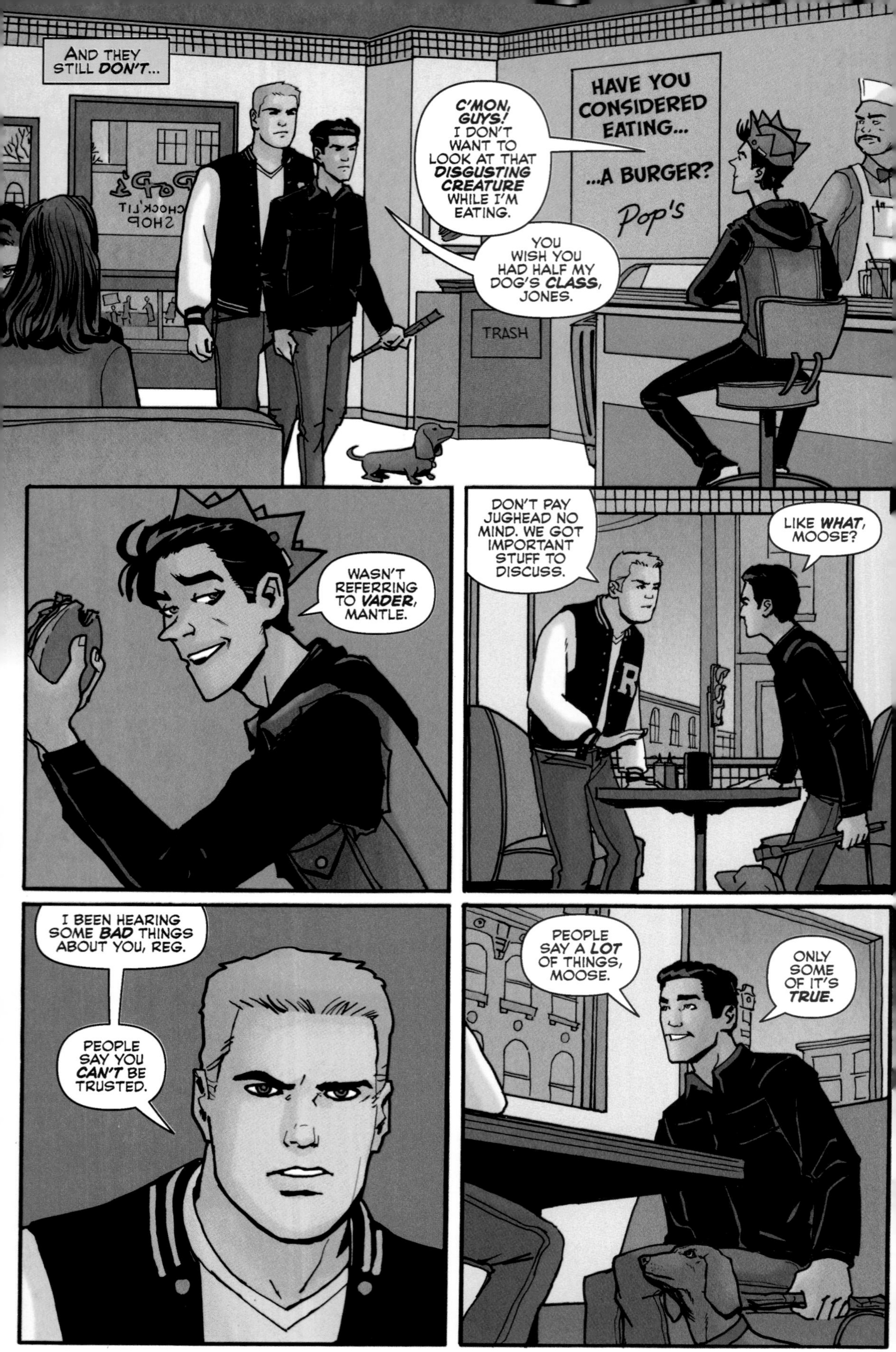
AND THEY STILL DON'T...
C'MON, GUYS! I DON'T WANT TO LOOK AT THAT DISGUSTING CREATURE WHILE I'M EATING.
HAVE YOU CONSIDERED EATING... ...A BURGER? Pop's
YOU WISH YOU HAD HALF MY DOG'S CLASS, JONES.
TRASH
WASN'T REFERRING TO VADER, MANTLE.
DON'T PAY JUGHEAD NO MIND. WE GOT IMPORTANT STUFF TO DISCUSS.
LIKE WHAT, MOOSE?
I BEEN HEARING SOME BAD THINGS ABOUT YOU, REG.
PEOPLE SAY YOU CAN'T BE TRUSTED.
PEOPLE SAY A LOT OF THINGS, MOOSE.
ONLY SOME OF IT'S TRUE.

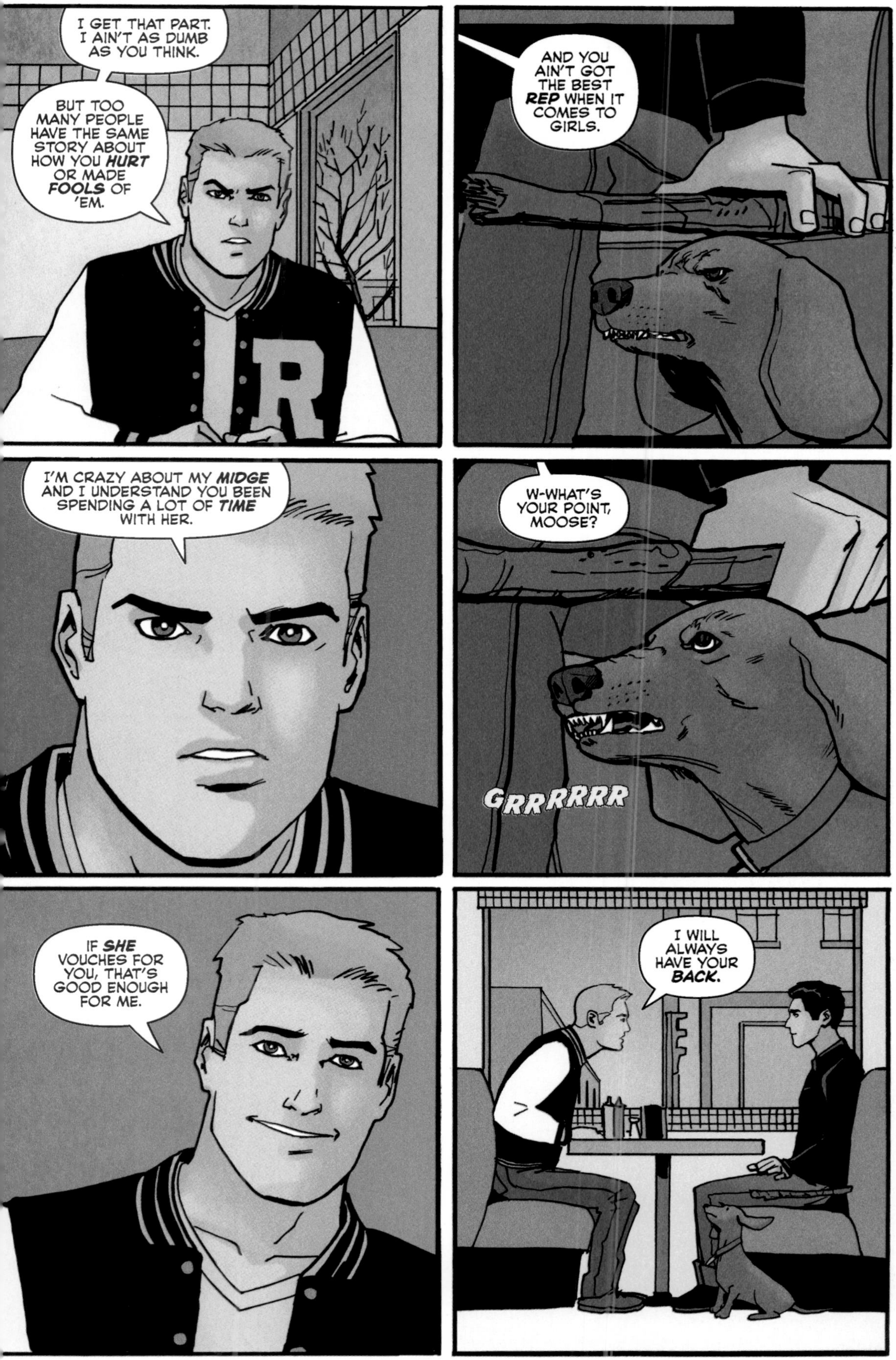
I GET THAT PART. I AIN'T AS DUMB AS YOU THINK.
BUT TOO MANY PEOPLE HAVE THE SAME STORY ABOUT HOW YOU HURT OR MADE FOOLS OF 'EM.
AND YOU AIN'T GOT THE BEST REP WHEN IT COMES TO GIRLS.
I'M CRAZY ABOUT MY MIDGE AND I UNDERSTAND YOU BEEN SPENDING A LOT OF TIME WITH HER.
W-WHAT'S YOUR POINT, MOOSE?
GRRRRRR
IF SHE VOUCHES FOR YOU, THAT'S GOOD ENOUGH FOR ME.
I WILL ALWAYS HAVE YOUR BACK.

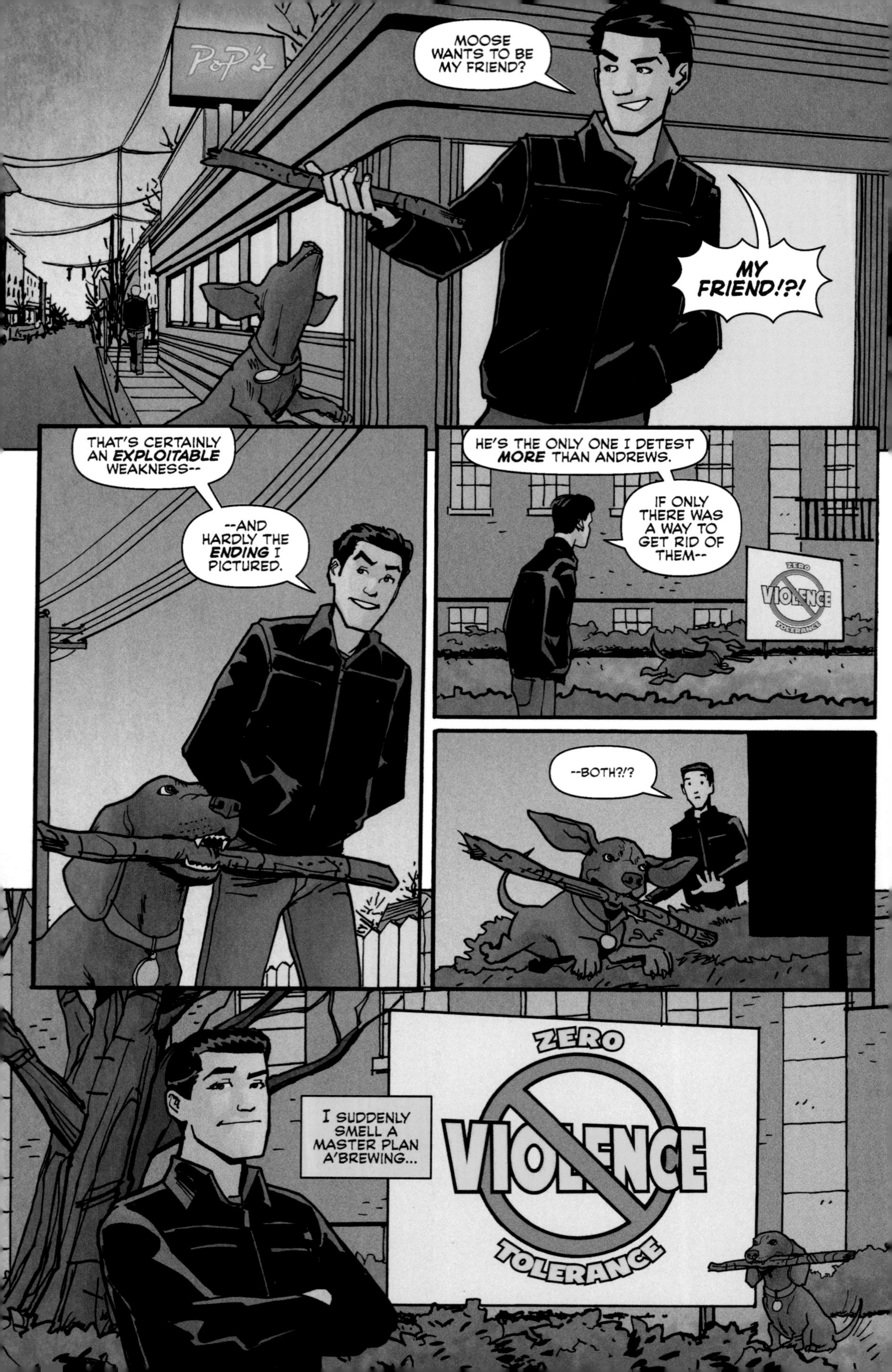
Pop's
MOOSE WANTS TO BE MY FRIEND?
MY FRIEND!?!
THAT'S CERTAINLY AN EXPLOITABLE WEAKNESS--
--AND HARDLY THE ENDING I PICTURED.
HE'S THE ONLY ONE I DETEST MORE THAN ANDREWS.
IF ONLY THERE WAS A WAY TO GET RID OF THEM--
ZERO VIOLENCE TOLERANCE
--BOTH?!?
I SUDDENLY SMELL A MASTER PLAN A'BREWING...
ZERO VIOLENCE TOLERANCE

TO BE CONTINUED...

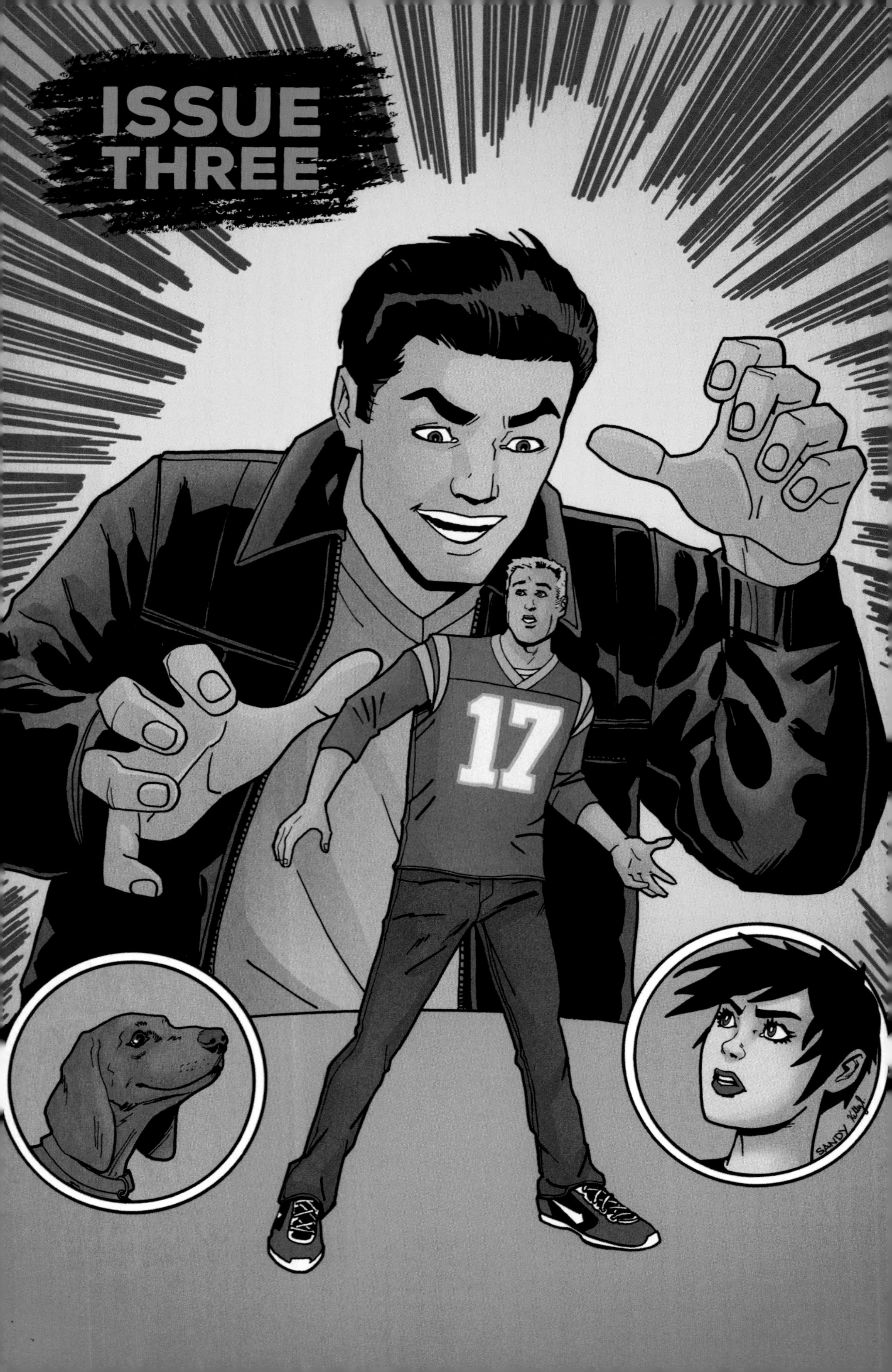
ISSUE
THREE
17

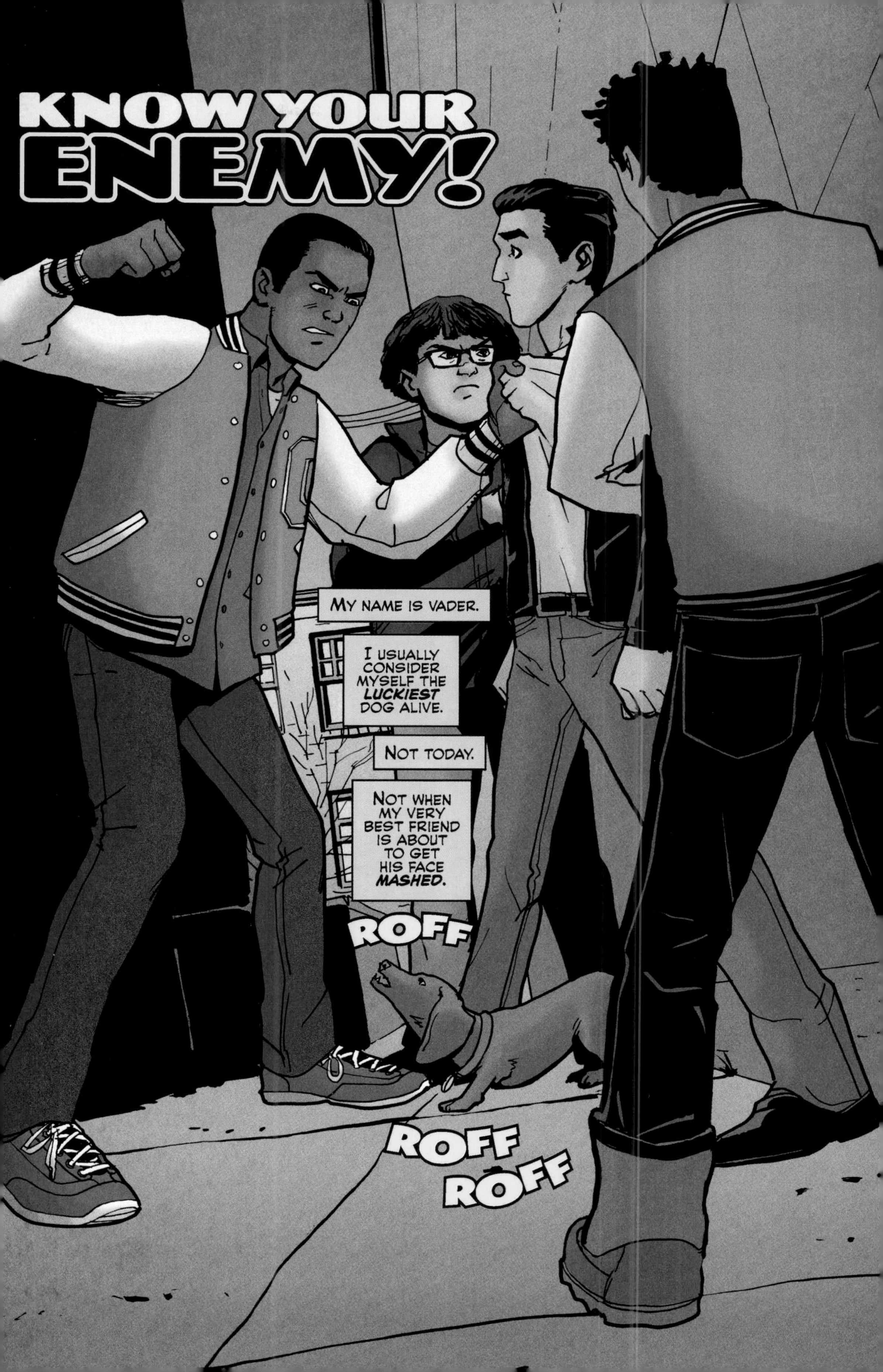
KNOW YOUR ENEMY!
MY NAME IS VADER.
I USUALLY CONSIDER MYSELF THE LUCKIEST DOG ALIVE.
NOT TODAY.
NOT WHEN MY VERY BEST FRIEND IS ABOUT TO GET HIS FACE MASHED.
ROFF
ROFF
ROFF

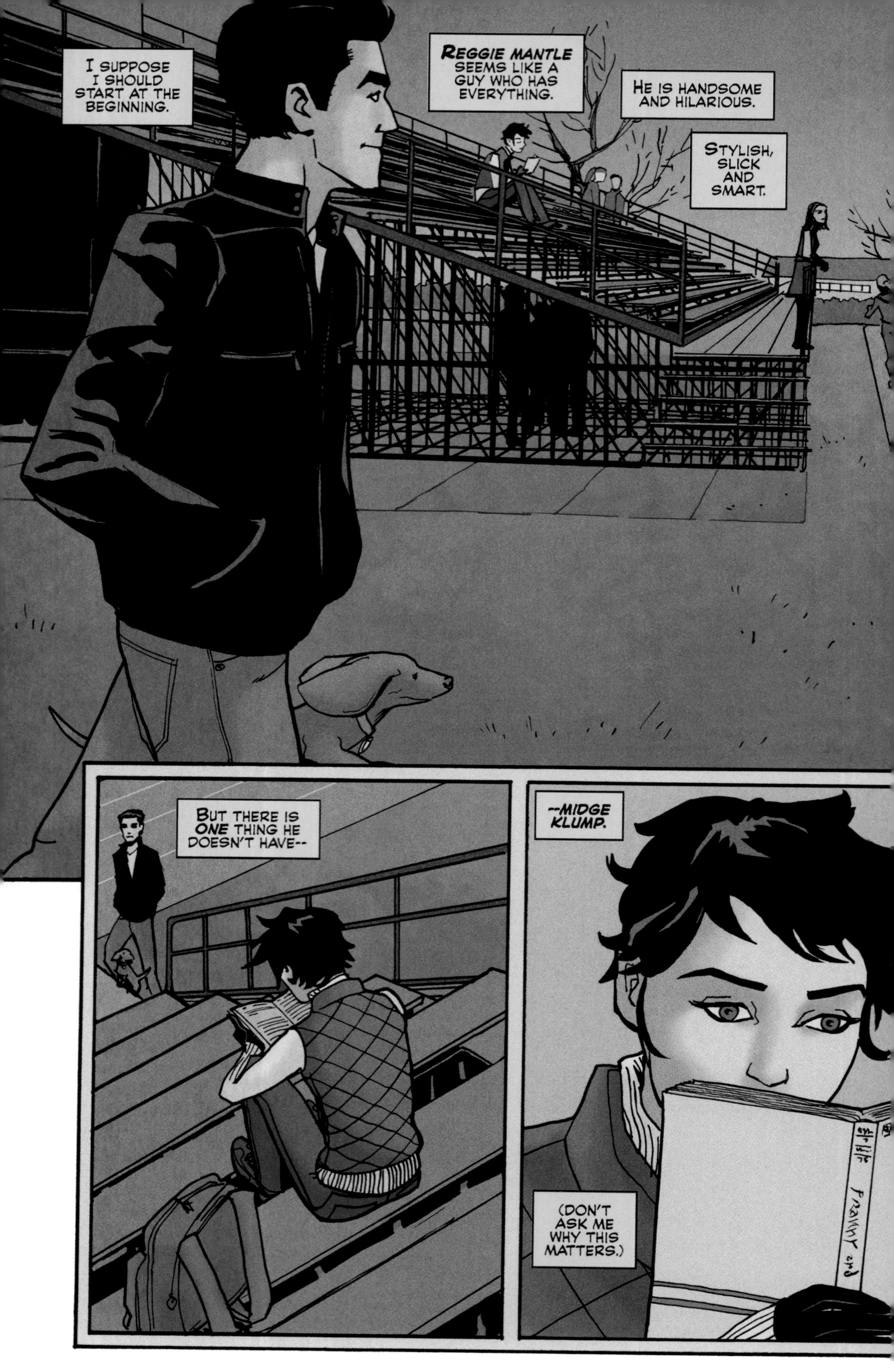
I SUPPOSE I SHOULD START AT THE BEGINNING.
REGGIE MANTLE SEEMS LIKE A GUY WHO HAS EVERYTHING.
HE IS HANDSOME AND HILARIOUS.
STYLISH, SLICK AND SMART.
BUT THERE IS ONE THING HE DOESN'T HAVE--
--MIDGE KLUMP.
(DON'T ASK ME WHY THIS MATTERS.)

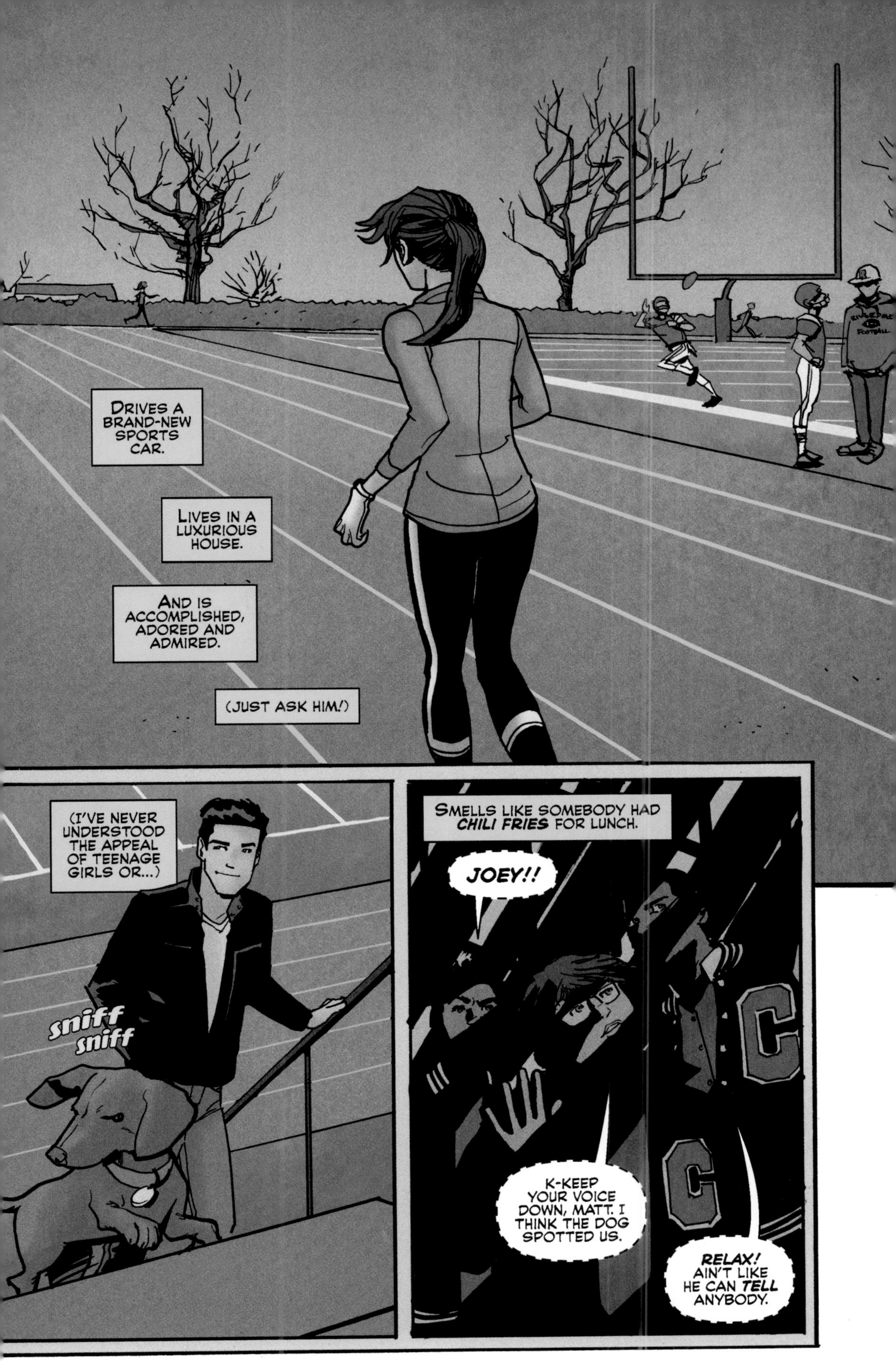

DRIVES A BRAND-NEW SPORTS CAR.
LIVES IN A LUXURIOUS HOUSE.
AND IS ACCOMPLISHED, ADORED AND ADMIRED.
(JUST ASK HIM!)
(I'VE NEVER UNDERSTOOD THE APPEAL OF TEENAGE GIRLS OR...)
sniff sniff
SMELLS LIKE SOMEBODY HAD CHILI FRIES FOR LUNCH.
JOEY!!
K-KEEP YOUR VOICE DOWN, MATT. I THINK THE DOG SPOTTED US.
RELAX! AIN'T LIKE HE CAN TELL ANYBODY.

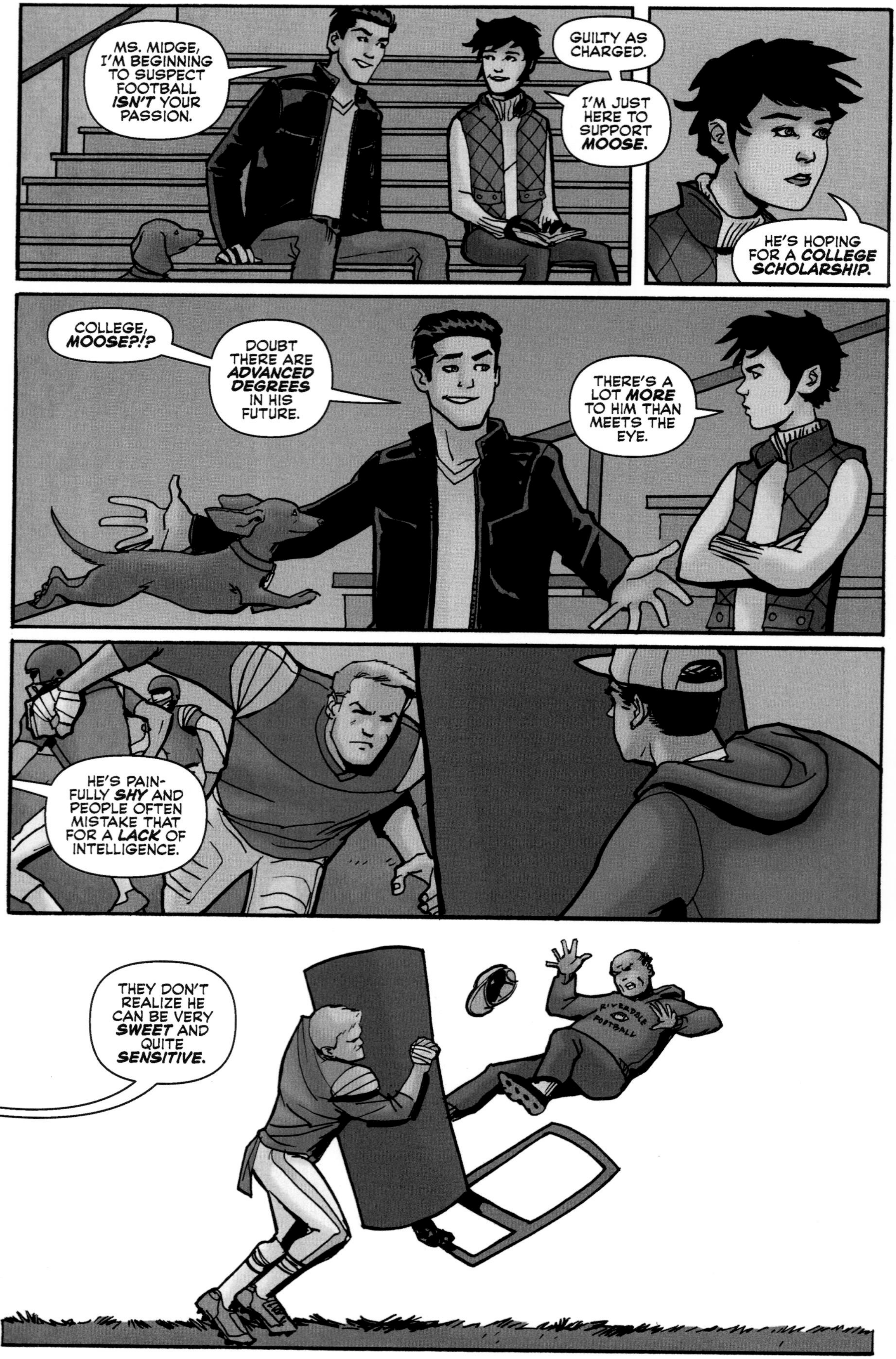
MS. MIDGE, I'M BEGINNING TO SUSPECT FOOTBALL ISN'T YOUR PASSION.
GUILTY AS CHARGED.
I'M JUST HERE TO SUPPORT MOOSE.
HE'S HOPING FOR A COLLEGE SCHOLARSHIP.
COLLEGE, MOOSE?!?
DOUBT THERE ARE ADVANCED DEGREES IN HIS FUTURE.
THERE'S A LOT MORE TO HIM THAN MEETS THE EYE.
HE'S PAIN-FULLY SHY AND PEOPLE OFTEN MISTAKE THAT FOR A LACK OF INTELLIGENCE.
THEY DON'T REALIZE HE CAN BE VERY SWEET AND QUITE SENSITIVE.
RIVERDALE FOOTBALL

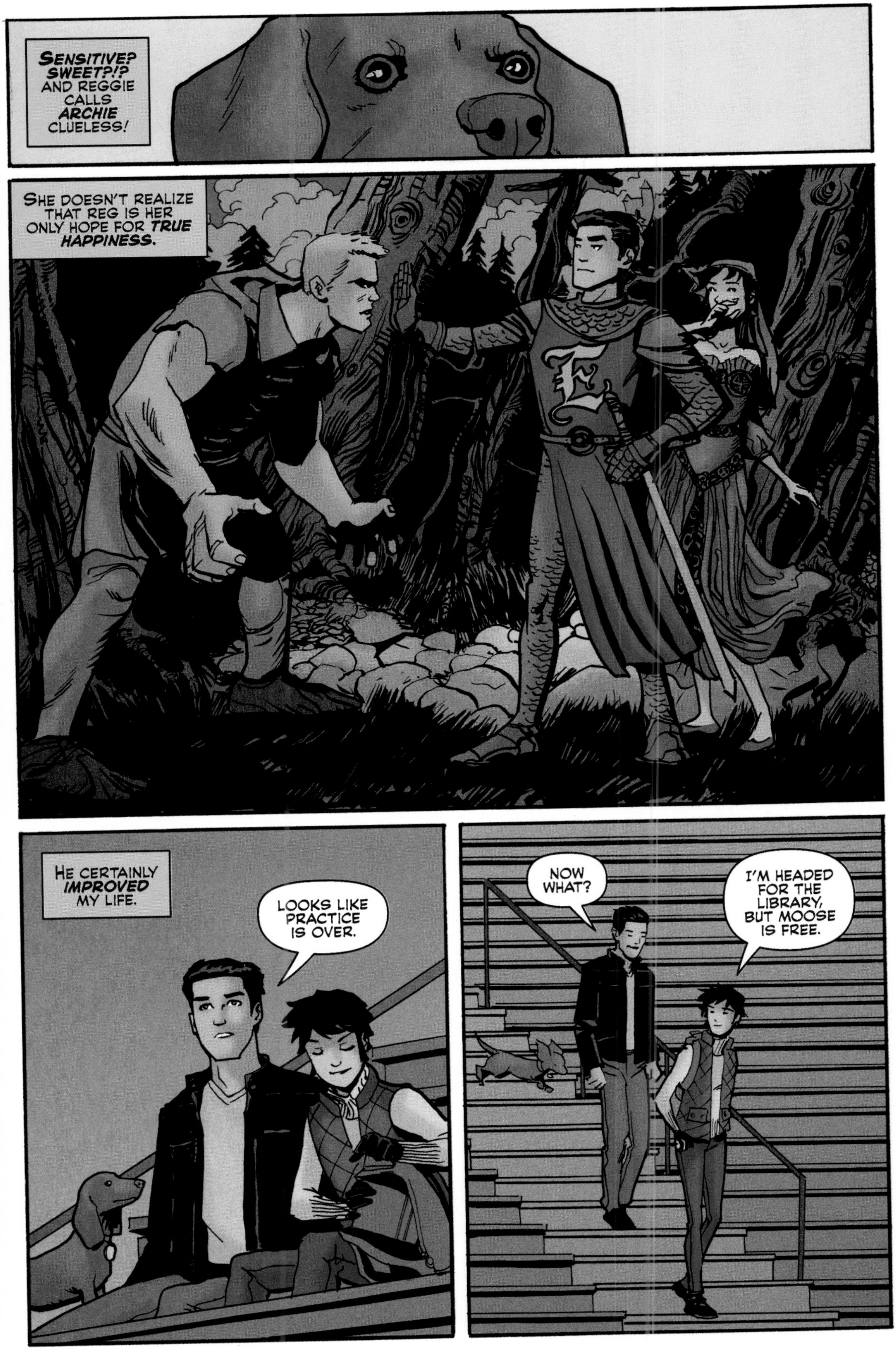
SENSITIVE? SWEET?!? AND REGGIE CALLS ARCHIE CLUELESS!
SHE DOESN'T REALIZE THAT REG IS HER ONLY HOPE FOR TRUE HAPPINESS.
HE CERTAINLY IMPROVED MY LIFE.
LOOKS LIKE PRACTICE IS OVER.
NOW WHAT?
I'M HEADED FOR THE LIBRARY, BUT MOOSE IS FREE.

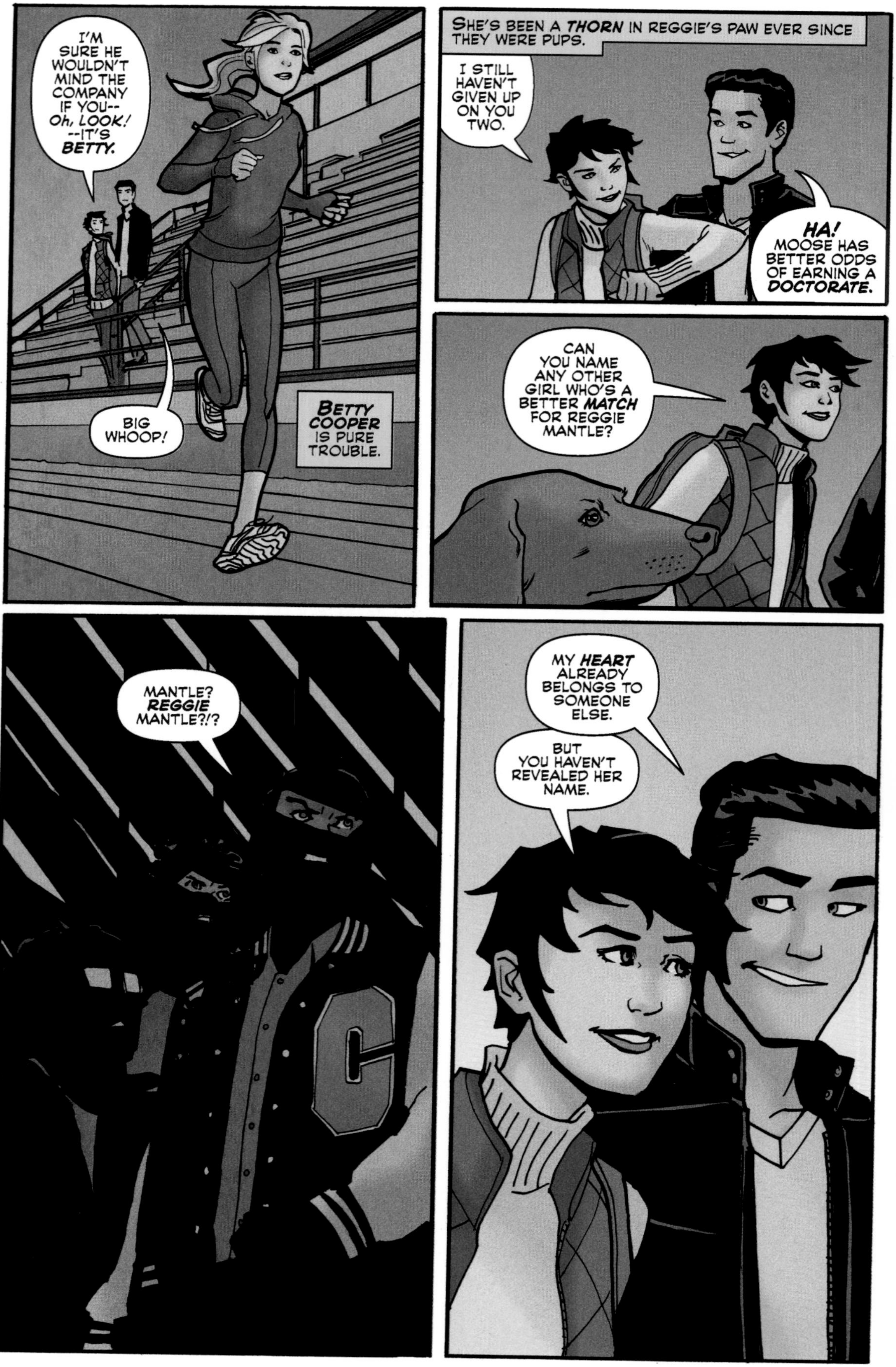
I'M SURE HE WOULDN'T MIND THE COMPANY IF YOU-- Oh, LOOK! --IT'S BETTY.
BIG WHOOP!
BETTY COOPER IS PURE TROUBLE.
SHE'S BEEN A THORN IN REGGIE'S PAW EVER SINCE THEY WERE PUPS.
I STILL HAVEN'T GIVEN UP ON YOU TWO.
HA! MOOSE HAS BETTER ODDS OF EARNING A DOCTORATE.
CAN YOU NAME ANY OTHER GIRL WHO'S A BETTER MATCH FOR REGGIE MANTLE?
MANTLE? REGGIE MANTLE?!?
MY HEART ALREADY BELONGS TO SOMEONE ELSE.
BUT YOU HAVEN'T REVEALED HER NAME.

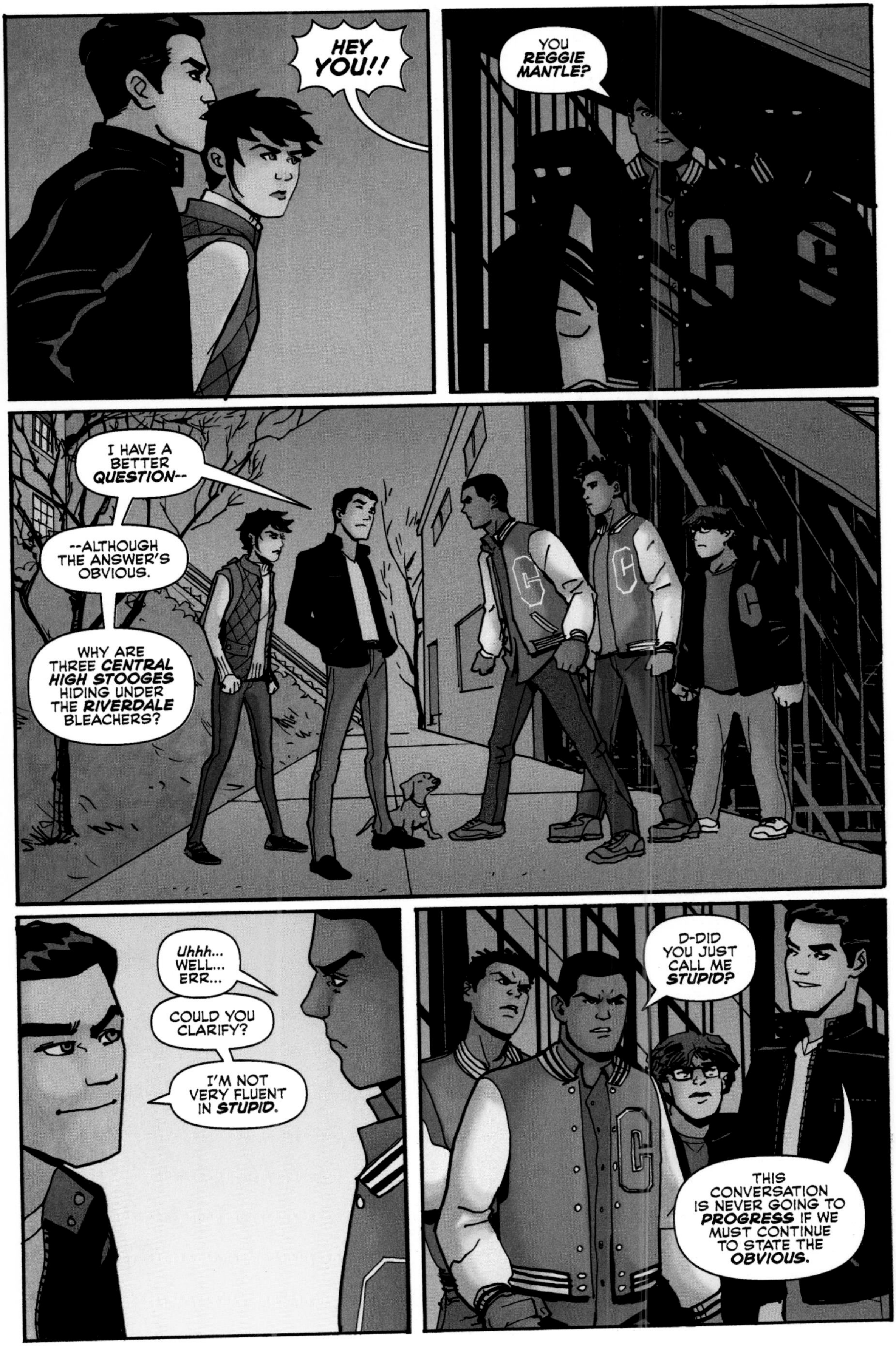
HEY YOU!!
YOU REGGIE MANTLE?
I HAVE A BETTER QUESTION--
--ALTHOUGH THE ANSWER'S OBVIOUS.
WHY ARE THREE CENTRAL HIGH STOOGES HIDING UNDER THE RIVERDALE BLEACHERS?
Uhhh... WELL... ERR...
COULD YOU CLARIFY?
I'M NOT VERY FLUENT IN STUPID.
D-DID YOU JUST CALL ME STUPID?
THIS CONVERSATION IS NEVER GOING TO PROGRESS IF WE MUST CONTINUE TO STATE THE OBVIOUS.

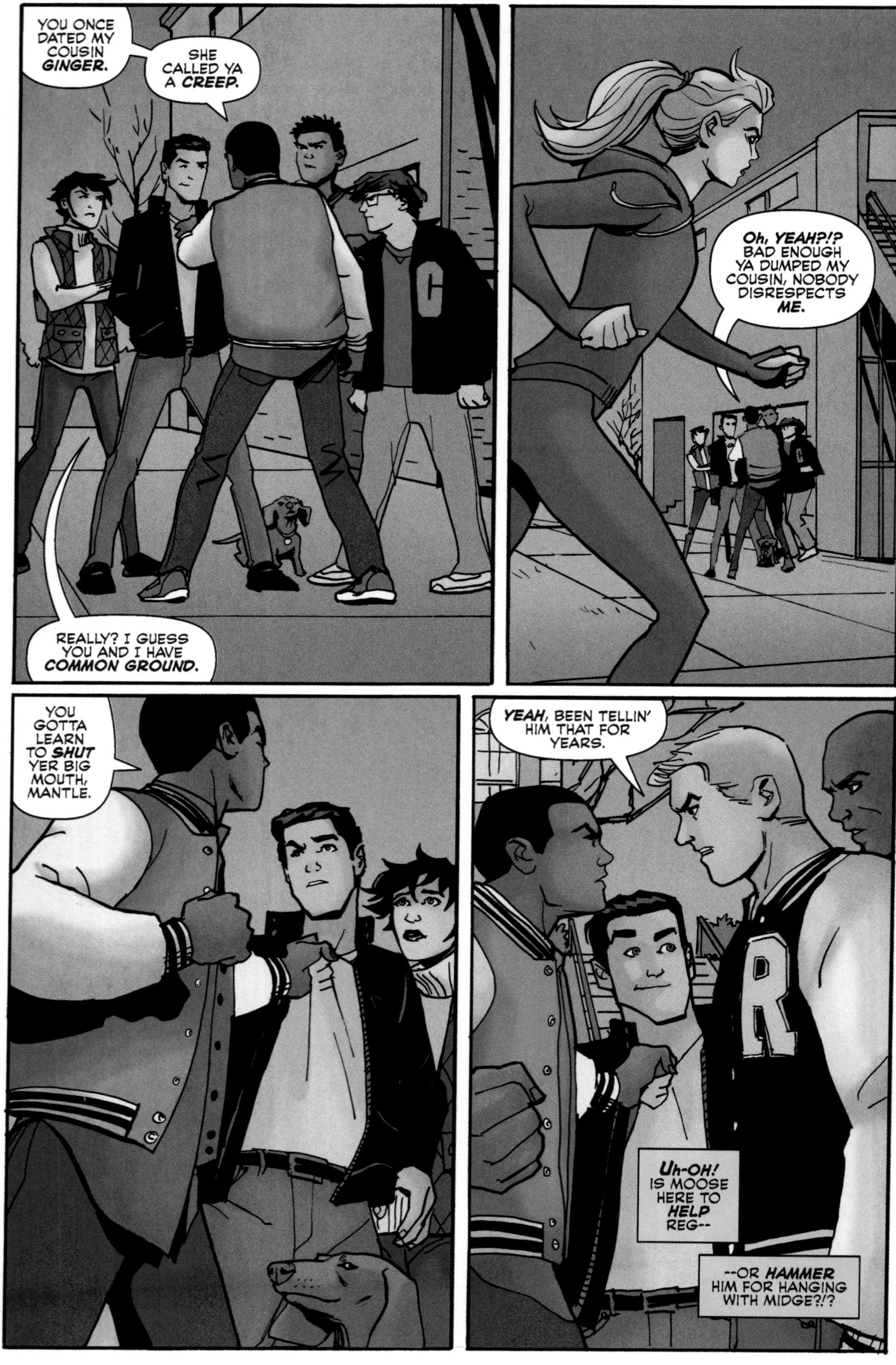
YOU ONCE DATED MY COUSIN **GINGER**.
SHE CALLED YA A **CREEP**.
REALLY? I GUESS YOU AND I HAVE **COMMON GROUND**.
Oh, YEAH?!? BAD ENOUGH YA DUMPED MY COUSIN, NOBODY DISRESPECTS **ME**.
YOU GOTTA LEARN TO **SHUT** YER BIG MOUTH, MANTLE.
YEAH, BEEN TELLIN' HIM THAT FOR YEARS.
Uh-OH! IS MOOSE HERE TO **HELP** REG--
--OR **HAMMER** HIM FOR HANGING WITH MIDGE?!?

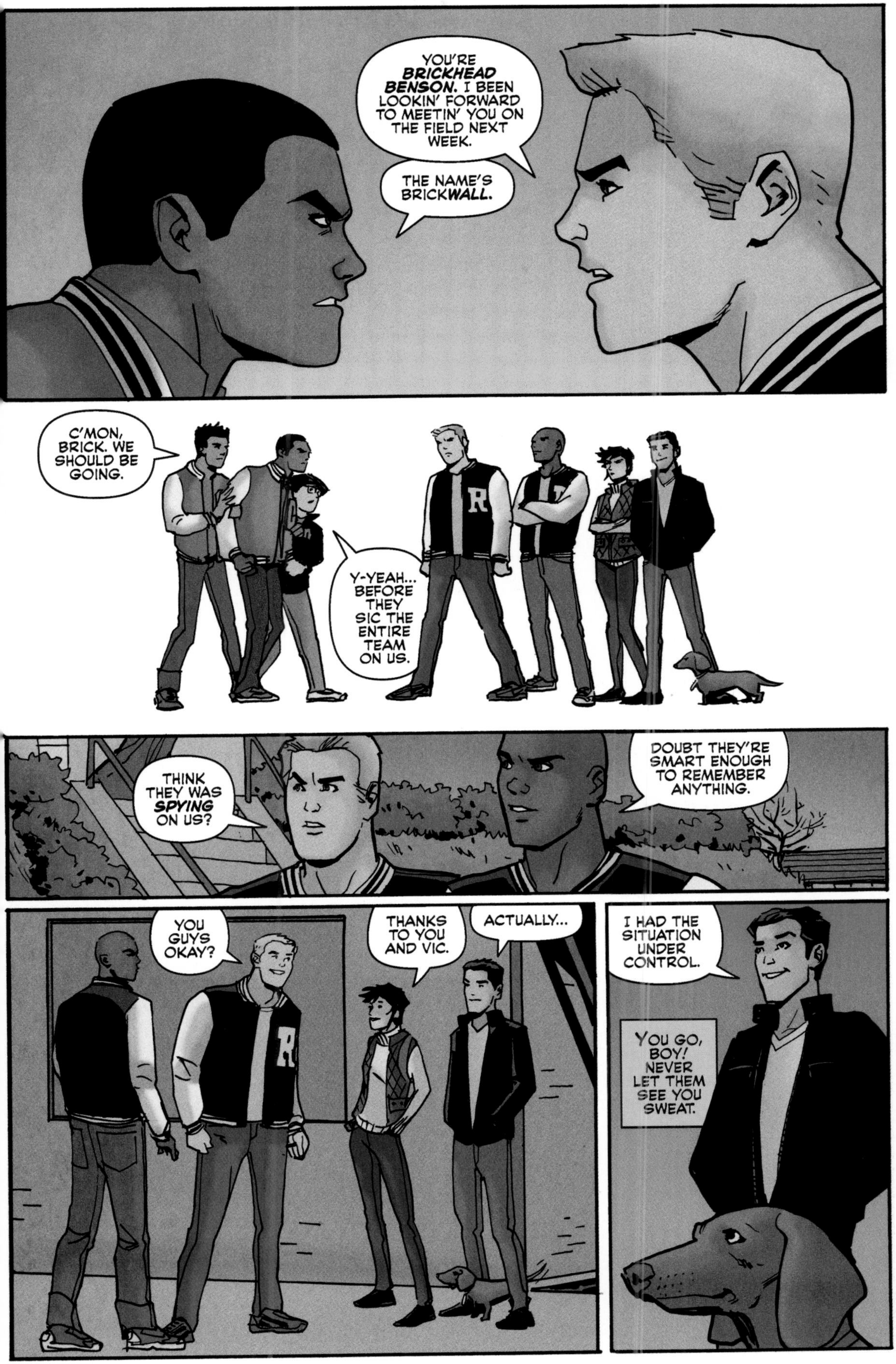
YOU'RE **BRICKHEAD BENSON.** I BEEN LOOKIN' FORWARD TO MEETIN' YOU ON THE FIELD NEXT WEEK.
THE NAME'S BRICK**WALL.**
C'MON, BRICK. WE SHOULD BE GOING.
Y-YEAH... BEFORE THEY SIC THE ENTIRE TEAM ON US.
THINK THEY WAS ***SPYING*** ON US?
DOUBT THEY'RE SMART ENOUGH TO REMEMBER ANYTHING.
YOU GUYS OKAY?
THANKS TO YOU AND VIC.
ACTUALLY...
I HAD THE SITUATION UNDER CONTROL.
YOU GO, BOY! NEVER LET THEM SEE YOU SWEAT.

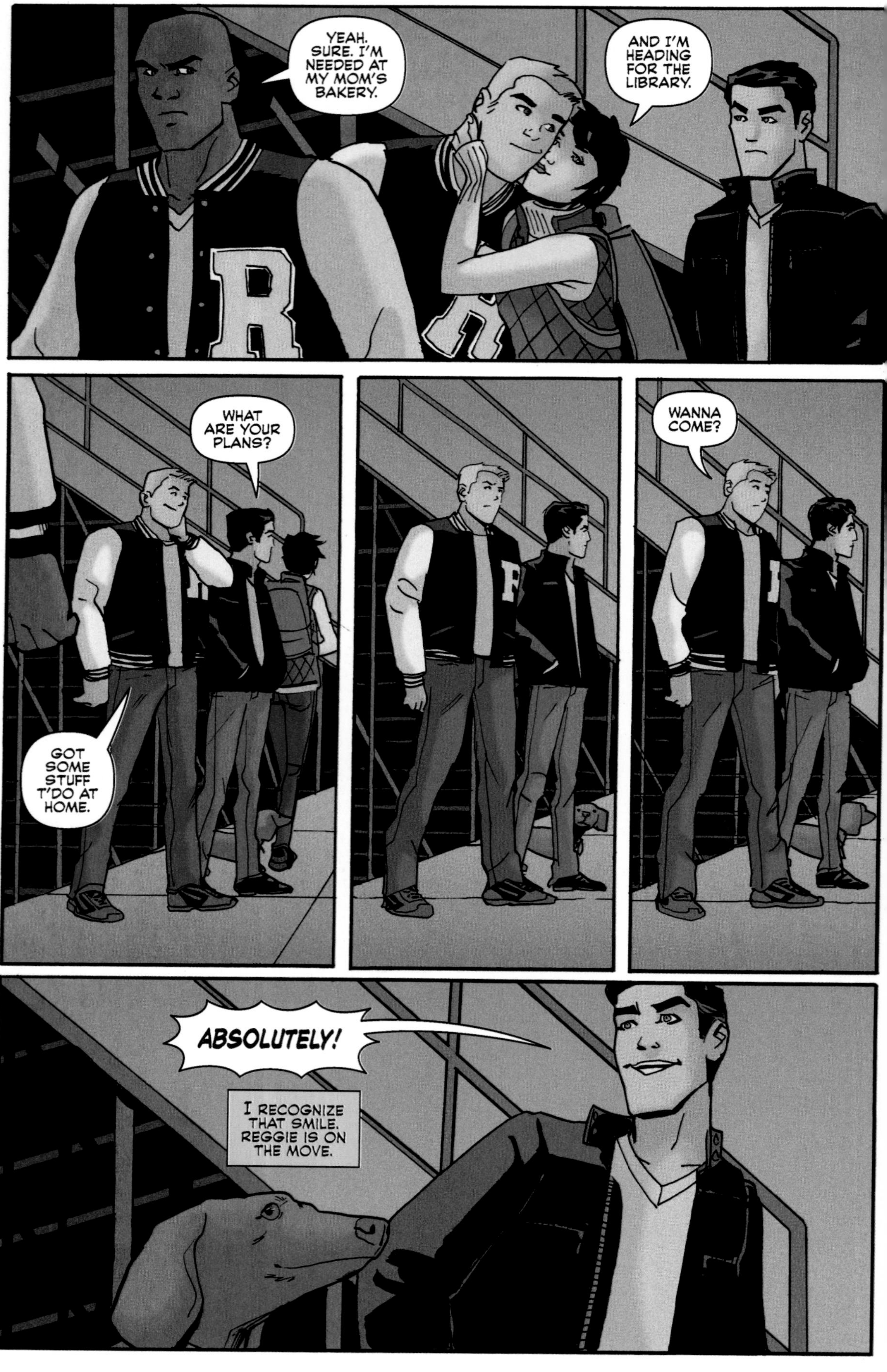
YEAH. SURE. I'M NEEDED AT MY MOM'S BAKERY.
AND I'M HEADING FOR THE LIBRARY.
WHAT ARE YOUR PLANS?
GOT SOME STUFF T'DO AT HOME.
WANNA COME?
ABSOLUTELY!
I RECOGNIZE THAT SMILE. REGGIE IS ON THE MOVE.

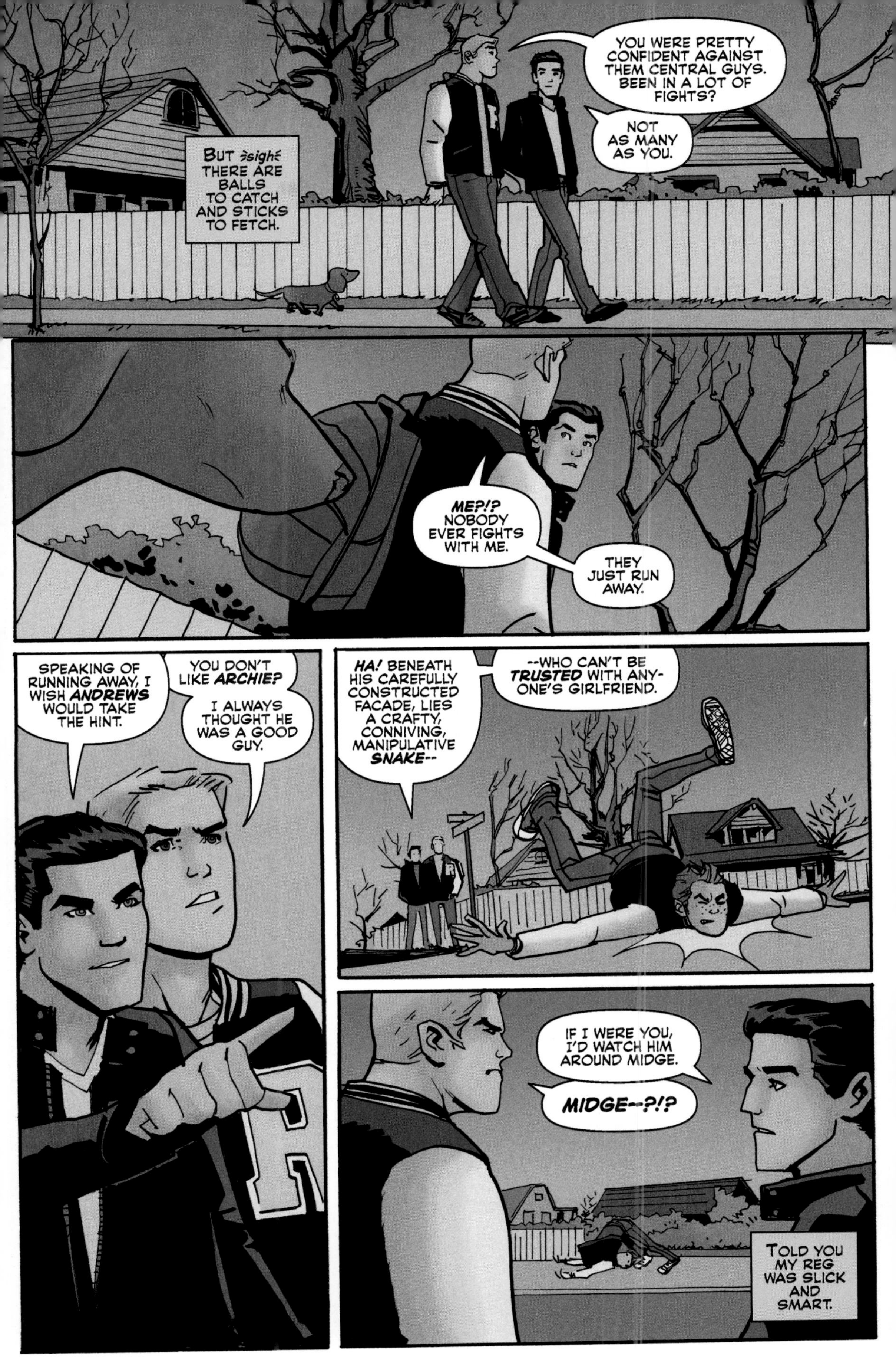

YOU WERE PRETTY CONFIDENT AGAINST THEM CENTRAL GUYS. BEEN IN A LOT OF FIGHTS?
NOT AS MANY AS YOU.
BUT ≥sigh≤ THERE ARE BALLS TO CATCH AND STICKS TO FETCH.
ME?!? NOBODY EVER FIGHTS WITH ME.
THEY JUST RUN AWAY.
SPEAKING OF RUNNING AWAY, I WISH ANDREWS WOULD TAKE THE HINT.
YOU DON'T LIKE ARCHIE?
I ALWAYS THOUGHT HE WAS A GOOD GUY.
HA! BENEATH HIS CAREFULLY CONSTRUCTED FACADE, LIES A CRAFTY, CONNIVING, MANIPULATIVE SNAKE--
--WHO CAN'T BE TRUSTED WITH ANYONE'S GIRLFRIEND.
IF I WERE YOU, I'D WATCH HIM AROUND MIDGE.
MIDGE--?!?
TOLD YOU MY REG WAS SLICK AND SMART.

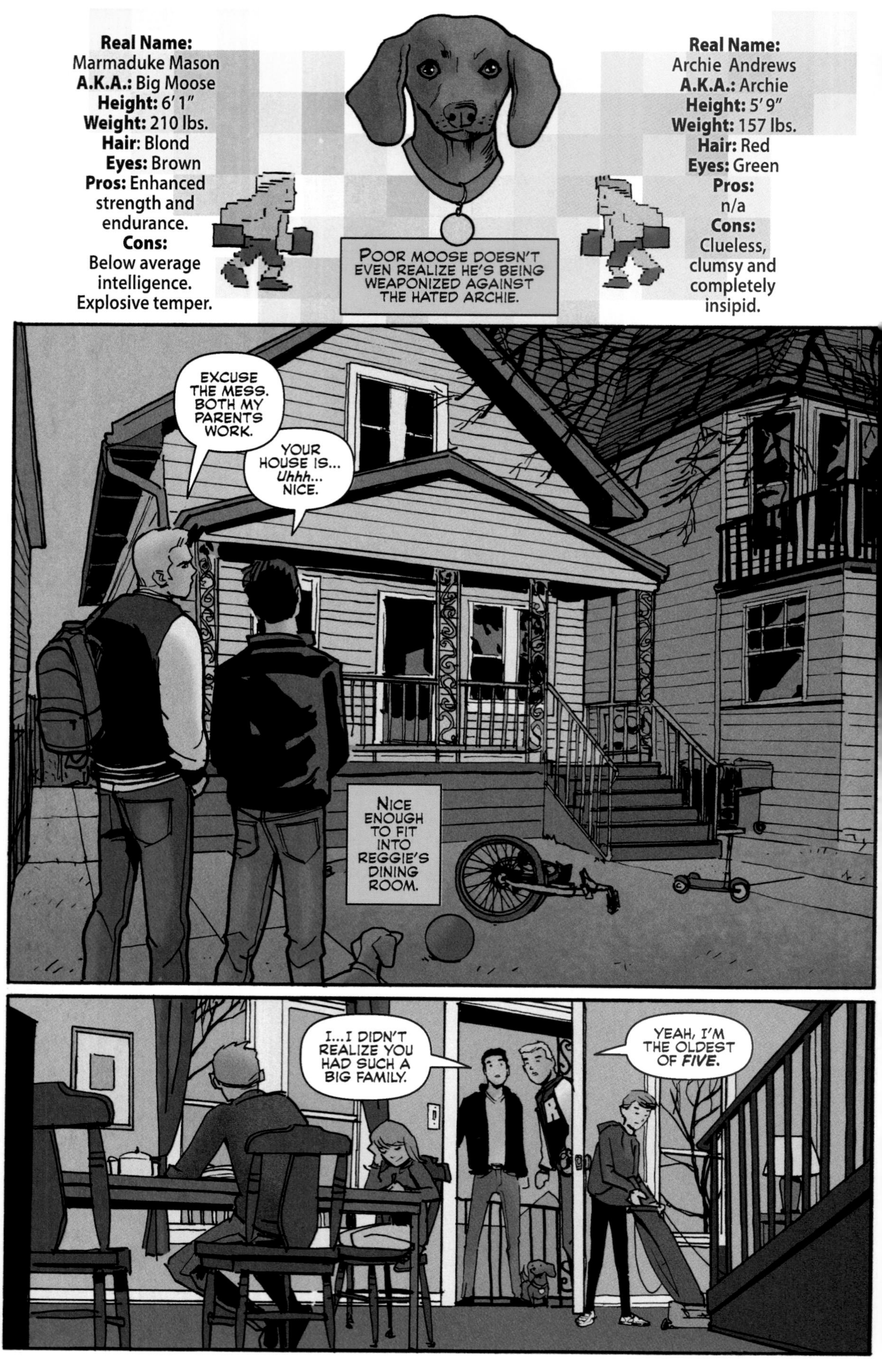
Real Name: Marmaduke Mason
A.K.A.: Big Moose
Height: 6′ 1″
Weight: 210 lbs.
Hair: Blond
Eyes: Brown
Pros: Enhanced strength and endurance.
Cons: Below average intelligence. Explosive temper.
POOR MOOSE DOESN'T EVEN REALIZE HE'S BEING WEAPONIZED AGAINST THE HATED ARCHIE.
Real Name: Archie Andrews
A.K.A.: Archie
Height: 5′ 9″
Weight: 157 lbs.
Hair: Red
Eyes: Green
Pros: n/a
Cons: Clueless, clumsy and completely insipid.
EXCUSE THE MESS. BOTH MY PARENTS WORK.
YOUR HOUSE IS... *Uhhh*... NICE.
NICE ENOUGH TO FIT INTO REGGIE'S DINING ROOM.
I...I DIDN'T REALIZE YOU HAD SUCH A BIG FAMILY.
YEAH, I'M THE OLDEST OF *FIVE*.

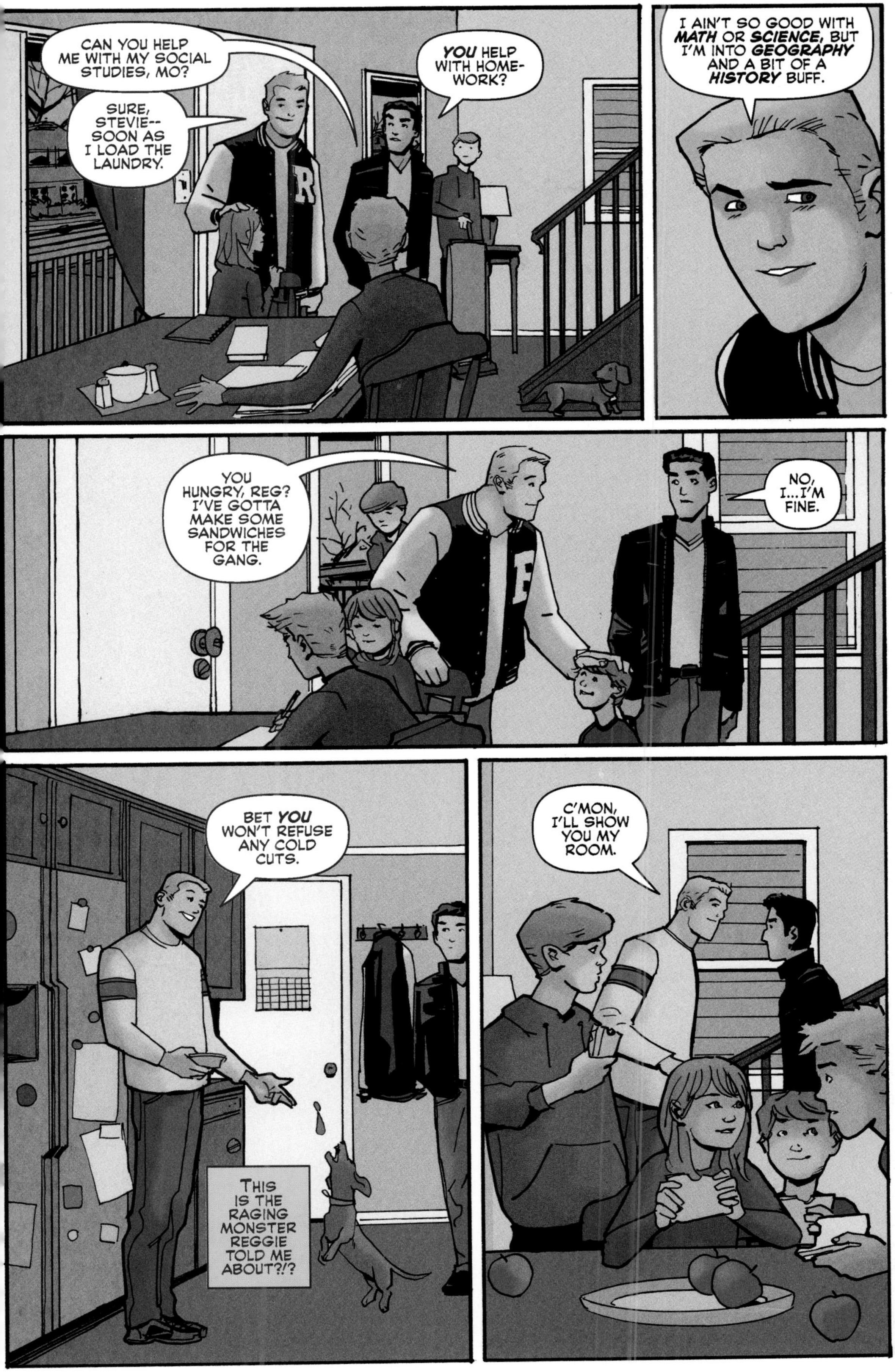

CAN YOU HELP ME WITH MY SOCIAL STUDIES, MO?
SURE, STEVIE-- SOON AS I LOAD THE LAUNDRY.
YOU HELP WITH HOME-WORK?
I AIN'T SO GOOD WITH *MATH* OR *SCIENCE*, BUT I'M INTO *GEOGRAPHY* AND A BIT OF A *HISTORY* BUFF.
YOU HUNGRY, REG? I'VE GOTTA MAKE SOME SANDWICHES FOR THE GANG.
NO, I...I'M FINE.
BET *YOU* WON'T REFUSE ANY COLD CUTS.
THIS IS THE RAGING MONSTER REGGIE TOLD ME ABOUT?!?
C'MON, I'LL SHOW YOU MY ROOM.

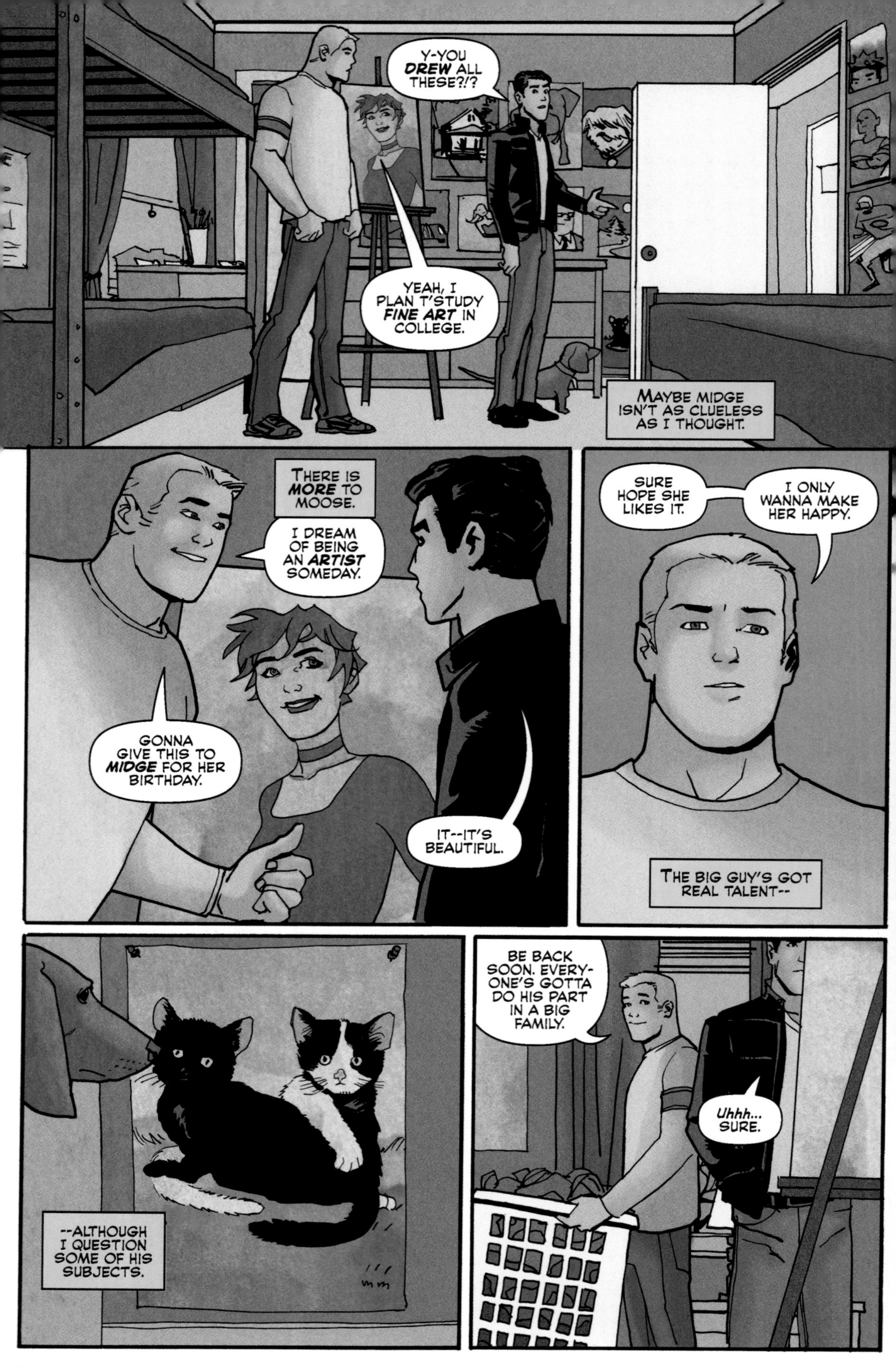
Y-YOU **DREW** ALL THESE?!?
YEAH, I PLAN T'STUDY **FINE ART** IN COLLEGE.
MAYBE MIDGE ISN'T AS CLUELESS AS I THOUGHT.
THERE IS **MORE** TO MOOSE.
I DREAM OF BEING AN **ARTIST** SOMEDAY.
GONNA GIVE THIS TO **MIDGE** FOR HER BIRTHDAY.
IT--IT'S BEAUTIFUL.
SURE HOPE SHE LIKES IT.
I ONLY WANNA MAKE HER HAPPY.
THE BIG GUY'S GOT REAL TALENT--
--ALTHOUGH I QUESTION SOME OF HIS SUBJECTS.
BE BACK SOON. EVERY-ONE'S GOTTA DO HIS PART IN A BIG FAMILY.
Uhhh... SURE.

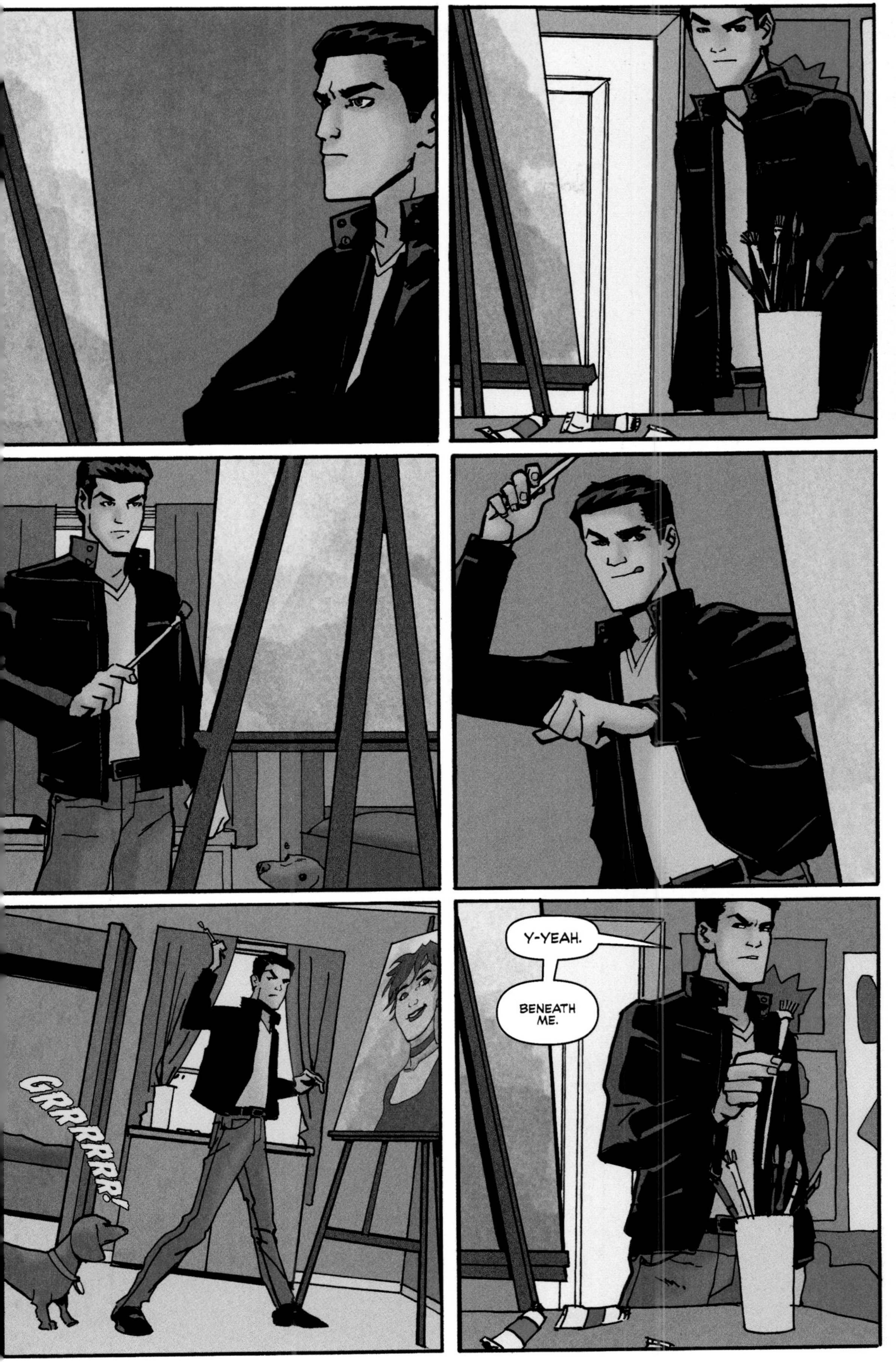
GRRRRRR!
Y-YEAH.
BENEATH ME.

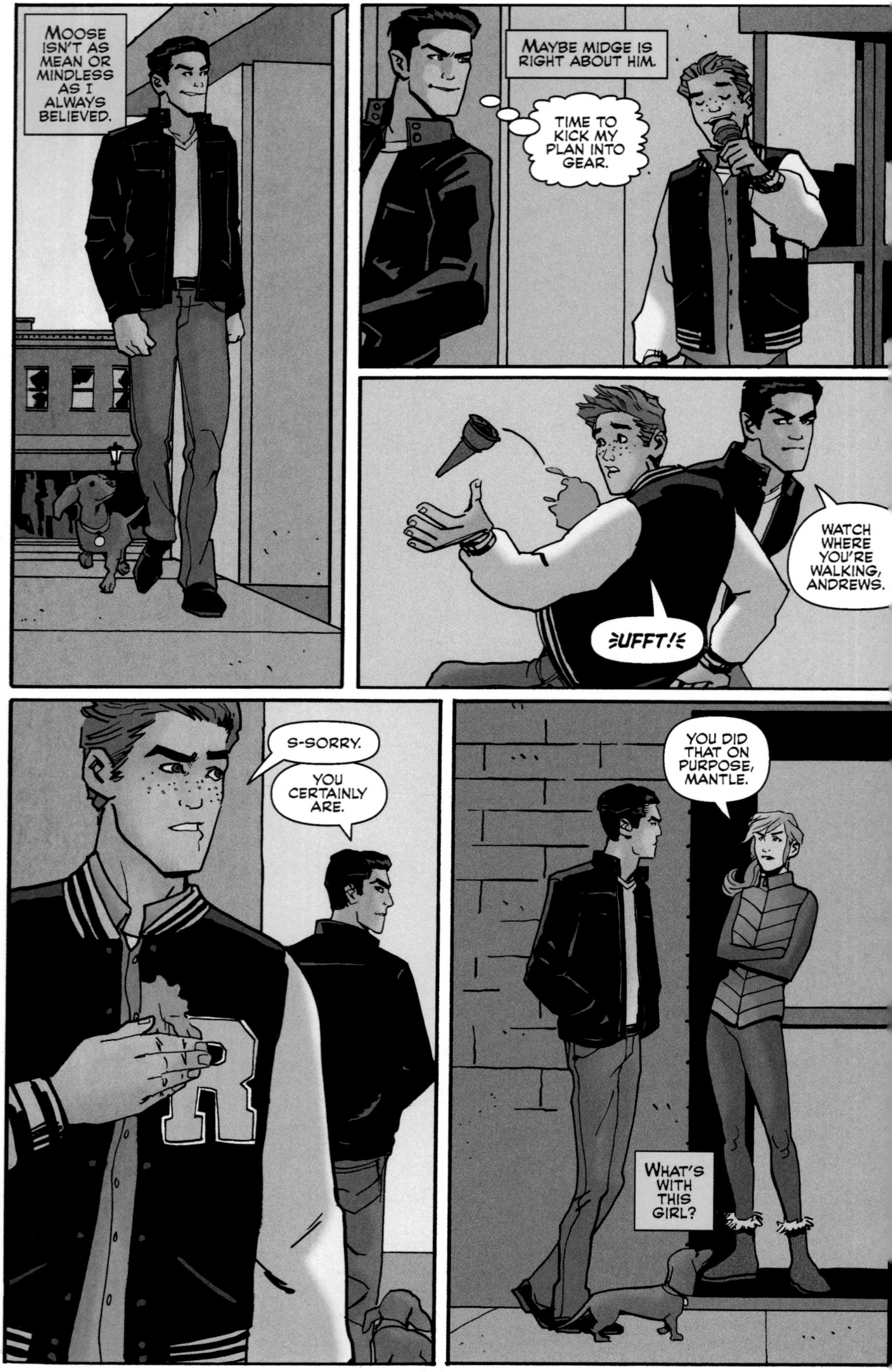
MOOSE ISN'T AS MEAN OR MINDLESS AS I ALWAYS BELIEVED.
MAYBE MIDGE IS RIGHT ABOUT HIM.
TIME TO KICK MY PLAN INTO GEAR.
WATCH WHERE YOU'RE WALKING, ANDREWS.
UFFT!
S-SORRY.
YOU CERTAINLY ARE.
YOU DID THAT ON PURPOSE, MANTLE.
WHAT'S WITH THIS GIRL?

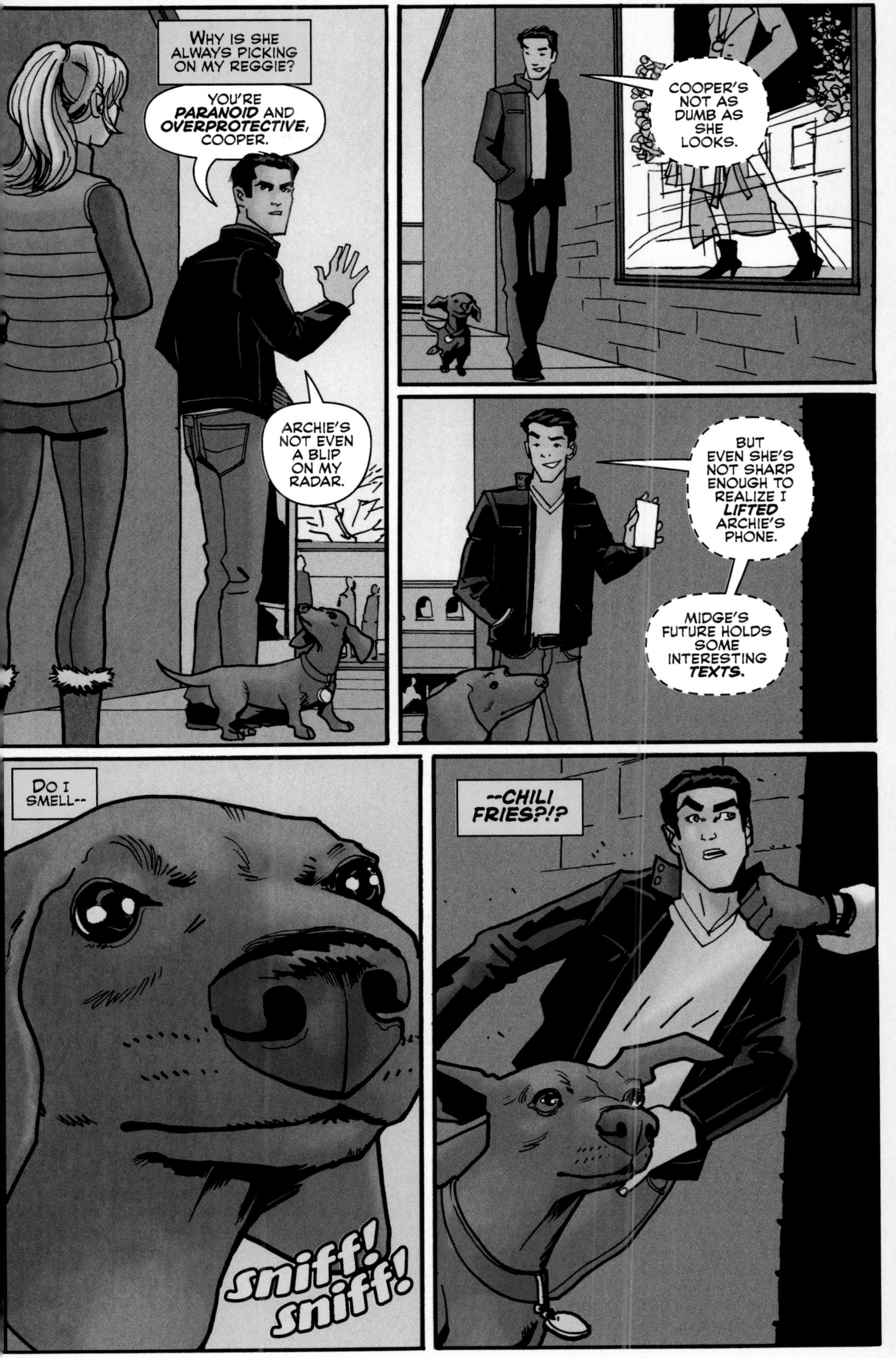
WHY IS SHE ALWAYS PICKING ON MY REGGIE?
YOU'RE **PARANOID** AND **OVERPROTECTIVE**, COOPER.
ARCHIE'S NOT EVEN A BLIP ON MY RADAR.
COOPER'S NOT AS DUMB AS SHE LOOKS.
BUT EVEN SHE'S NOT SHARP ENOUGH TO REALIZE I **LIFTED** ARCHIE'S PHONE.
MIDGE'S FUTURE HOLDS SOME INTERESTING **TEXTS**.
DO I SMELL--
sniff! sniff!
--CHILI FRIES?!?

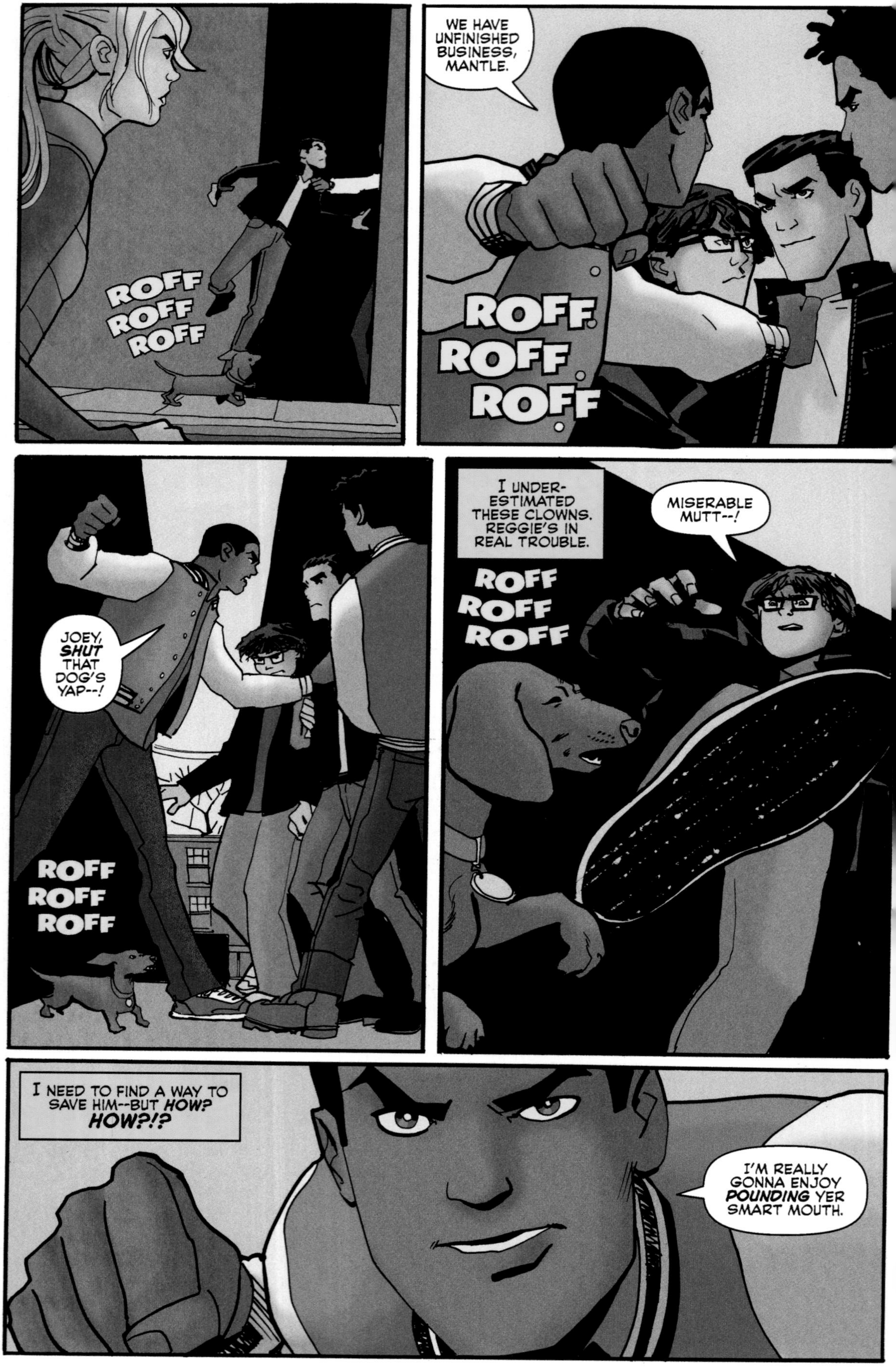

ROFF
ROFF
ROFF
WE HAVE UNFINISHED BUSINESS, MANTLE.
ROFF
ROFF
ROFF
JOEY, **SHUT** THAT DOG'S YAP--!
ROFF
ROFF
ROFF
I UNDER-ESTIMATED THESE CLOWNS. REGGIE'S IN REAL TROUBLE.
MISERABLE MUTT--!
ROFF
ROFF
ROFF
I NEED TO FIND A WAY TO SAVE HIM--BUT ***HOW? HOW?!?***
I'M REALLY GONNA ENJOY ***POUNDING*** YER SMART MOUTH.

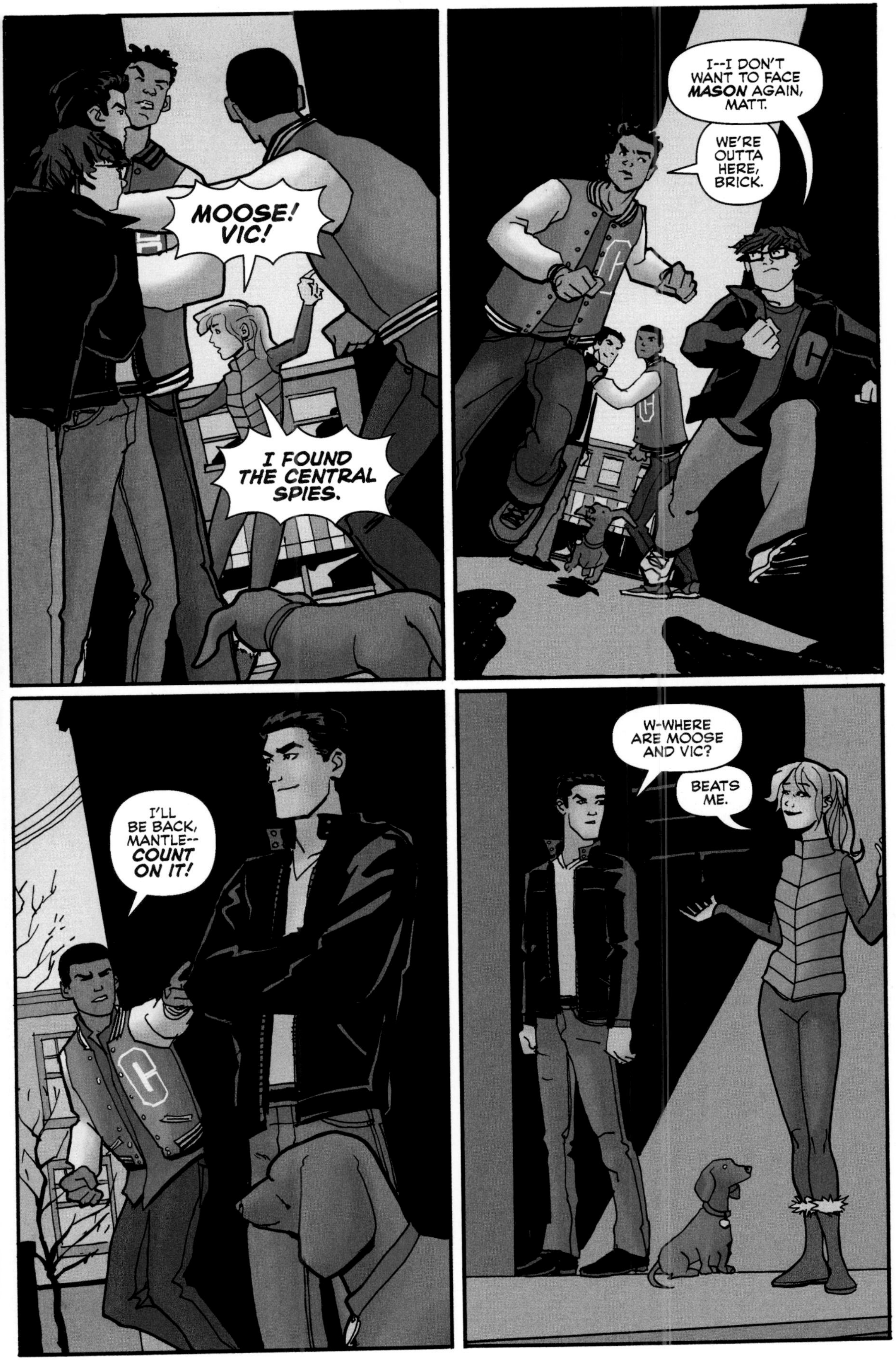
MOOSE! VIC!
I FOUND THE CENTRAL SPIES.
I--I DON'T WANT TO FACE MASON AGAIN, MATT.
WE'RE OUTTA HERE, BRICK.
I'LL BE BACK, MANTLE-- COUNT ON IT!
W-WHERE ARE MOOSE AND VIC?
BEATS ME.

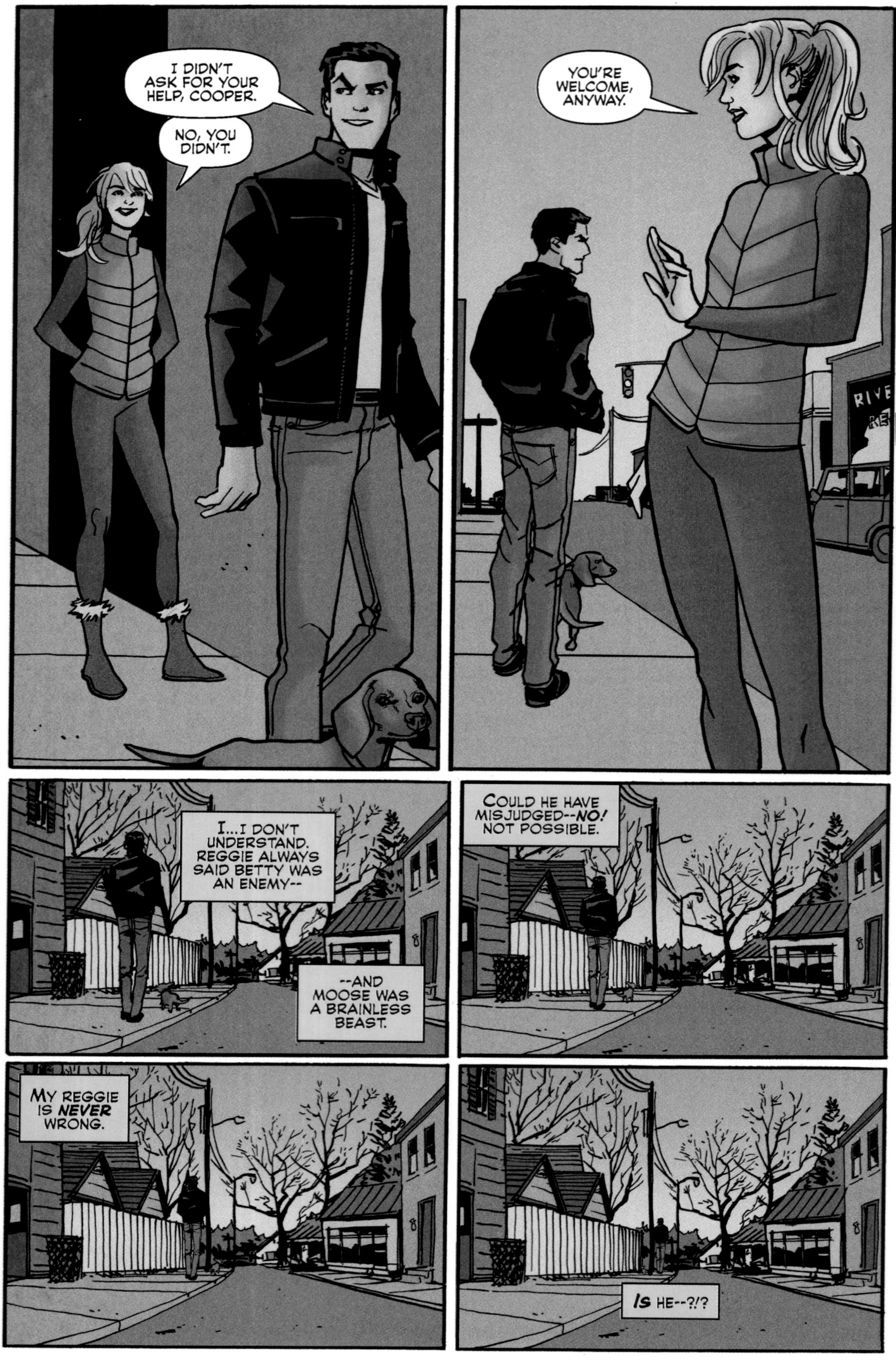

I DIDN'T ASK FOR YOUR HELP, COOPER.
NO, YOU DIDN'T.
YOU'RE WELCOME, ANYWAY.
RIVE
I...I DON'T UNDERSTAND. REGGIE ALWAYS SAID BETTY WAS AN ENEMY--
--AND MOOSE WAS A BRAINLESS BEAST.
COULD HE HAVE MISJUDGED--***NO!*** NOT POSSIBLE.
MY REGGIE IS ***NEVER*** WRONG.
IS HE--?!?

TO BE CONTINUED...

ISSUE FOUR

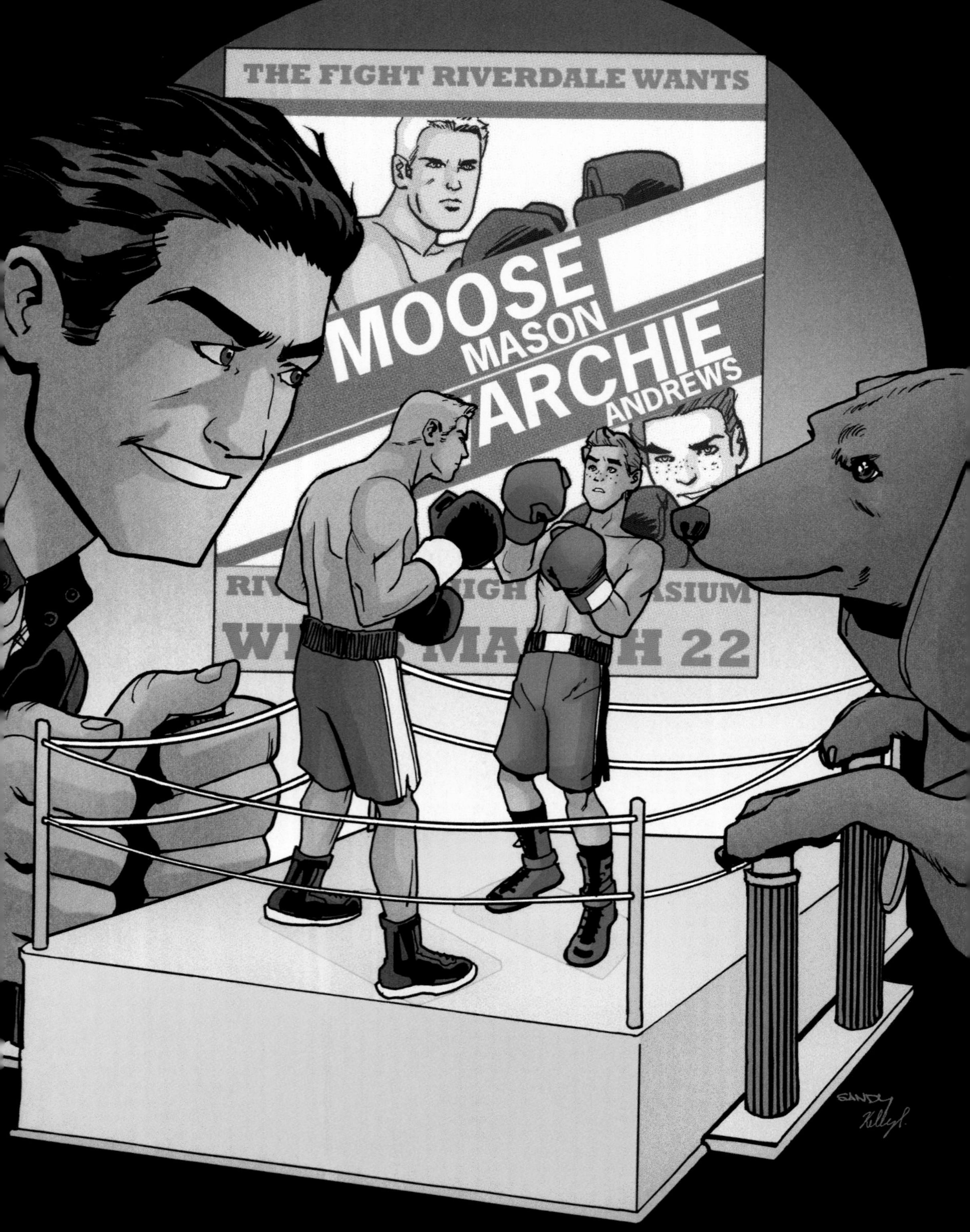

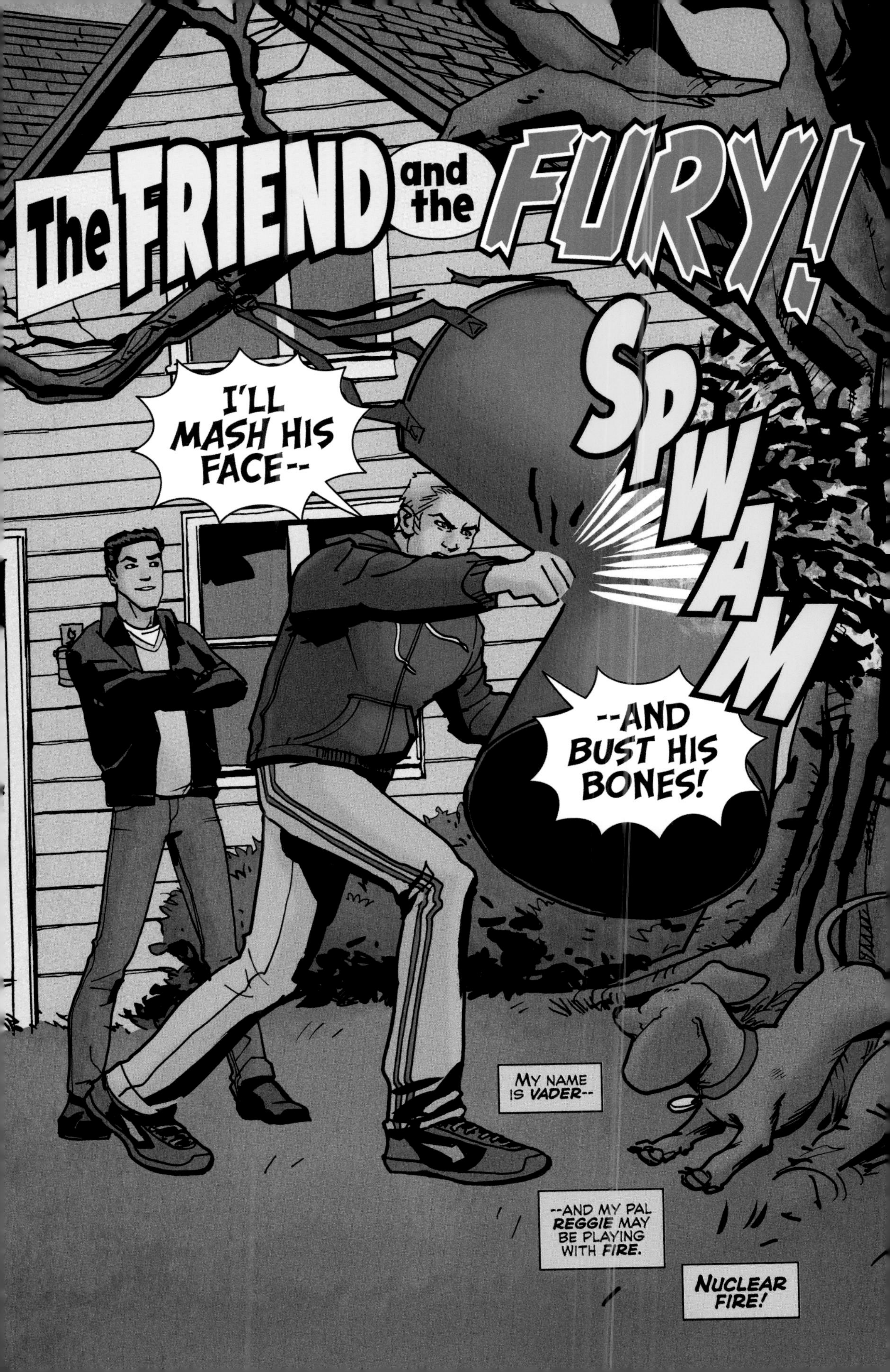
The FRIEND and the FURY!
SPWAM
I'LL MASH HIS FACE--
--AND BUST HIS BONES!
MY NAME IS VADER--
--AND MY PAL REGGIE MAY BE PLAYING WITH FIRE.
NUCLEAR FIRE!

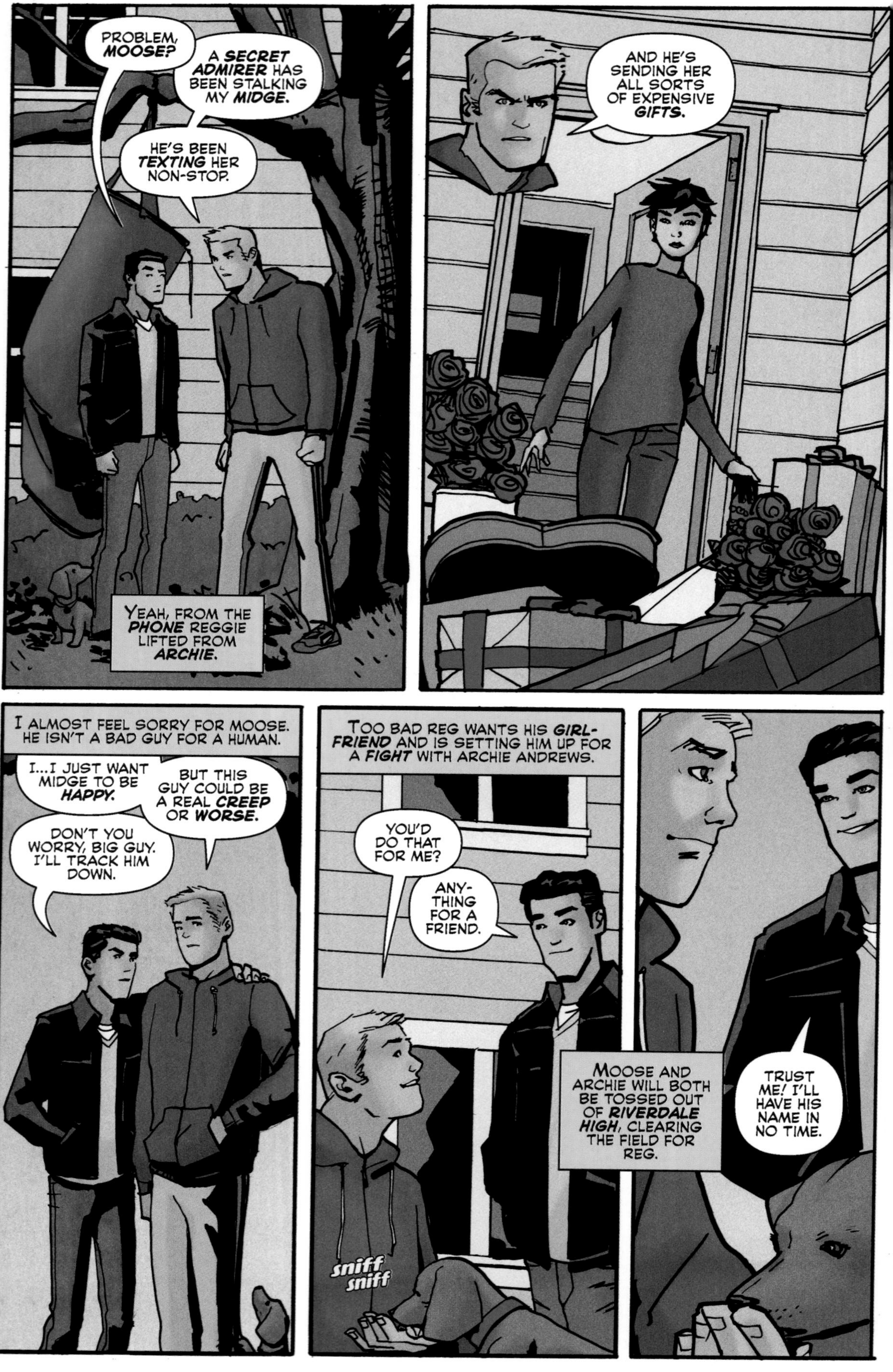
PROBLEM, MOOSE?
A SECRET ADMIRER HAS BEEN STALKING MY MIDGE.
HE'S BEEN TEXTING HER NON-STOP.
YEAH, FROM THE PHONE REGGIE LIFTED FROM ARCHIE.
AND HE'S SENDING HER ALL SORTS OF EXPENSIVE GIFTS.
I ALMOST FEEL SORRY FOR MOOSE. HE ISN'T A BAD GUY FOR A HUMAN.
I...I JUST WANT MIDGE TO BE HAPPY.
BUT THIS GUY COULD BE A REAL CREEP OR WORSE.
DON'T YOU WORRY, BIG GUY. I'LL TRACK HIM DOWN.
TOO BAD REG WANTS HIS GIRLFRIEND AND IS SETTING HIM UP FOR A FIGHT WITH ARCHIE ANDREWS.
YOU'D DO THAT FOR ME?
ANYTHING FOR A FRIEND.
sniff sniff
MOOSE AND ARCHIE WILL BOTH BE TOSSED OUT OF RIVERDALE HIGH, CLEARING THE FIELD FOR REG.
TRUST ME! I'LL HAVE HIS NAME IN NO TIME.

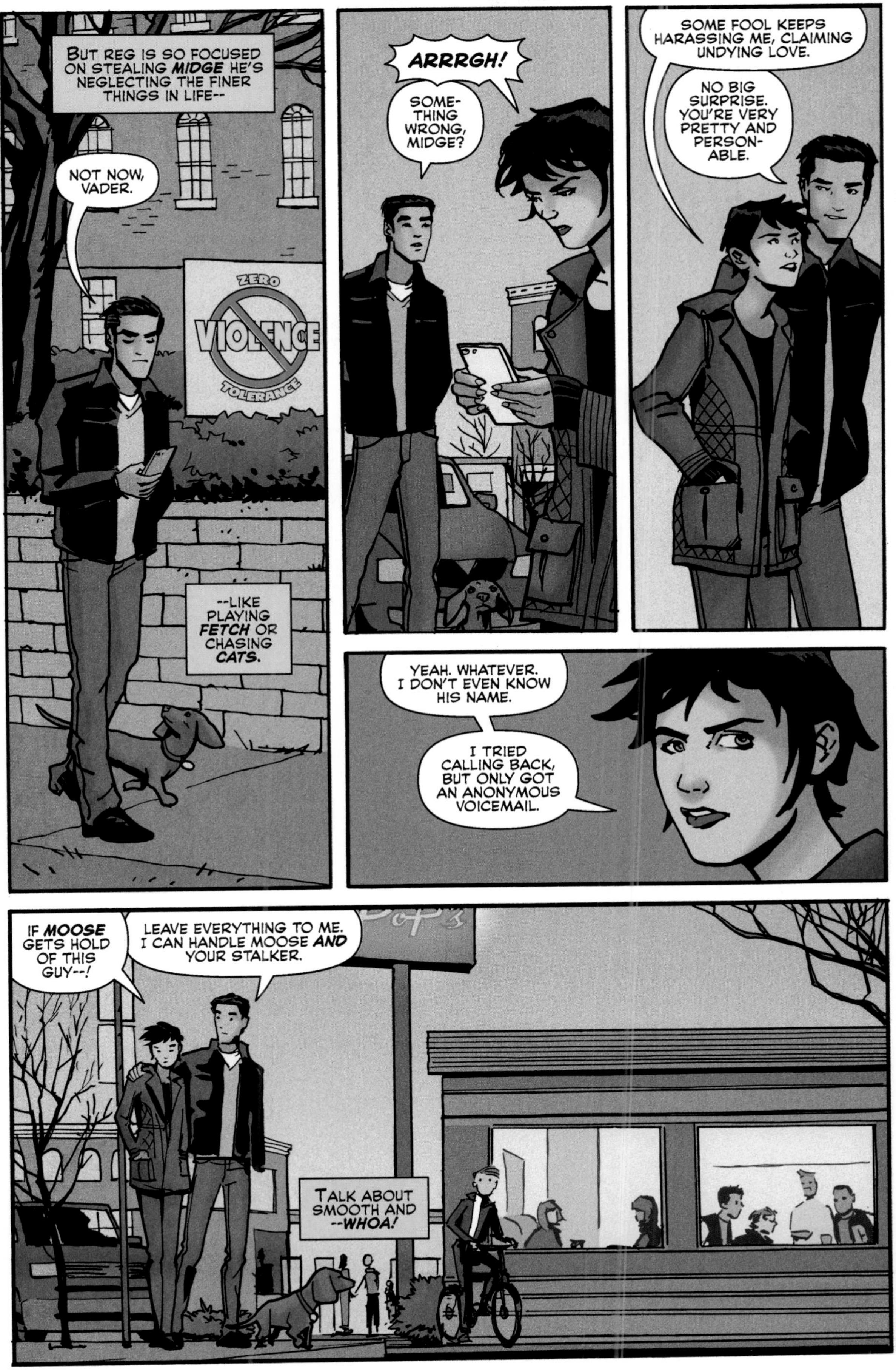

BUT REG IS SO FOCUSED ON STEALING MIDGE HE'S NEGLECTING THE FINER THINGS IN LIFE--
NOT NOW, VADER.
ZERO VIOLENCE TOLERANCE
--LIKE PLAYING FETCH OR CHASING CATS.
ARRRGH!
SOME-THING WRONG, MIDGE?
SOME FOOL KEEPS HARASSING ME, CLAIMING UNDYING LOVE.
NO BIG SURPRISE. YOU'RE VERY PRETTY AND PERSON-ABLE.
YEAH. WHATEVER. I DON'T EVEN KNOW HIS NAME.
I TRIED CALLING BACK, BUT ONLY GOT AN ANONYMOUS VOICEMAIL.
IF MOOSE GETS HOLD OF THIS GUY--!
LEAVE EVERYTHING TO ME. I CAN HANDLE MOOSE AND YOUR STALKER.
TALK ABOUT SMOOTH AND --WHOA!

DO I SMELL *CHILI FRIES?!?*

JOEY!

TALK TO HIM, BRICK--WE CAN'T TAKE HIM ANY-WHERE.

CHILL, MATT! I JUST SPOTTED *MANTLE.*

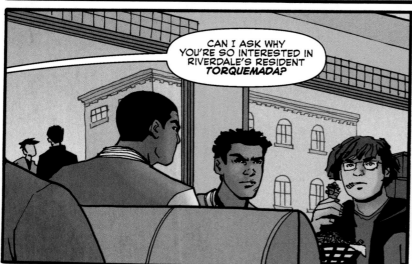

CAN I ASK WHY YOU'RE SO INTERESTED IN RIVERDALE'S RESIDENT *TORQUEMADA?*

NOT THAT IT'S ANY OF YOUR BUSINESS, BUT I OWE HIM FOR DISRESPECTING MY COUSIN--

--AND *MOUTHING OFF* TO ME.

NOW *BACK OFF,* BLONDIE--YOU'RE RUINING THE AMBIANCE.

NAME'S *BETTY*... NOT BLONDIE... AND REGGIE MANTLE IS A CLASSMATE.

THAT MAKES HIM MY BUSINESS.

WHO'S YOUR *COUSIN?* WE MAY HAVE A LOT IN COMMON.

WHY IS *BETTY COOPER* HANGING WITH THE GUYS WHO THREATENED MY REGGIE?

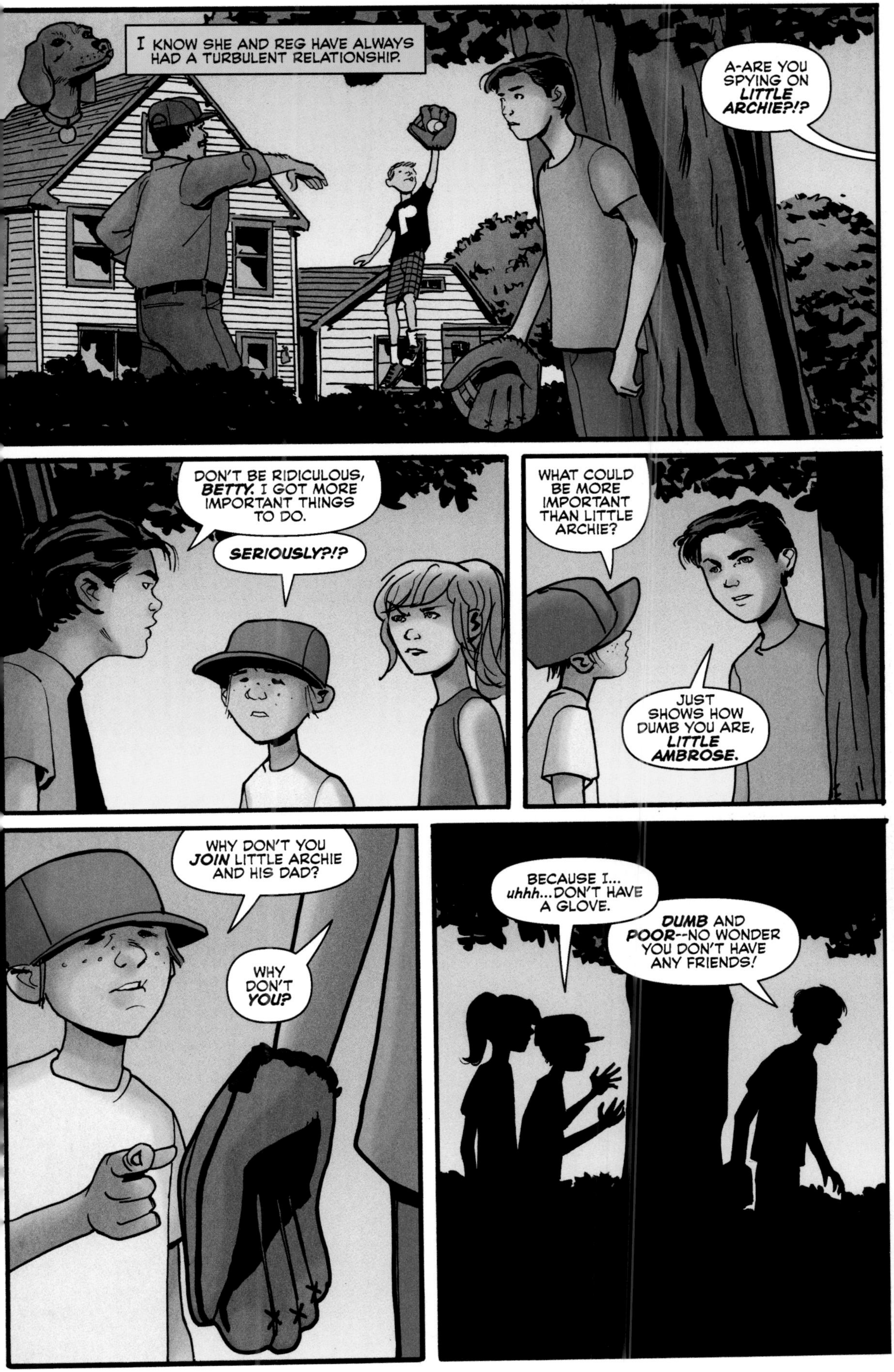
I KNOW SHE AND REG HAVE ALWAYS HAD A TURBULENT RELATIONSHIP.
A-ARE YOU SPYING ON LITTLE ARCHIE?!?
DON'T BE RIDICULOUS, BETTY. I GOT MORE IMPORTANT THINGS TO DO.
SERIOUSLY?!?
WHAT COULD BE MORE IMPORTANT THAN LITTLE ARCHIE?
JUST SHOWS HOW DUMB YOU ARE, LITTLE AMBROSE.
WHY DON'T YOU JOIN LITTLE ARCHIE AND HIS DAD?
WHY DON'T YOU?
BECAUSE I... uhhh...DON'T HAVE A GLOVE.
DUMB AND POOR--NO WONDER YOU DON'T HAVE ANY FRIENDS!

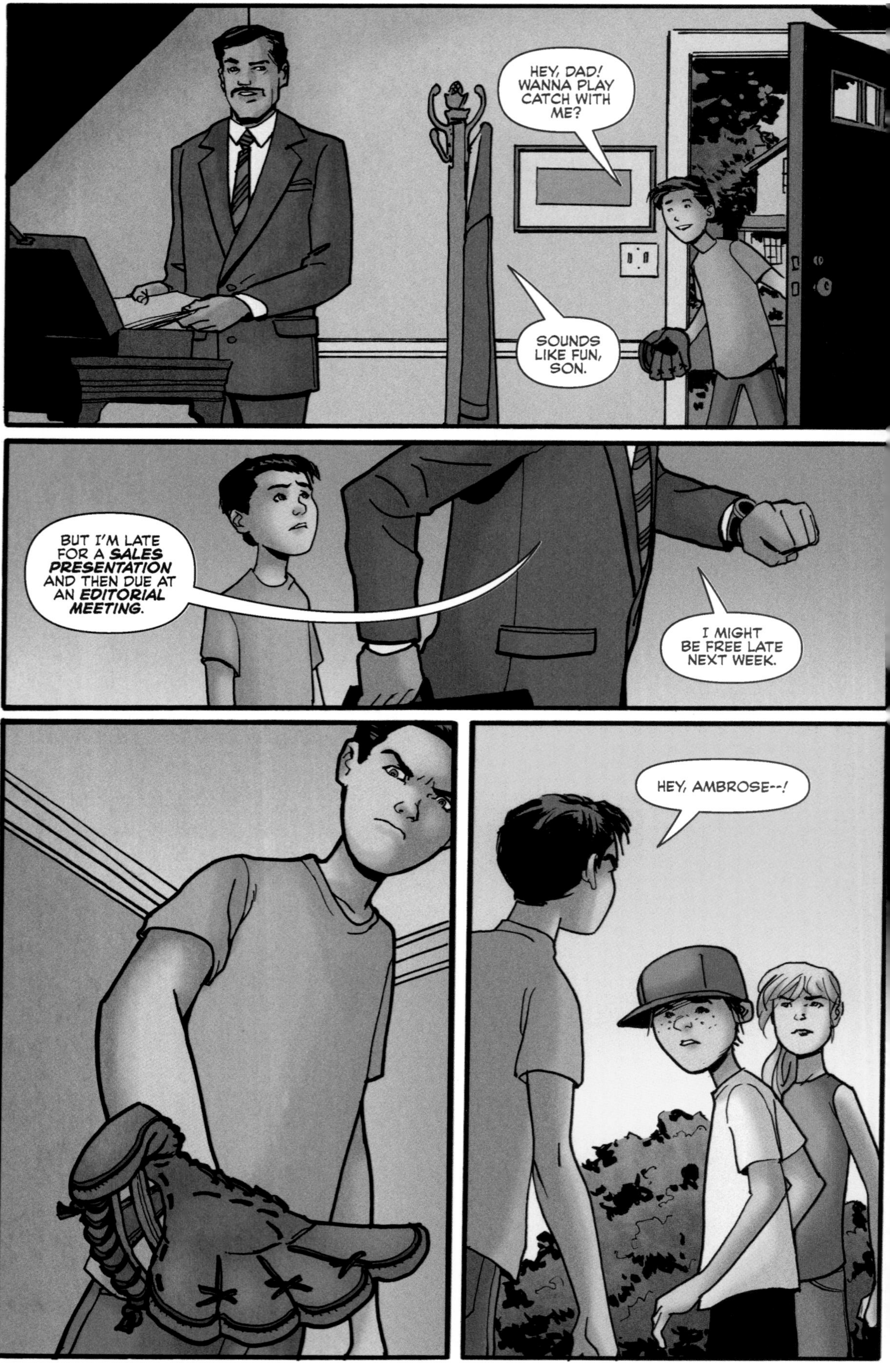
HEY, DAD! WANNA PLAY CATCH WITH ME?
SOUNDS LIKE FUN, SON.
BUT I'M LATE FOR A **SALES PRESENTATION** AND THEN DUE AT AN **EDITORIAL MEETING**.
I MIGHT BE FREE LATE NEXT WEEK.
HEY, AMBROSE--!

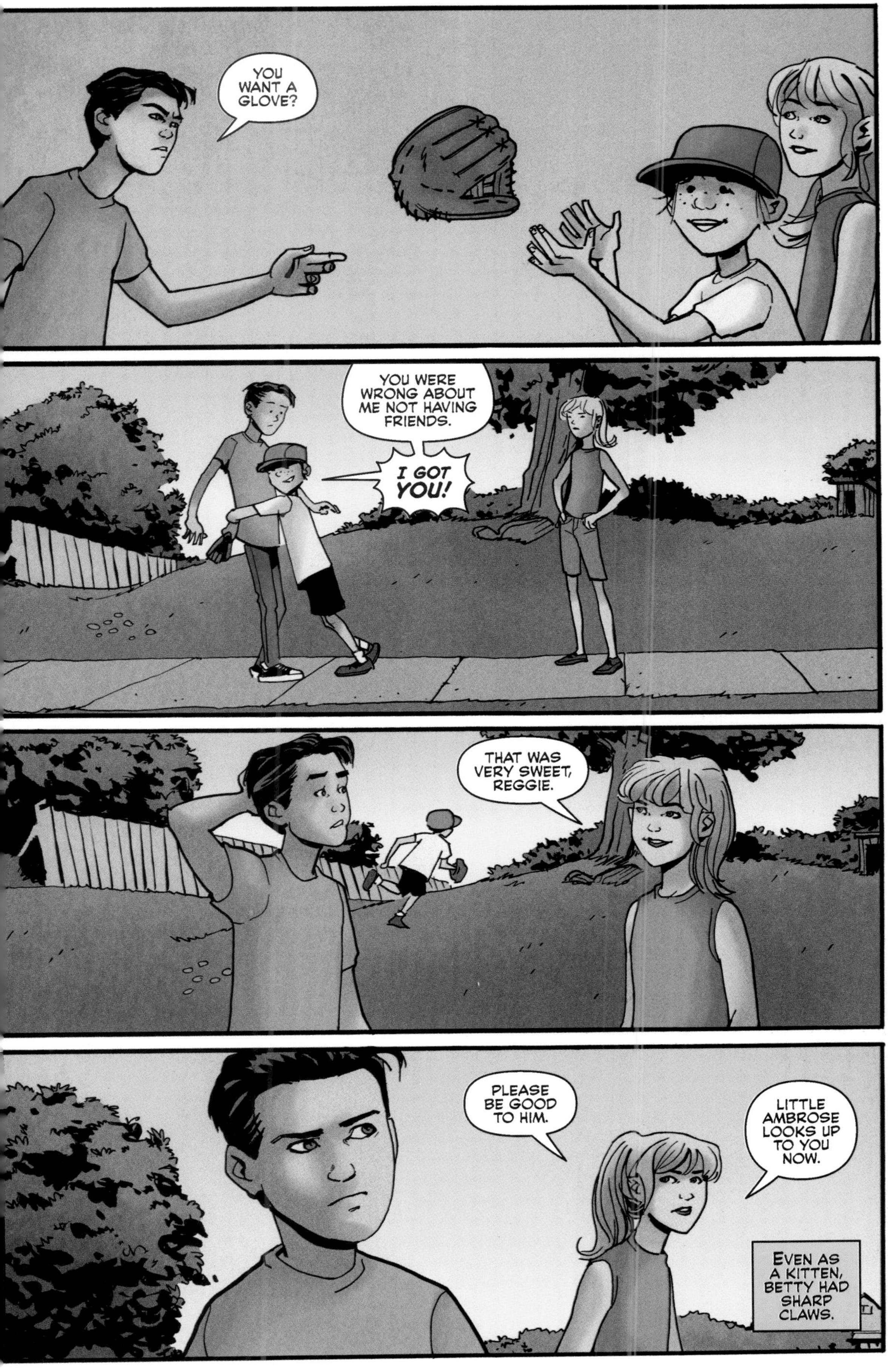
YOU WANT A GLOVE?
YOU WERE WRONG ABOUT ME NOT HAVING FRIENDS.
I GOT YOU!
THAT WAS VERY SWEET, REGGIE.
PLEASE BE GOOD TO HIM.
LITTLE AMBROSE LOOKS UP TO YOU NOW.
EVEN AS A KITTEN, BETTY HAD SHARP CLAWS.

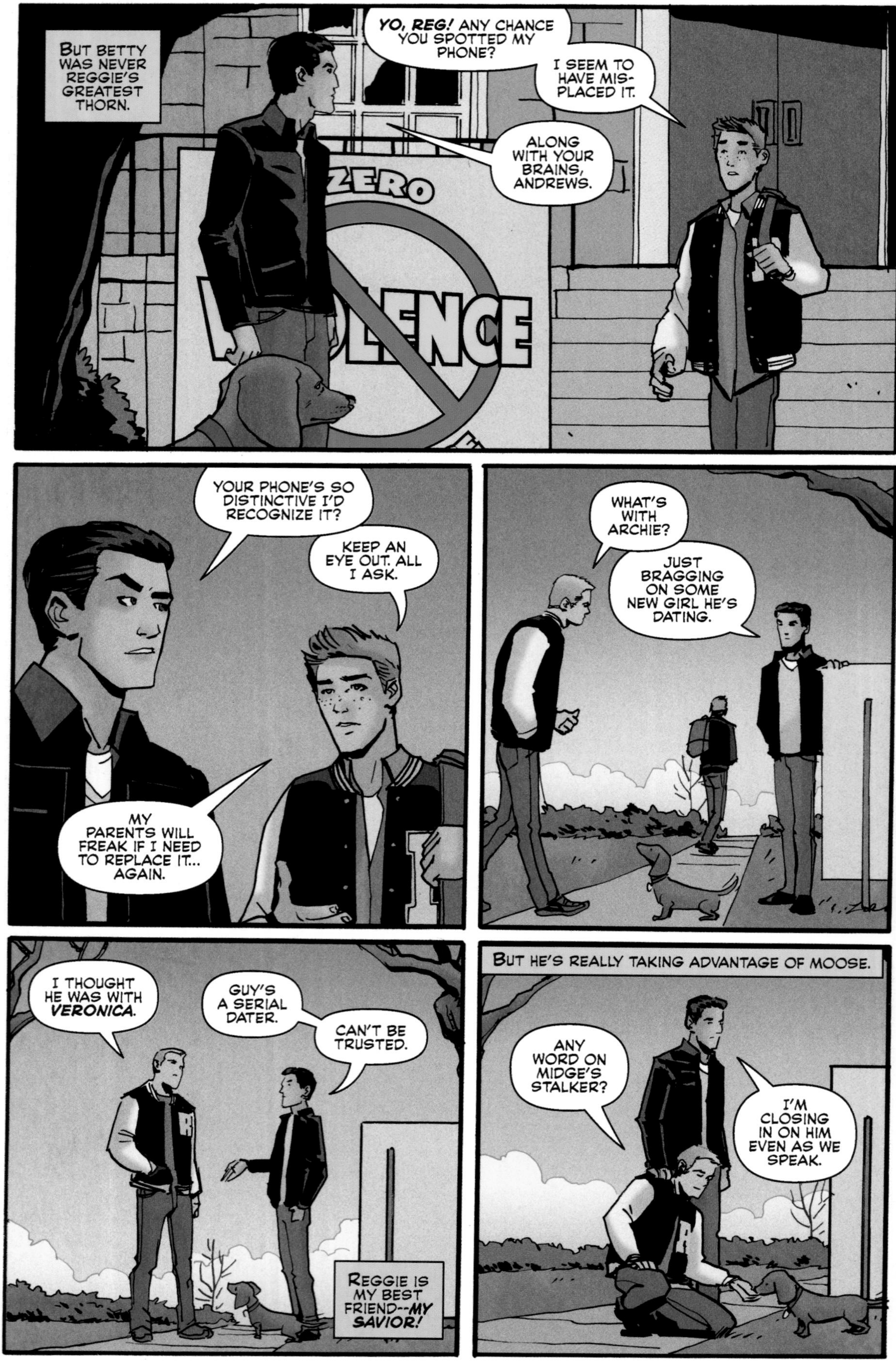
But Betty was never Reggie's greatest thorn.
YO, REG! ANY CHANCE YOU SPOTTED MY PHONE?
I SEEM TO HAVE MIS-PLACED IT.
ALONG WITH YOUR BRAINS, ANDREWS.
ZERO
LENCE
YOUR PHONE'S SO DISTINCTIVE I'D RECOGNIZE IT?
KEEP AN EYE OUT. ALL I ASK.
MY PARENTS WILL FREAK IF I NEED TO REPLACE IT... AGAIN.
WHAT'S WITH ARCHIE?
JUST BRAGGING ON SOME NEW GIRL HE'S DATING.
I THOUGHT HE WAS WITH VERONICA.
GUY'S A SERIAL DATER.
CAN'T BE TRUSTED.
Reggie is my best friend--my savior!
But he's really taking advantage of Moose.
ANY WORD ON MIDGE'S STALKER?
I'M CLOSING IN ON HIM EVEN AS WE SPEAK.

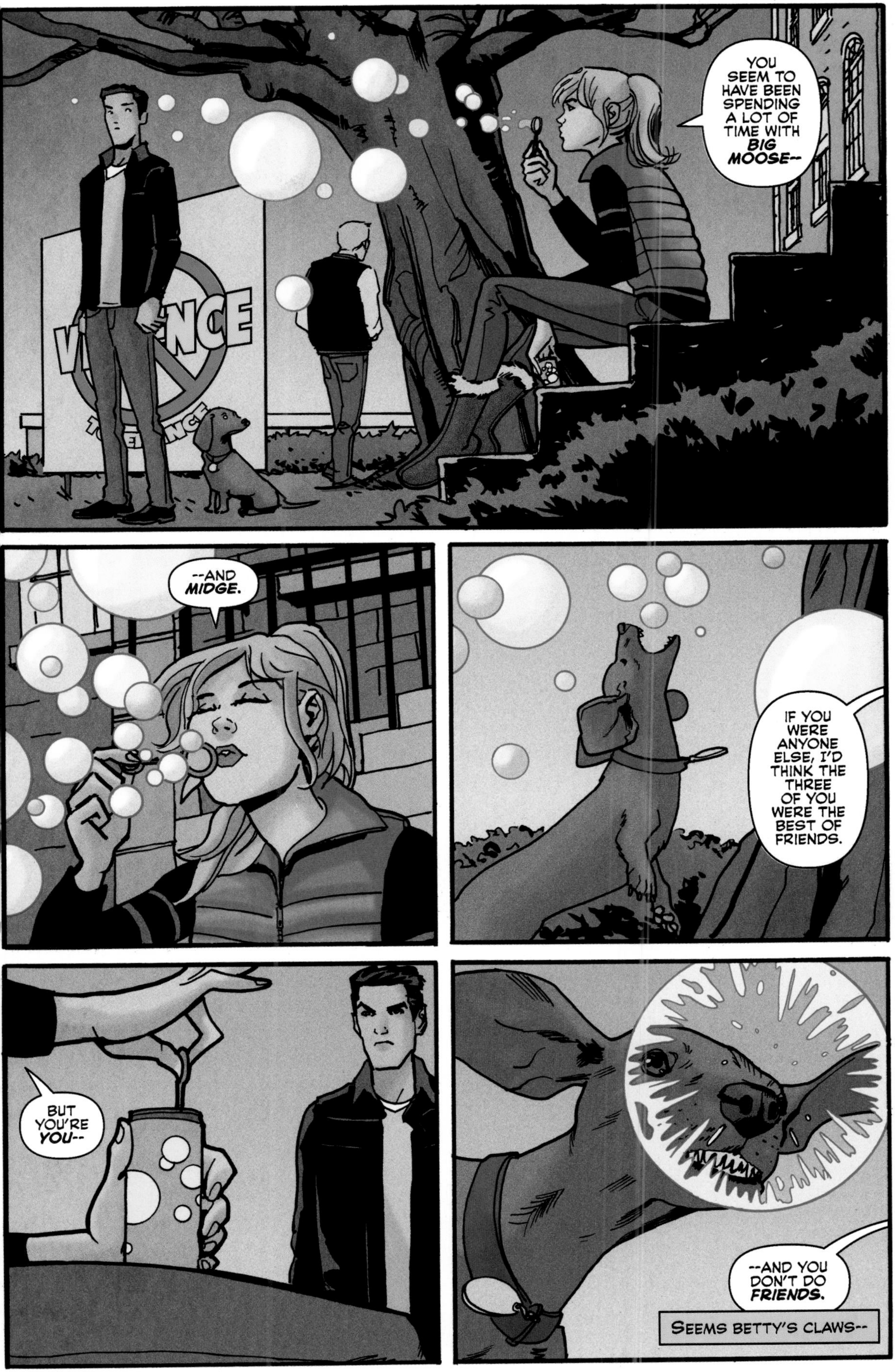
YOU SEEM TO HAVE BEEN SPENDING A LOT OF TIME WITH BIG MOOSE--
--AND MIDGE.
IF YOU WERE ANYONE ELSE, I'D THINK THE THREE OF YOU WERE THE BEST OF FRIENDS.
BUT YOU'RE YOU--
--AND YOU DON'T DO FRIENDS.
SEEMS BETTY'S CLAWS--

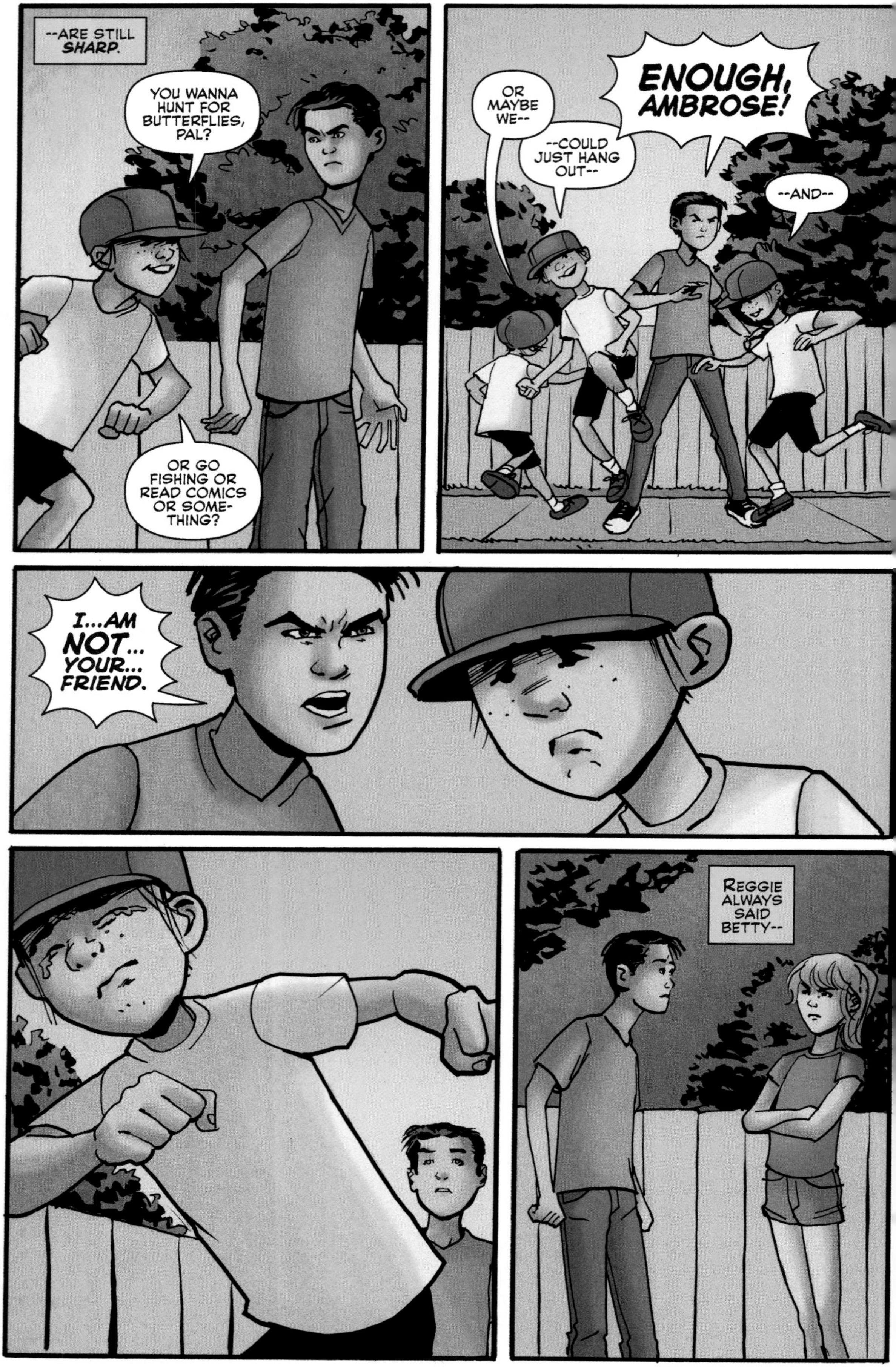
--ARE STILL SHARP.
YOU WANNA HUNT FOR BUTTERFLIES, PAL?
OR GO FISHING OR READ COMICS OR SOMETHING?
OR MAYBE WE--
--COULD JUST HANG OUT--
ENOUGH, AMBROSE!
--AND--
I...AM NOT... YOUR... FRIEND.
REGGIE ALWAYS SAID BETTY--

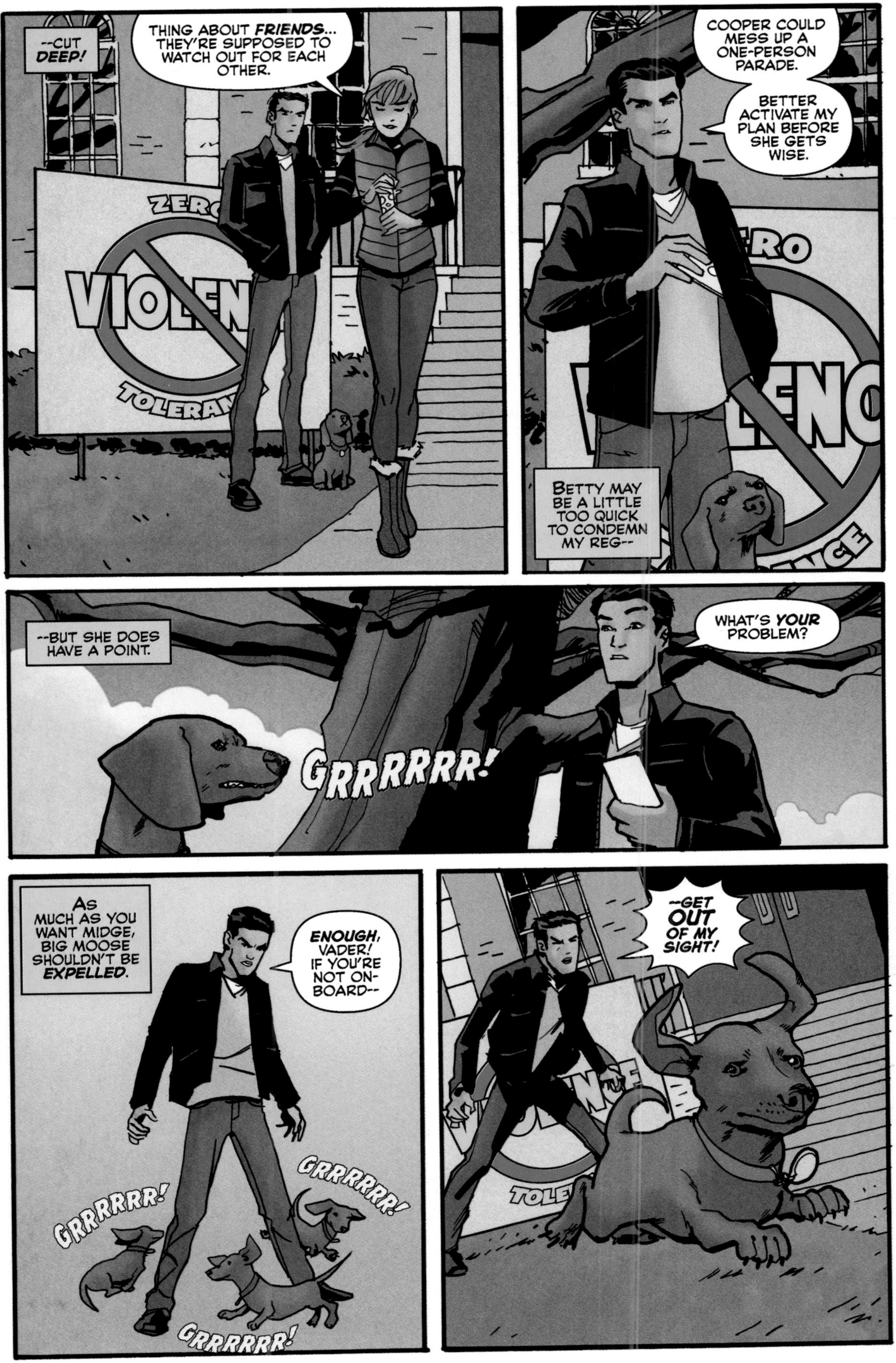
--CUT DEEP!
THING ABOUT FRIENDS... THEY'RE SUPPOSED TO WATCH OUT FOR EACH OTHER.
ZERO
VIOLEN
TOLERAN
COOPER COULD MESS UP A ONE-PERSON PARADE.
BETTER ACTIVATE MY PLAN BEFORE SHE GETS WISE.
ERO
LENC
BETTY MAY BE A LITTLE TOO QUICK TO CONDEMN MY REG--
--BUT SHE DOES HAVE A POINT.
WHAT'S YOUR PROBLEM?
GRRRRRR!
AS MUCH AS YOU WANT MIDGE, BIG MOOSE SHOULDN'T BE EXPELLED.
ENOUGH, VADER! IF YOU'RE NOT ON-BOARD--
GRRRRRR!
GRRRRRR!
GRRRRRR!
--GET OUT OF MY SIGHT!
TOLE

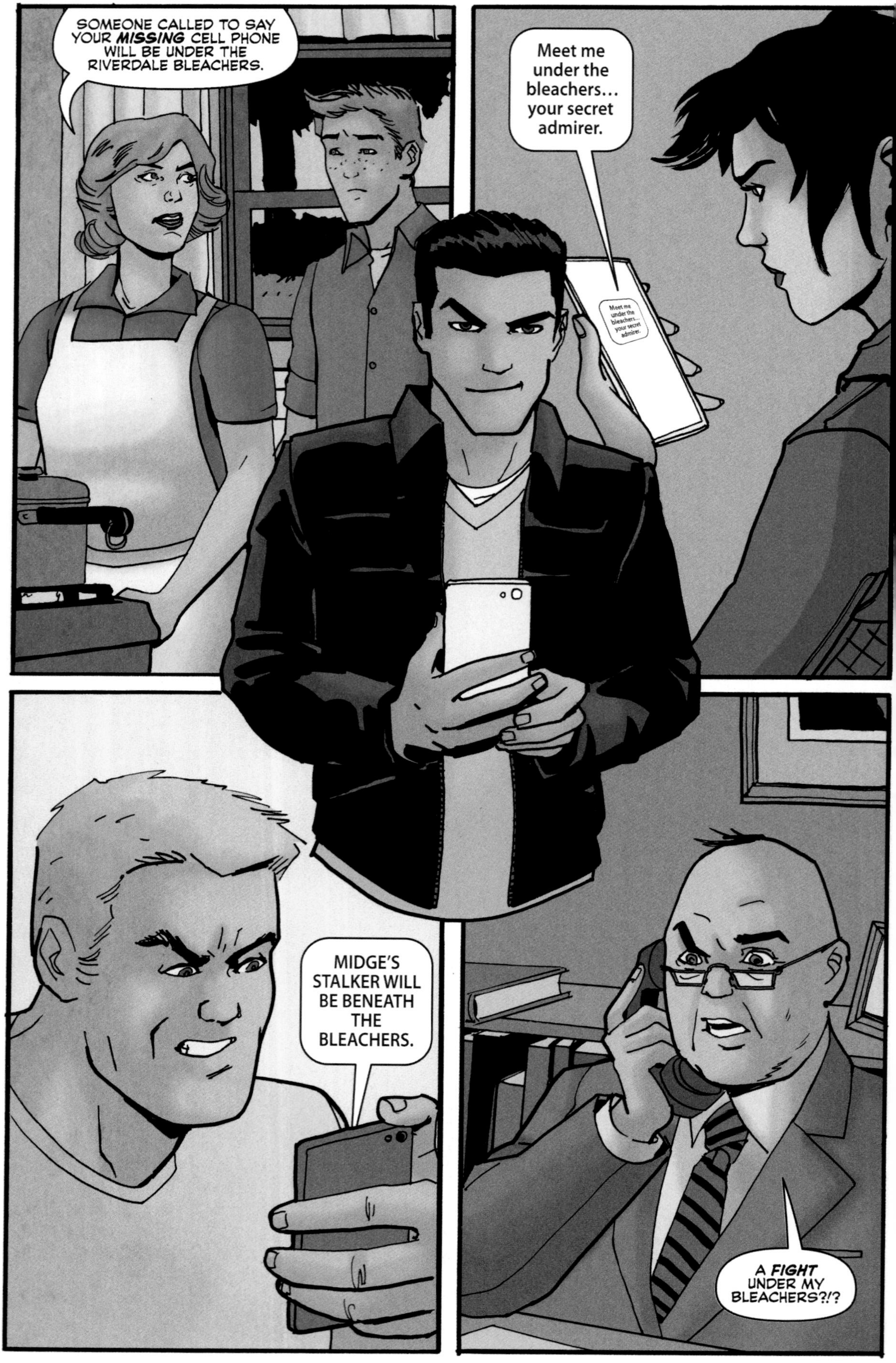
SOMEONE CALLED TO SAY YOUR MISSING CELL PHONE WILL BE UNDER THE RIVERDALE BLEACHERS.
Meet me under the bleachers… your secret admirer.
Meet me under the bleachers… your secret admirer.
MIDGE'S STALKER WILL BE BENEATH THE BLEACHERS.
A FIGHT UNDER MY BLEACHERS?!?

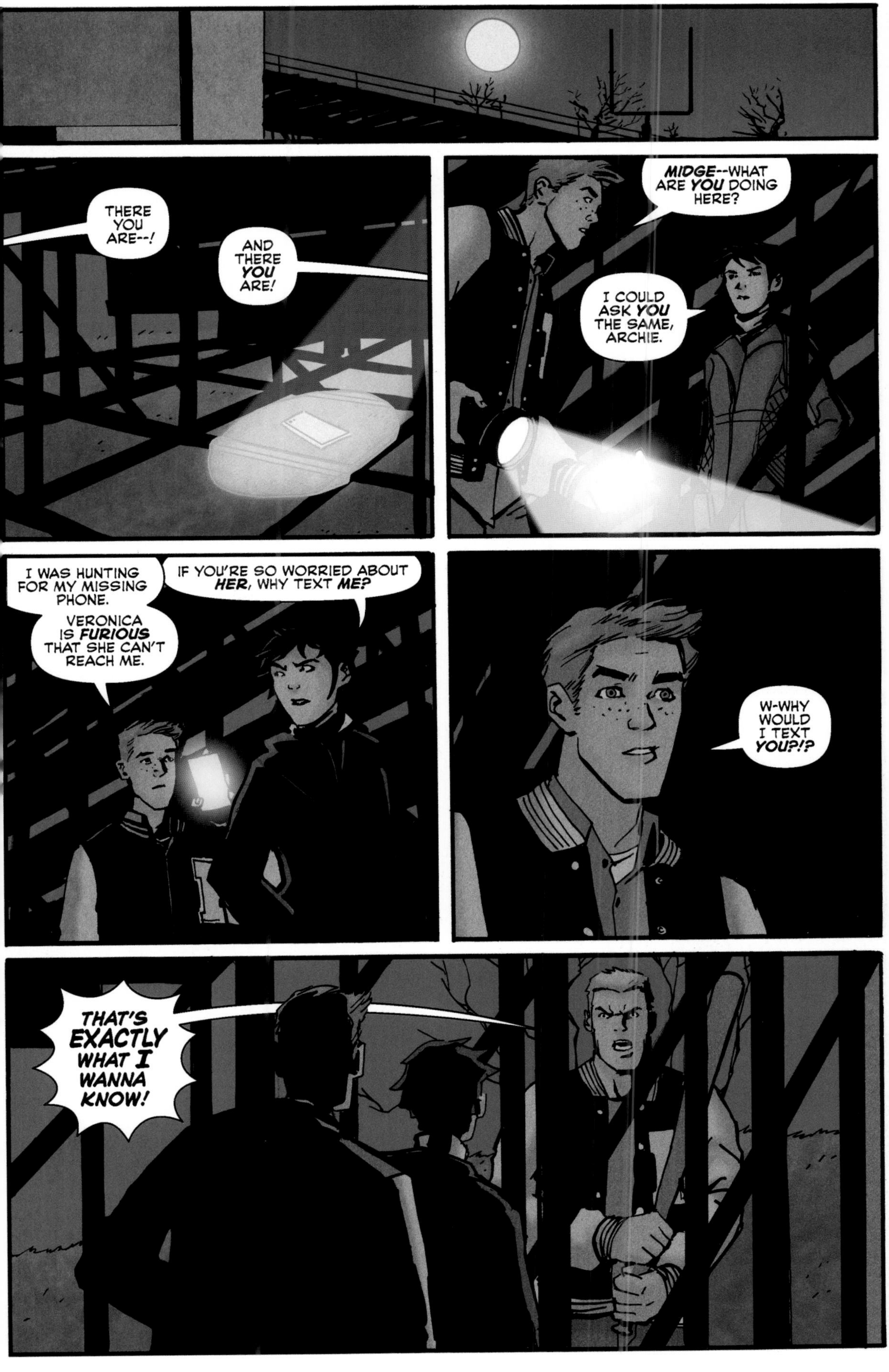
THERE YOU ARE--!
AND THERE YOU ARE!
MIDGE--WHAT ARE YOU DOING HERE?
I COULD ASK YOU THE SAME, ARCHIE.
I WAS HUNTING FOR MY MISSING PHONE.
VERONICA IS FURIOUS THAT SHE CAN'T REACH ME.
IF YOU'RE SO WORRIED ABOUT HER, WHY TEXT ME?
W-WHY WOULD I TEXT YOU?!?
THAT'S EXACTLY WHAT I WANNA KNOW!

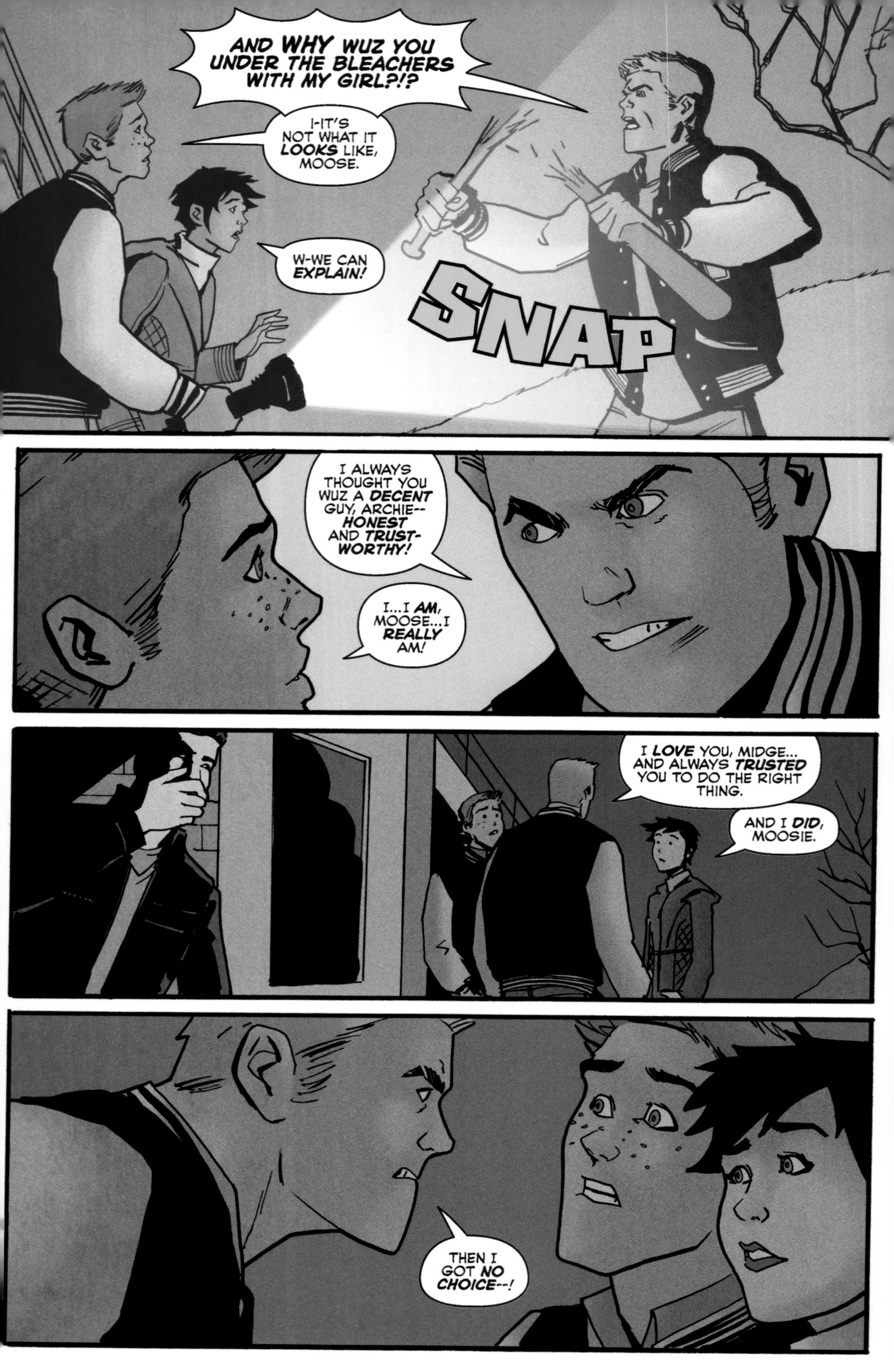
AND WHY WUZ YOU UNDER THE BLEACHERS WITH MY GIRL?!?
I-IT'S NOT WHAT IT LOOKS LIKE, MOOSE.
W-WE CAN EXPLAIN!
SNAP
I ALWAYS THOUGHT YOU WUZ A DECENT GUY, ARCHIE-- HONEST AND TRUST-WORTHY!
I...I AM, MOOSE...I REALLY AM!
I LOVE YOU, MIDGE... AND ALWAYS TRUSTED YOU TO DO THE RIGHT THING.
AND I DID, MOOSIE.
THEN I GOT NO CHOICE--!

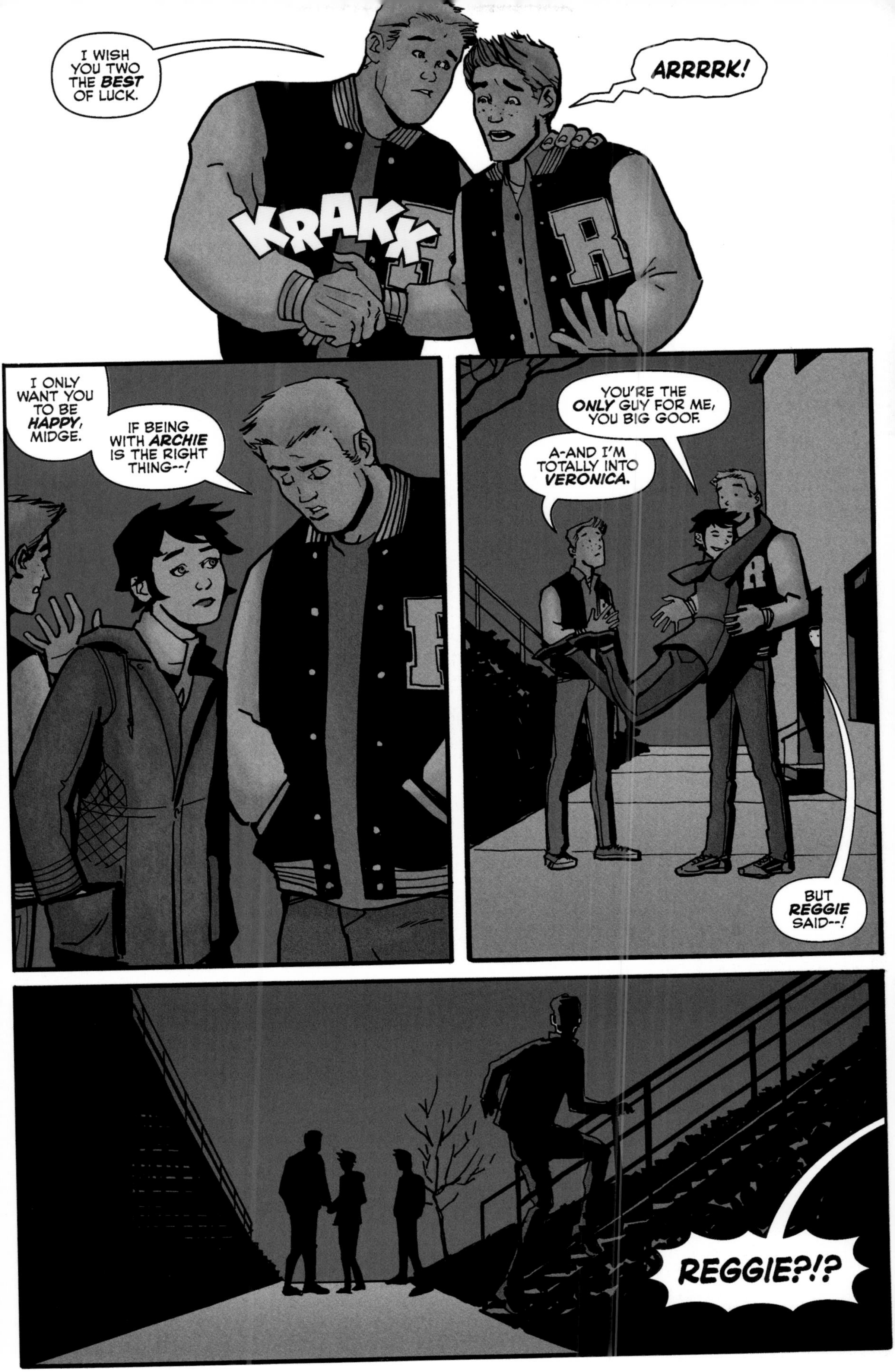
I WISH YOU TWO THE BEST OF LUCK.
KRAKK
ARRRRK!
I ONLY WANT YOU TO BE HAPPY, MIDGE.
IF BEING WITH ARCHIE IS THE RIGHT THING--!
YOU'RE THE ONLY GUY FOR ME, YOU BIG GOOF.
A-AND I'M TOTALLY INTO VERONICA.
BUT REGGIE SAID--!
REGGIE?!?

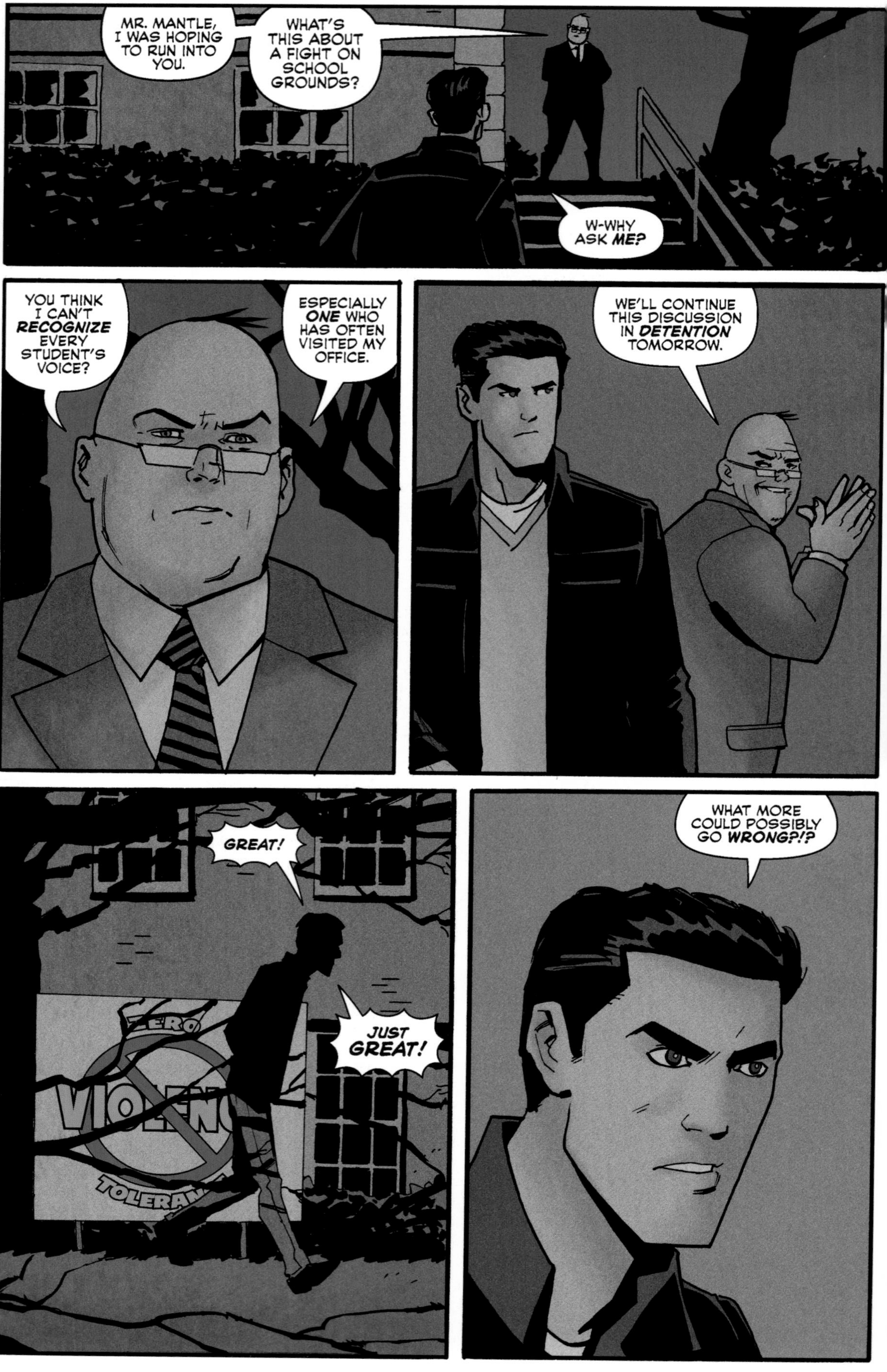
MR. MANTLE, I WAS HOPING TO RUN INTO YOU.
WHAT'S THIS ABOUT A FIGHT ON SCHOOL GROUNDS?
W-WHY ASK ME?
YOU THINK I CAN'T RECOGNIZE EVERY STUDENT'S VOICE?
ESPECIALLY ONE WHO HAS OFTEN VISITED MY OFFICE.
WE'LL CONTINUE THIS DISCUSSION IN DETENTION TOMORROW.
GREAT!
ZERO
VIOLENC
TOLERAN
JUST GREAT!
WHAT MORE COULD POSSIBLY GO WRONG?!?

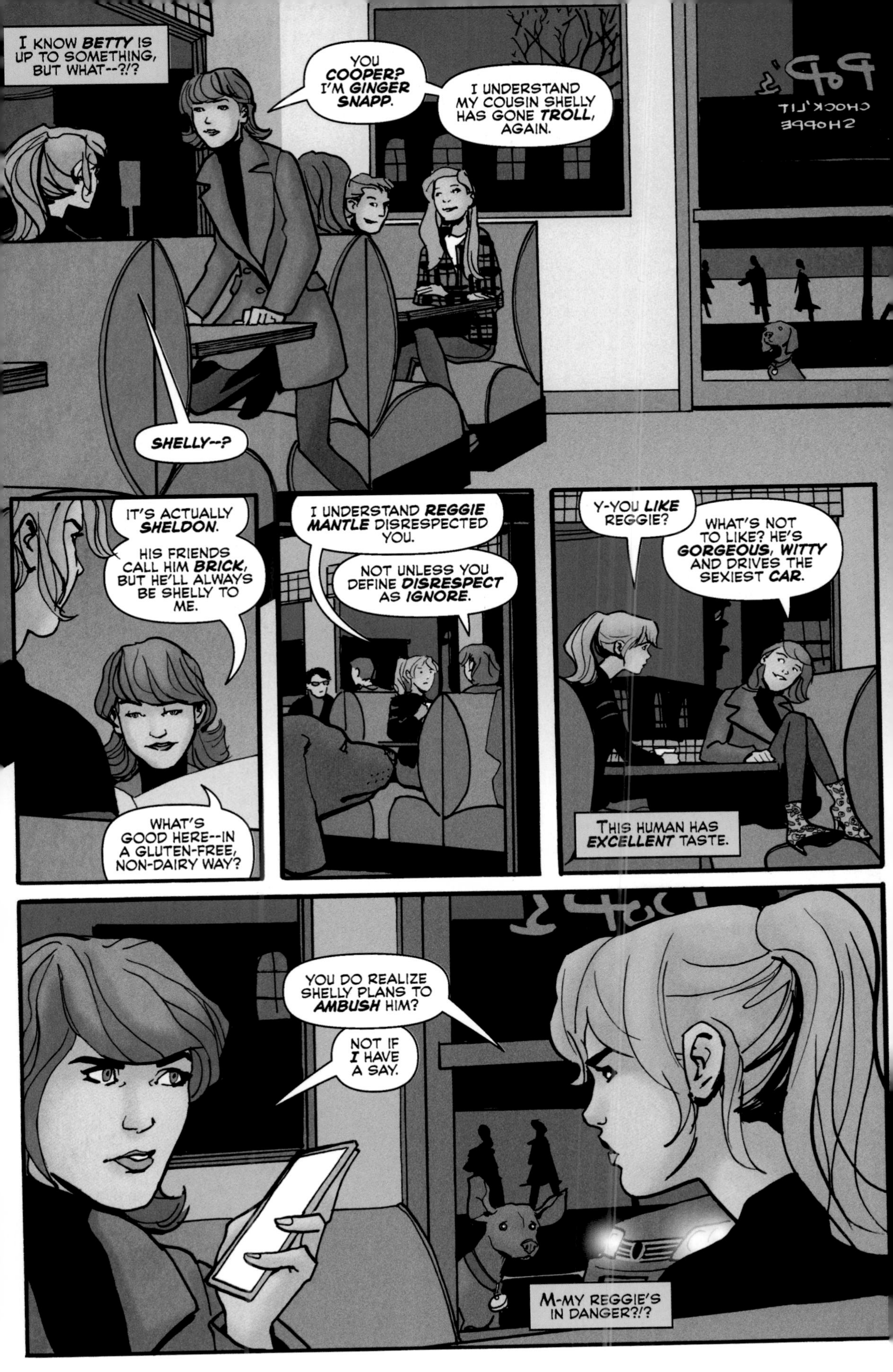
I KNOW BETTY IS UP TO SOMETHING, BUT WHAT--?!?
YOU COOPER? I'M GINGER SNAPP.
I UNDERSTAND MY COUSIN SHELLY HAS GONE TROLL, AGAIN.
POP'S CHOCK'LIT SHOPPE
SHELLY--?
IT'S ACTUALLY SHELDON.
HIS FRIENDS CALL HIM BRICK, BUT HE'LL ALWAYS BE SHELLY TO ME.
WHAT'S GOOD HERE--IN A GLUTEN-FREE, NON-DAIRY WAY?
I UNDERSTAND REGGIE MANTLE DISRESPECTED YOU.
NOT UNLESS YOU DEFINE DISRESPECT AS IGNORE.
Y-YOU LIKE REGGIE?
WHAT'S NOT TO LIKE? HE'S GORGEOUS, WITTY AND DRIVES THE SEXIEST CAR.
THIS HUMAN HAS EXCELLENT TASTE.
YOU DO REALIZE SHELLY PLANS TO AMBUSH HIM?
NOT IF I HAVE A SAY.
M-MY REGGIE'S IN DANGER?!?

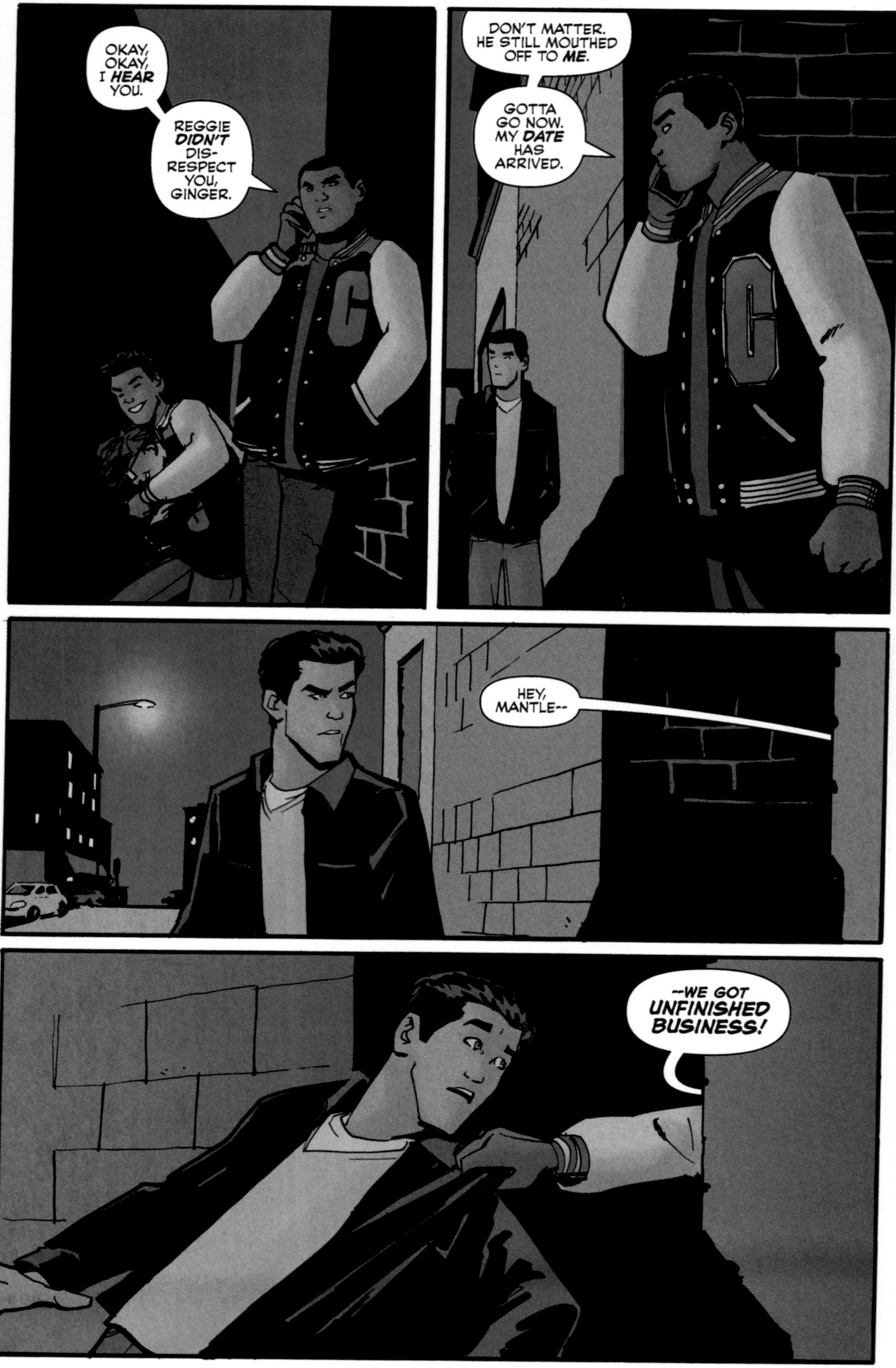
OKAY, OKAY, I HEAR YOU.
REGGIE DIDN'T DIS-RESPECT YOU, GINGER.
DON'T MATTER. HE STILL MOUTHED OFF TO ME.
GOTTA GO NOW. MY DATE HAS ARRIVED.
HEY, MANTLE--
--WE GOT UNFINISHED BUSINESS!

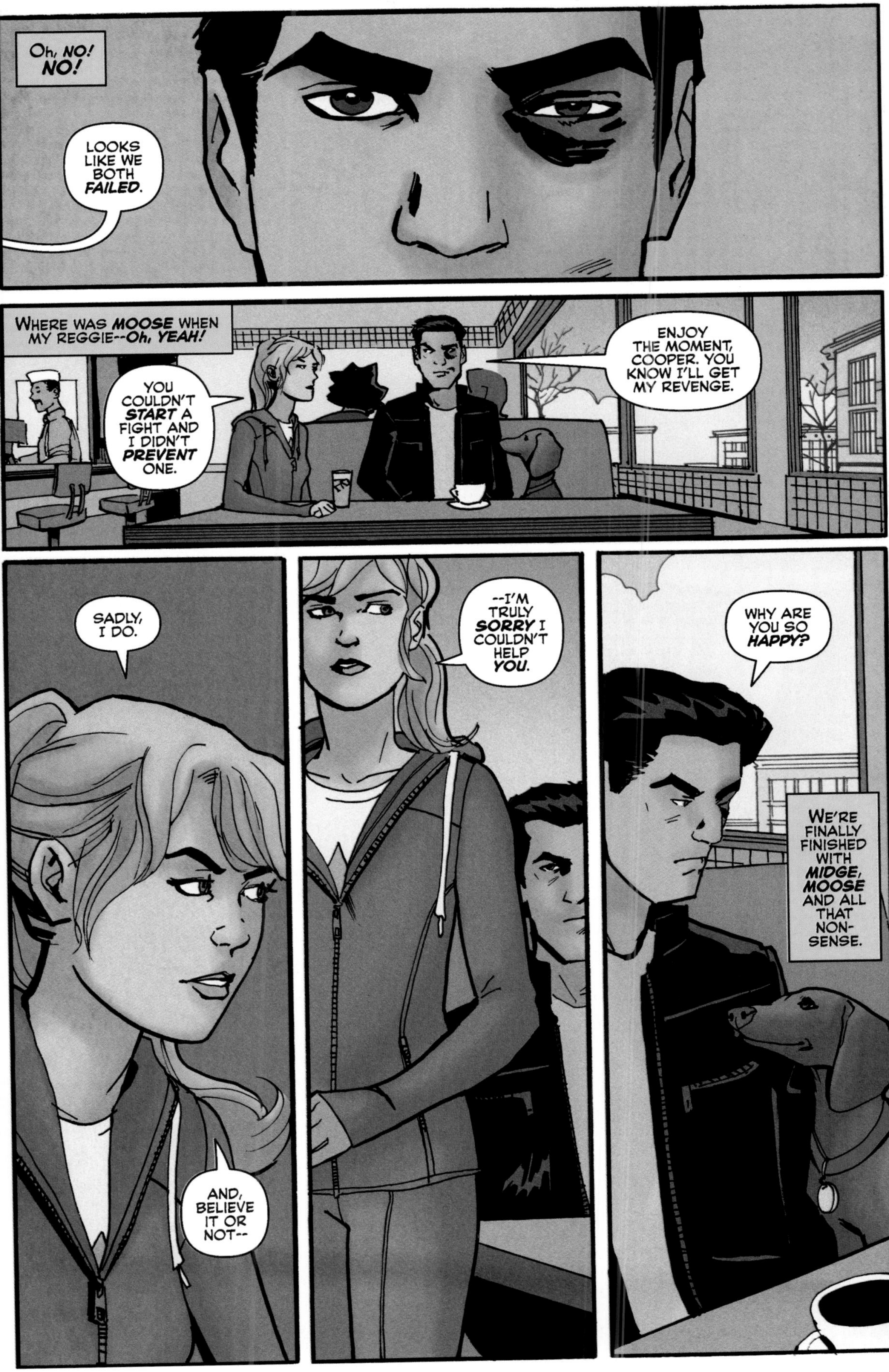
Oh, NO! NO!
LOOKS LIKE WE BOTH FAILED.
WHERE WAS MOOSE WHEN MY REGGIE--Oh, YEAH!
YOU COULDN'T START A FIGHT AND I DIDN'T PREVENT ONE.
ENJOY THE MOMENT, COOPER. YOU KNOW I'LL GET MY REVENGE.
SADLY, I DO.
AND, BELIEVE IT OR NOT--
--I'M TRULY SORRY I COULDN'T HELP YOU.
WHY ARE YOU SO HAPPY?
WE'RE FINALLY FINISHED WITH MIDGE, MOOSE AND ALL THAT NON-SENSE.

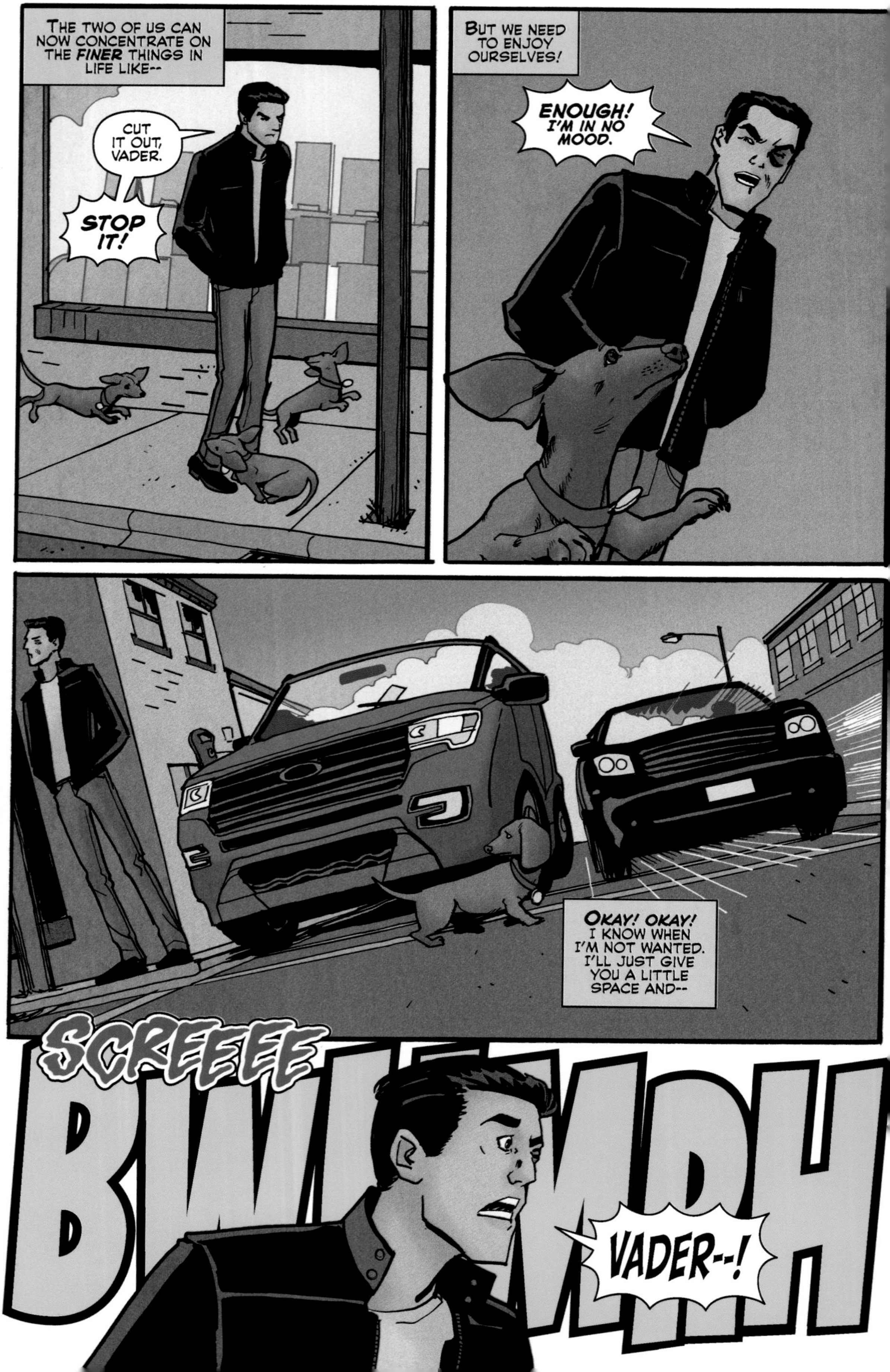
THE TWO OF US CAN NOW CONCENTRATE ON THE *FINER* THINGS IN LIFE LIKE--
CUT IT OUT, VADER.
STOP IT!
BUT WE NEED TO ENJOY OURSELVES!
ENOUGH! I'M IN NO MOOD.
OKAY! OKAY! I KNOW WHEN I'M NOT WANTED. I'LL JUST GIVE YOU A LITTLE SPACE AND--
SCREEEEE
VADER--!

TO BE CONTINUED...

ISSUE FIVE

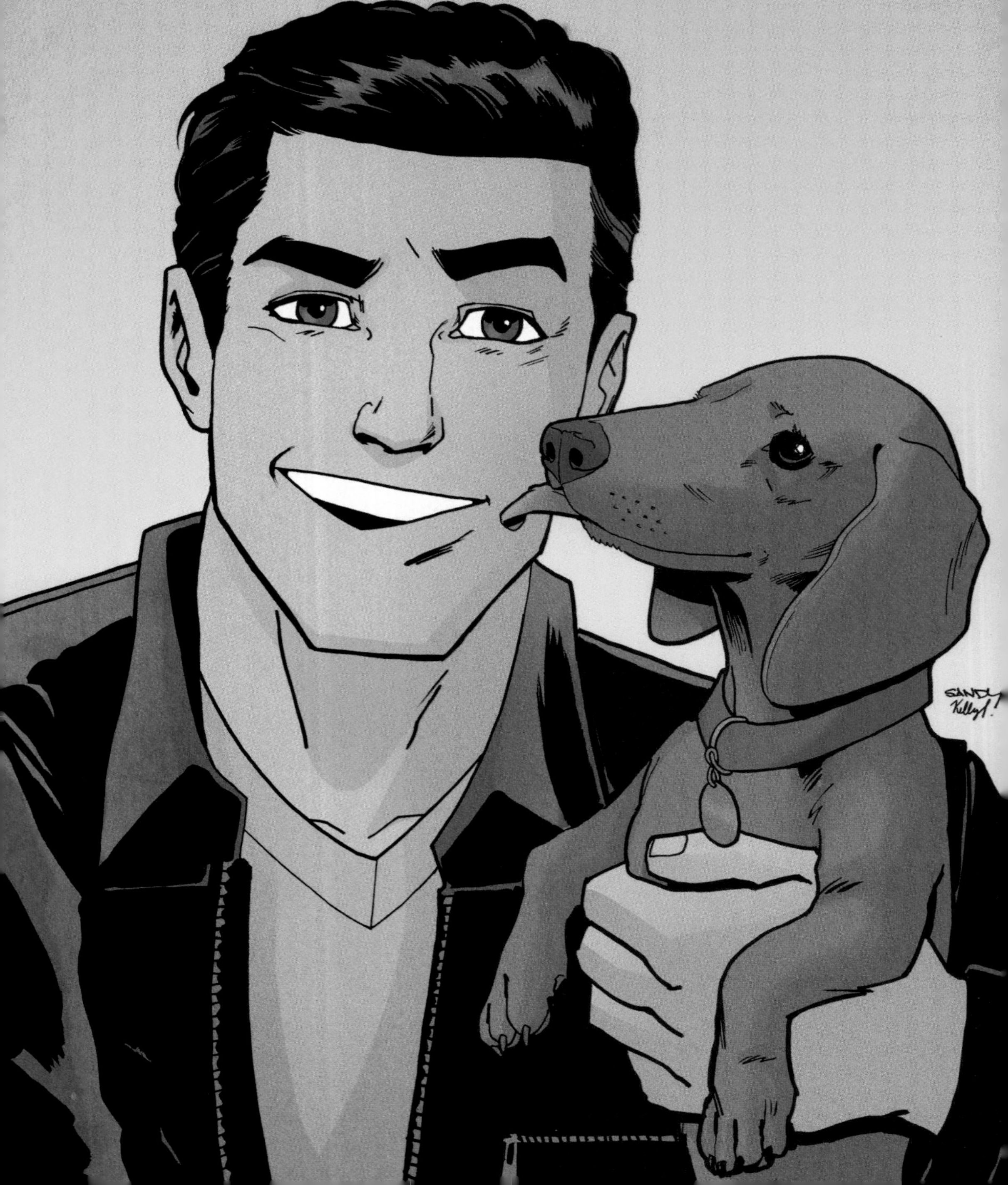

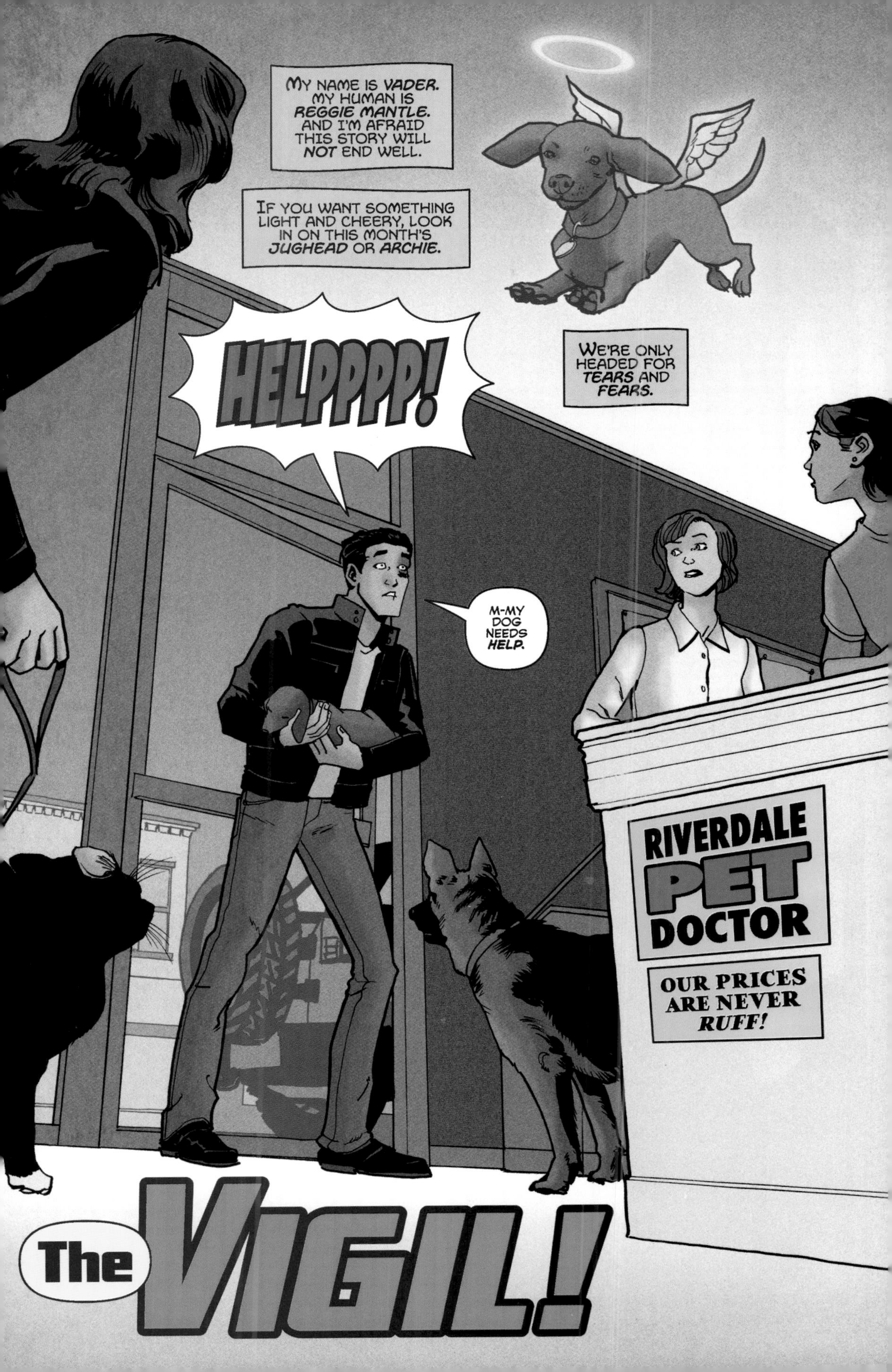
MY NAME IS VADER. MY HUMAN IS REGGIE MANTLE. AND I'M AFRAID THIS STORY WILL NOT END WELL.
IF YOU WANT SOMETHING LIGHT AND CHEERY, LOOK IN ON THIS MONTH'S JUGHEAD OR ARCHIE.
HELPPPP!
WE'RE ONLY HEADED FOR TEARS AND FEARS.
M-MY DOG NEEDS HELP.
RIVERDALE PET DOCTOR
OUR PRICES ARE NEVER RUFF!
The VIGIL!

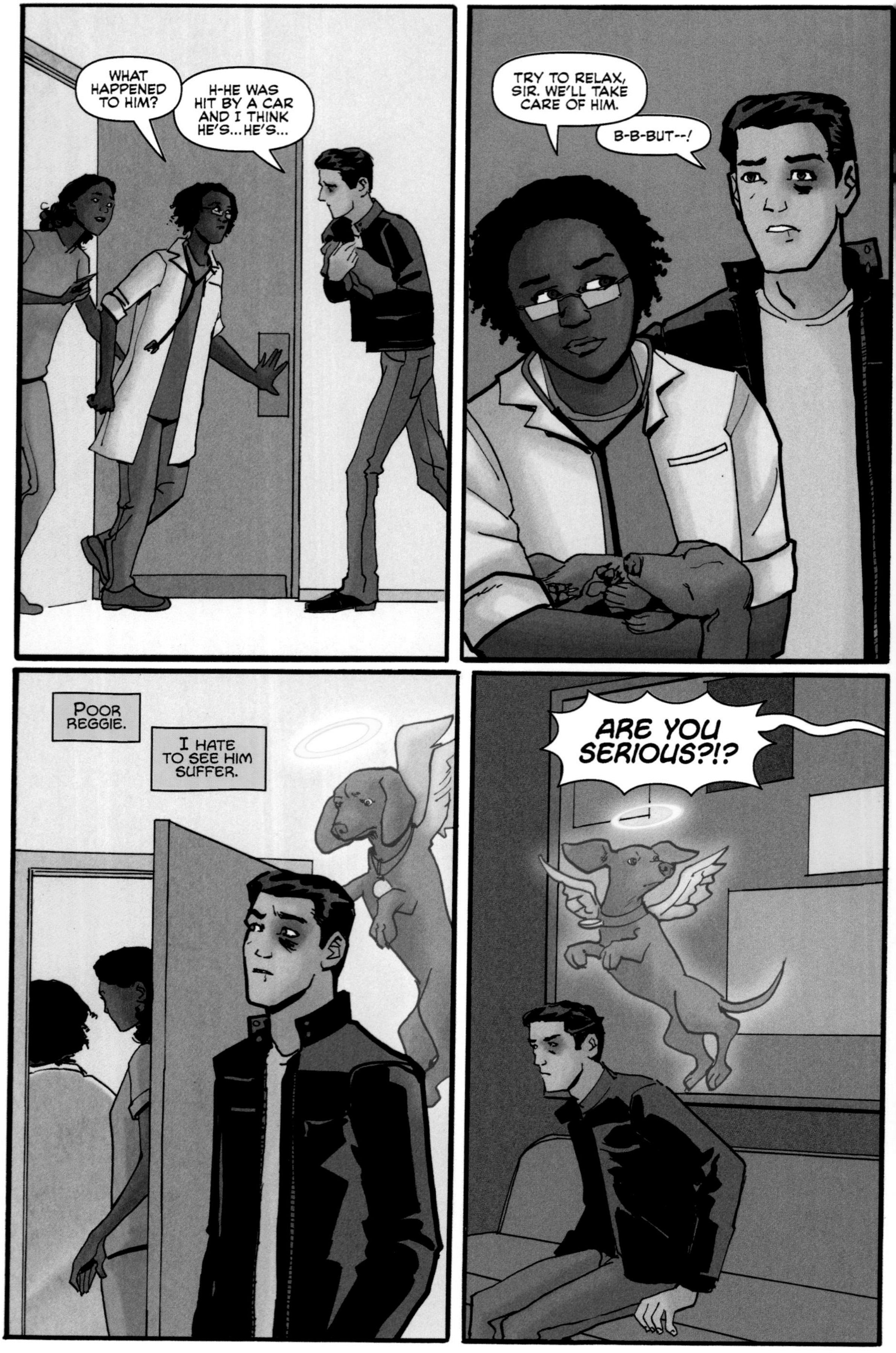
WHAT HAPPENED TO HIM?
H-HE WAS HIT BY A CAR AND I THINK HE'S...HE'S...
TRY TO RELAX, SIR. WE'LL TAKE CARE OF HIM.
B-B-BUT--!
POOR REGGIE.
I HATE TO SEE HIM SUFFER.
ARE YOU SERIOUS?!?

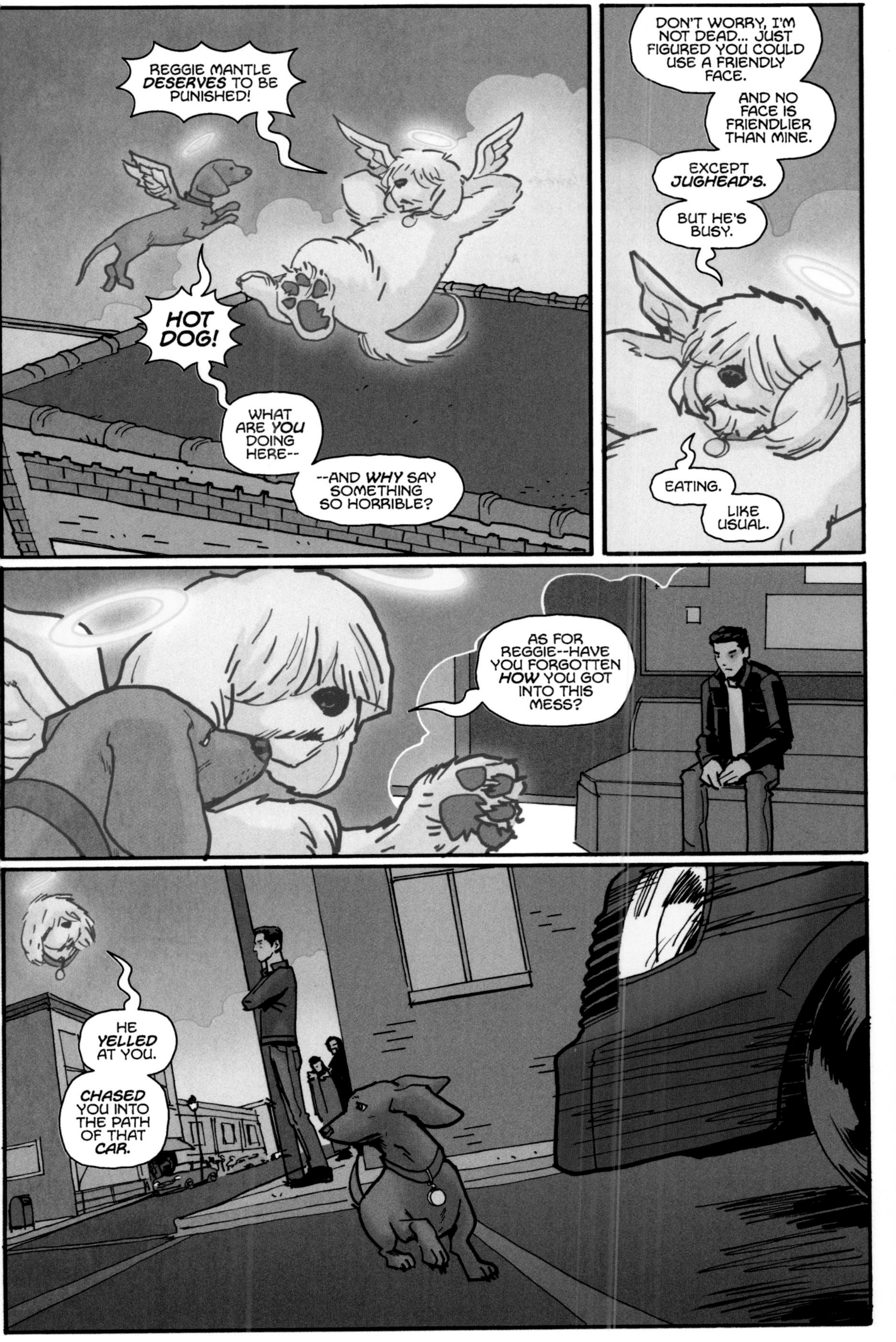

REGGIE MANTLE *DESERVES* TO BE PUNISHED!
HOT DOG!
WHAT ARE *YOU* DOING HERE--
--AND *WHY* SAY SOMETHING SO HORRIBLE?
DON'T WORRY, I'M NOT DEAD... JUST FIGURED YOU COULD USE A FRIENDLY FACE.
AND NO FACE IS FRIENDLIER THAN MINE.
EXCEPT *JUGHEAD'S.*
BUT HE'S BUSY.
EATING.
LIKE USUAL.
AS FOR REGGIE--HAVE YOU FORGOTTEN *HOW* YOU GOT INTO THIS MESS?
HE *YELLED* AT YOU.
CHASED YOU INTO THE PATH OF THAT *CAR.*

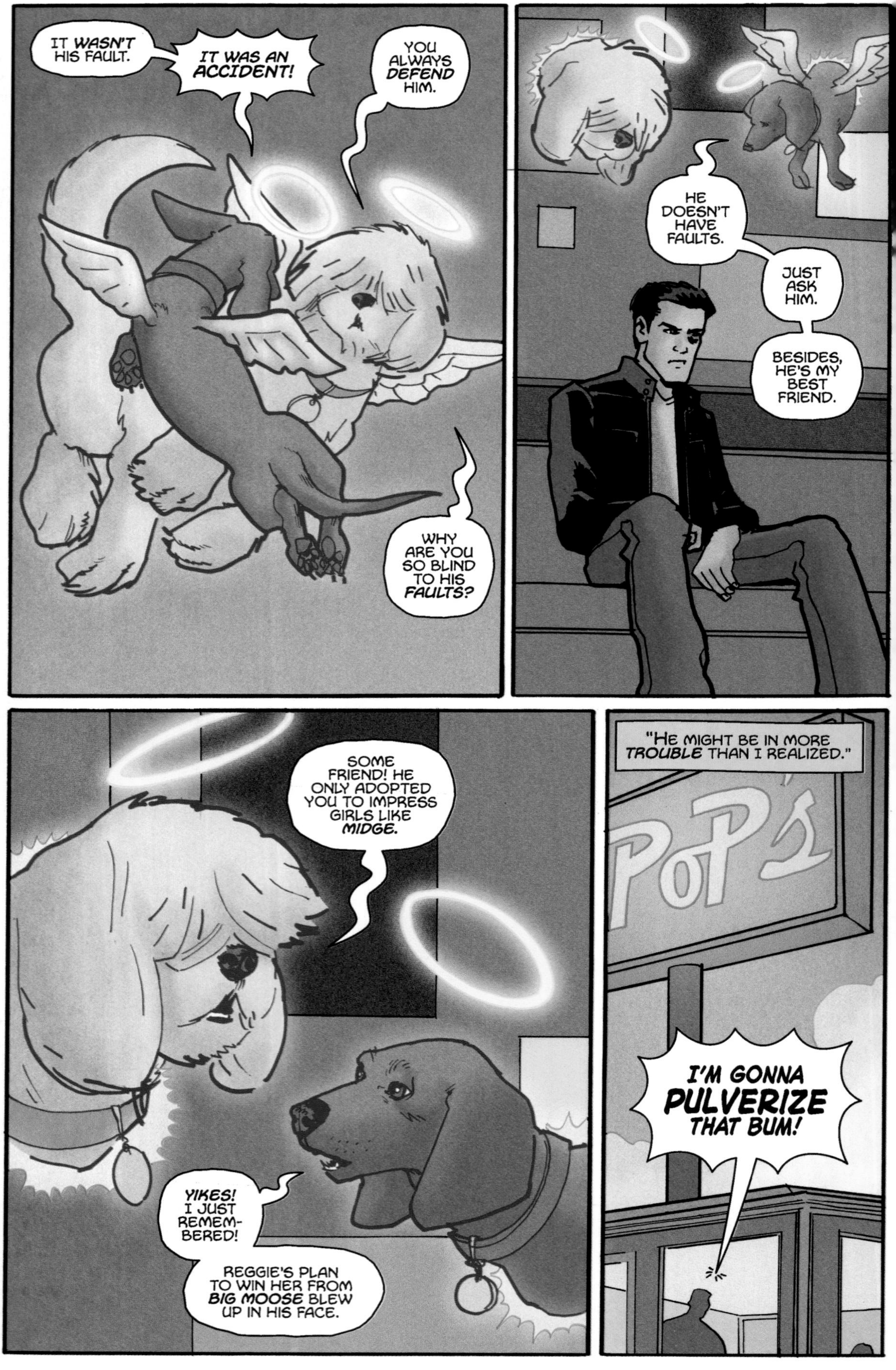
IT WASN'T HIS FAULT.
IT WAS AN ACCIDENT!
YOU ALWAYS DEFEND HIM.
WHY ARE YOU SO BLIND TO HIS FAULTS?
HE DOESN'T HAVE FAULTS.
JUST ASK HIM.
BESIDES, HE'S MY BEST FRIEND.
SOME FRIEND! HE ONLY ADOPTED YOU TO IMPRESS GIRLS LIKE MIDGE.
YIKES! I JUST REMEM-BERED!
REGGIE'S PLAN TO WIN HER FROM BIG MOOSE BLEW UP IN HIS FACE.
"HE MIGHT BE IN MORE TROUBLE THAN I REALIZED."
POP'S
I'M GONNA PULVERIZE THAT BUM!

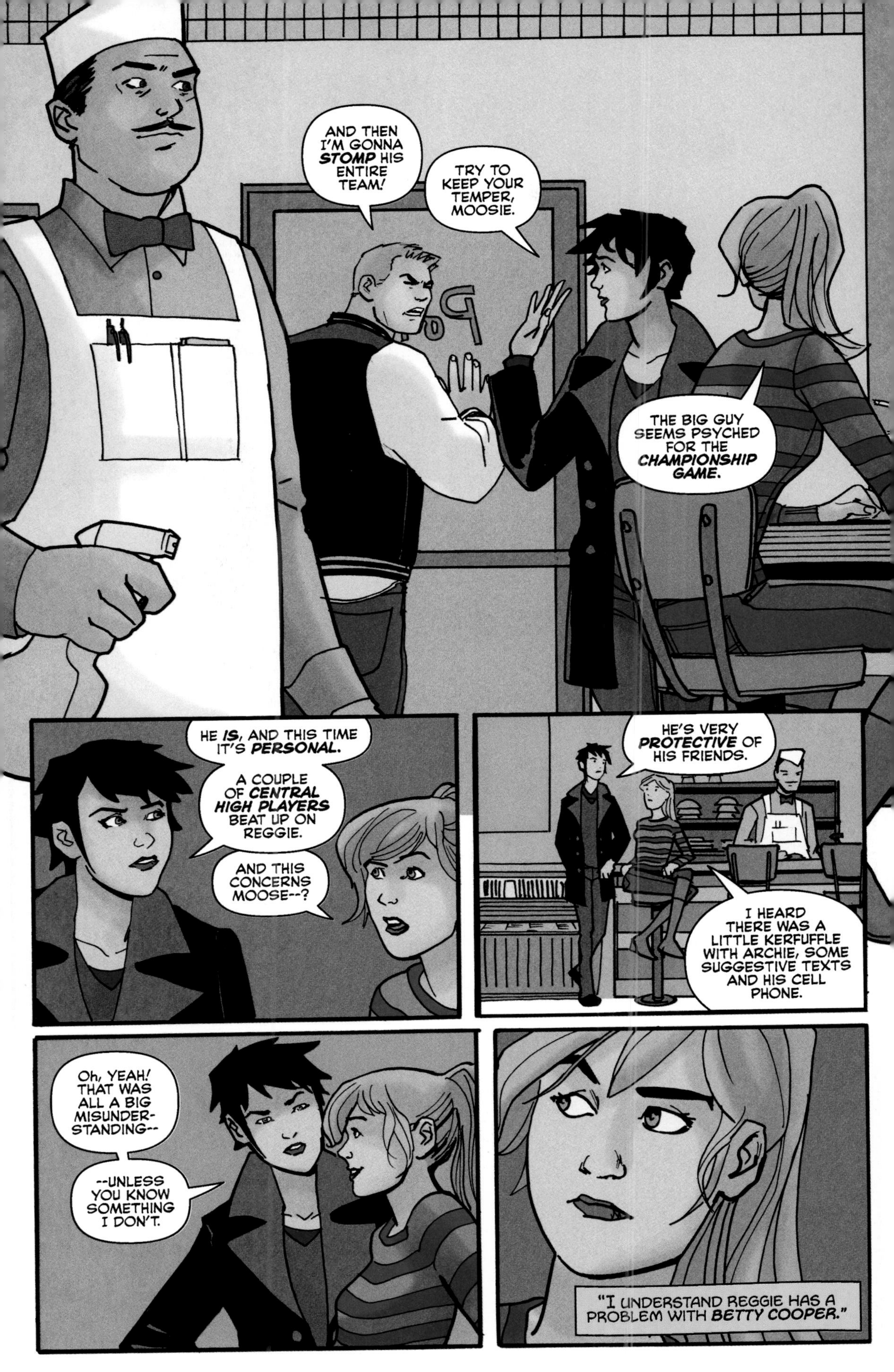

AND THEN I'M GONNA STOMP HIS ENTIRE TEAM!
TRY TO KEEP YOUR TEMPER, MOOSIE.
THE BIG GUY SEEMS PSYCHED FOR THE CHAMPIONSHIP GAME.
HE IS, AND THIS TIME IT'S PERSONAL.
A COUPLE OF CENTRAL HIGH PLAYERS BEAT UP ON REGGIE.
AND THIS CONCERNS MOOSE--?
HE'S VERY PROTECTIVE OF HIS FRIENDS.
I HEARD THERE WAS A LITTLE KERFUFFLE WITH ARCHIE, SOME SUGGESTIVE TEXTS AND HIS CELL PHONE.
Oh, YEAH! THAT WAS ALL A BIG MISUNDERSTANDING--
--UNLESS YOU KNOW SOMETHING I DON'T.
"I UNDERSTAND REGGIE HAS A PROBLEM WITH BETTY COOPER."

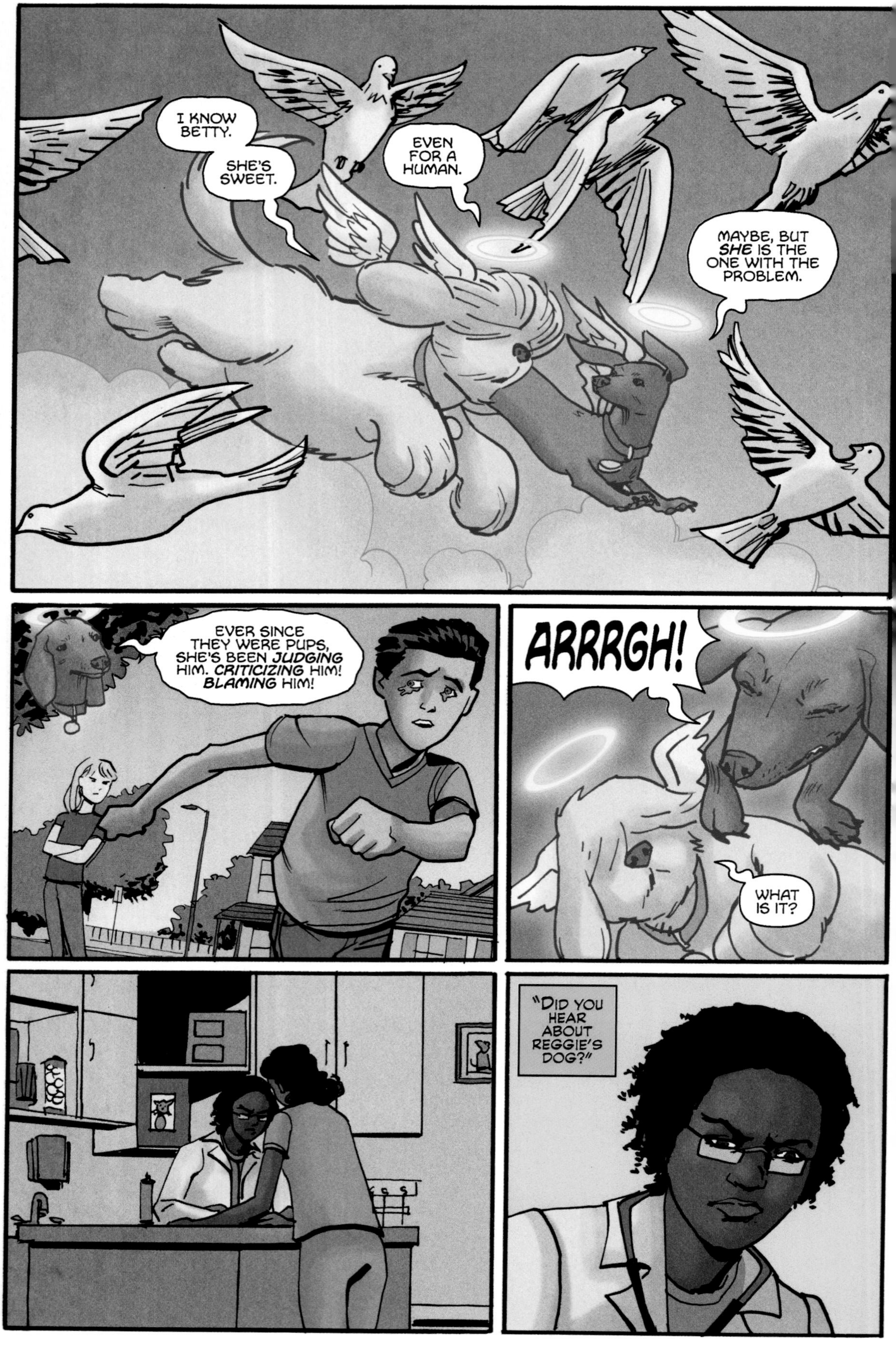
I KNOW BETTY.
SHE'S SWEET.
EVEN FOR A HUMAN.
MAYBE, BUT *SHE* IS THE ONE WITH THE PROBLEM.
EVER SINCE THEY WERE PUPS, SHE'S BEEN *JUDGING* HIM. *CRITICIZING* HIM! *BLAMING* HIM!
ARRRGH!
WHAT IS IT?
"DID YOU HEAR ABOUT REGGIE'S DOG?"

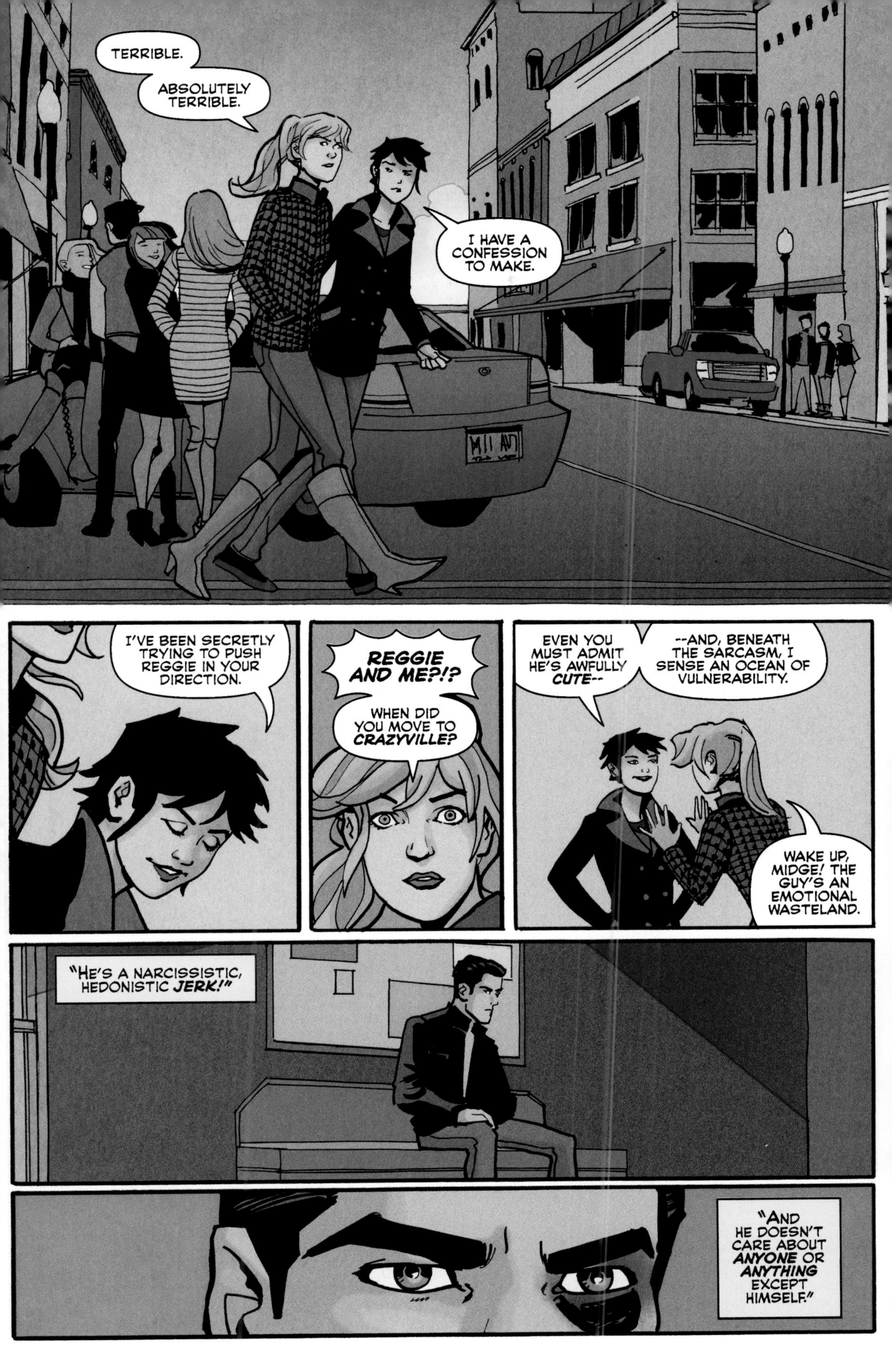
TERRIBLE.
ABSOLUTELY TERRIBLE.
I HAVE A CONFESSION TO MAKE.
I'VE BEEN SECRETLY TRYING TO PUSH REGGIE IN YOUR DIRECTION.
REGGIE AND ME?!?
WHEN DID YOU MOVE TO CRAZYVILLE?
EVEN YOU MUST ADMIT HE'S AWFULLY CUTE--
--AND, BENEATH THE SARCASM, I SENSE AN OCEAN OF VULNERABILITY.
WAKE UP, MIDGE! THE GUY'S AN EMOTIONAL WASTELAND.
"HE'S A NARCISSISTIC, HEDONISTIC JERK!"
"AND HE DOESN'T CARE ABOUT ANYONE OR ANYTHING EXCEPT HIMSELF."

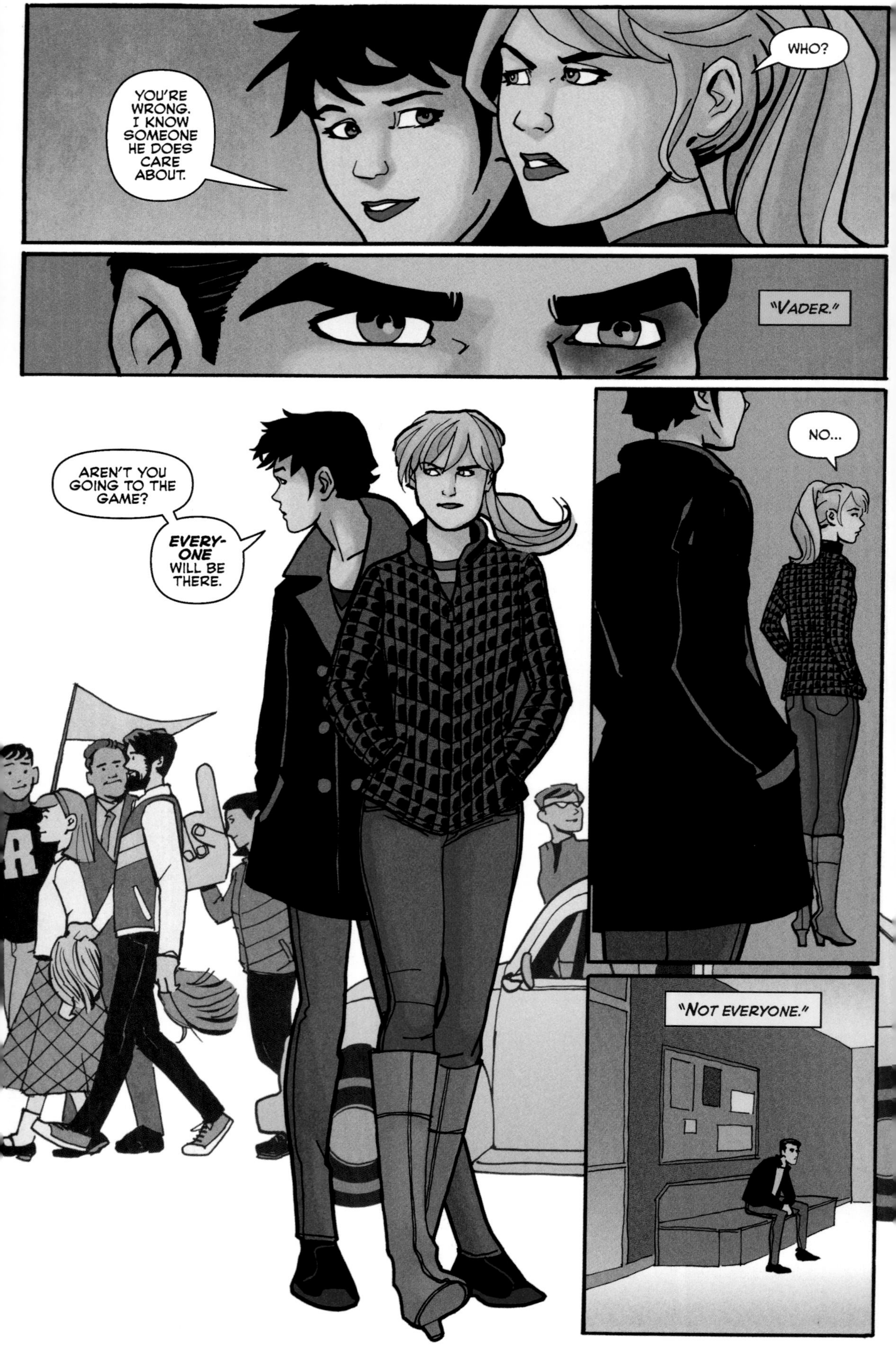
YOU'RE WRONG. I KNOW SOMEONE HE DOES CARE ABOUT.
WHO?
"VADER."
AREN'T YOU GOING TO THE GAME?
EVERY-ONE WILL BE THERE.
NO...
"NOT EVERYONE."

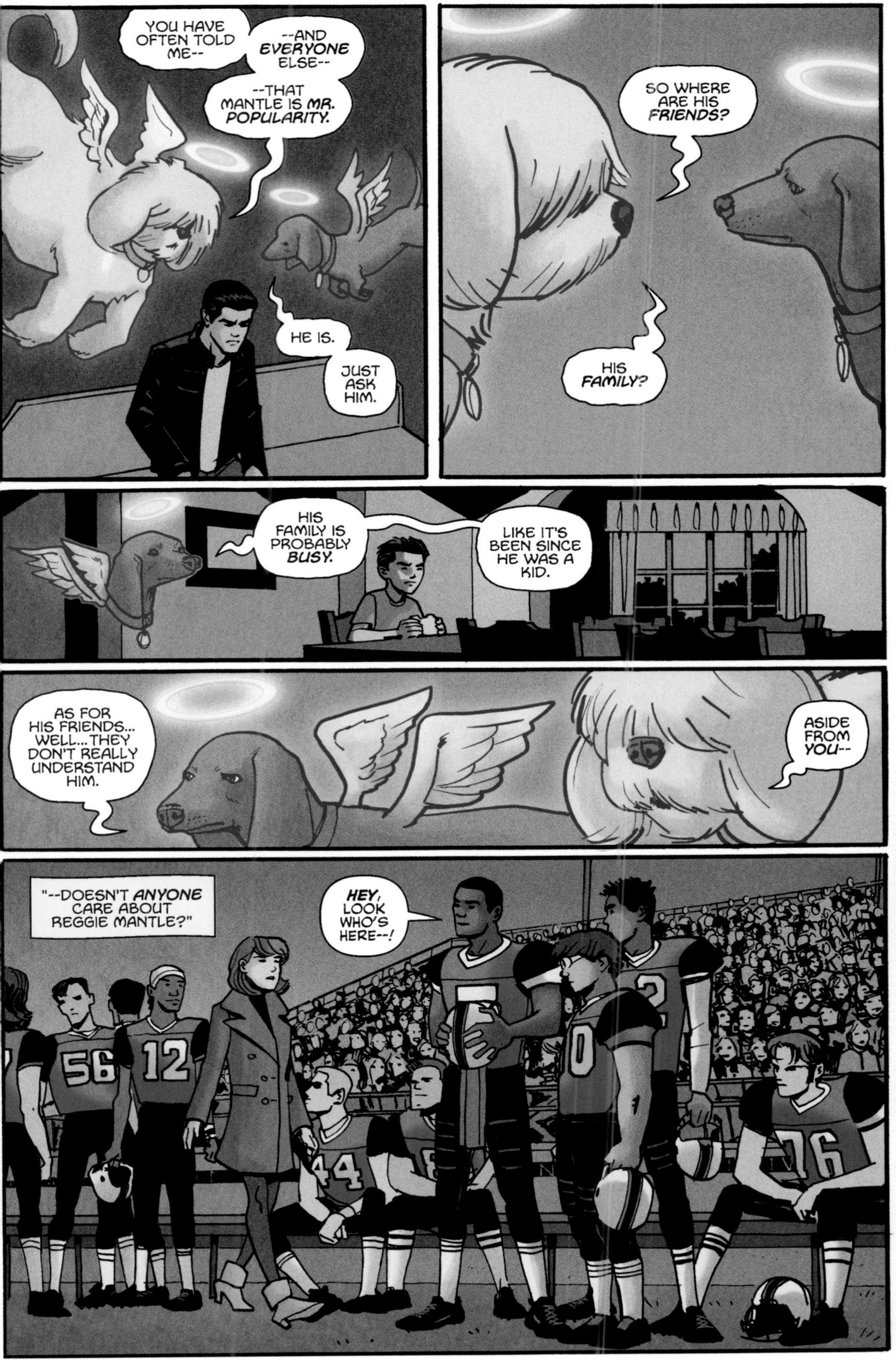

YOU HAVE OFTEN TOLD ME--
--AND EVERYONE ELSE--
--THAT MANTLE IS MR. POPULARITY.
HE IS.
JUST ASK HIM.
SO WHERE ARE HIS FRIENDS?
HIS FAMILY?
HIS FAMILY IS PROBABLY BUSY.
LIKE IT'S BEEN SINCE HE WAS A KID.
AS FOR HIS FRIENDS... WELL... THEY DON'T REALLY UNDERSTAND HIM.
ASIDE FROM YOU--
"--DOESN'T ANYONE CARE ABOUT REGGIE MANTLE?"
HEY, LOOK WHO'S HERE--!

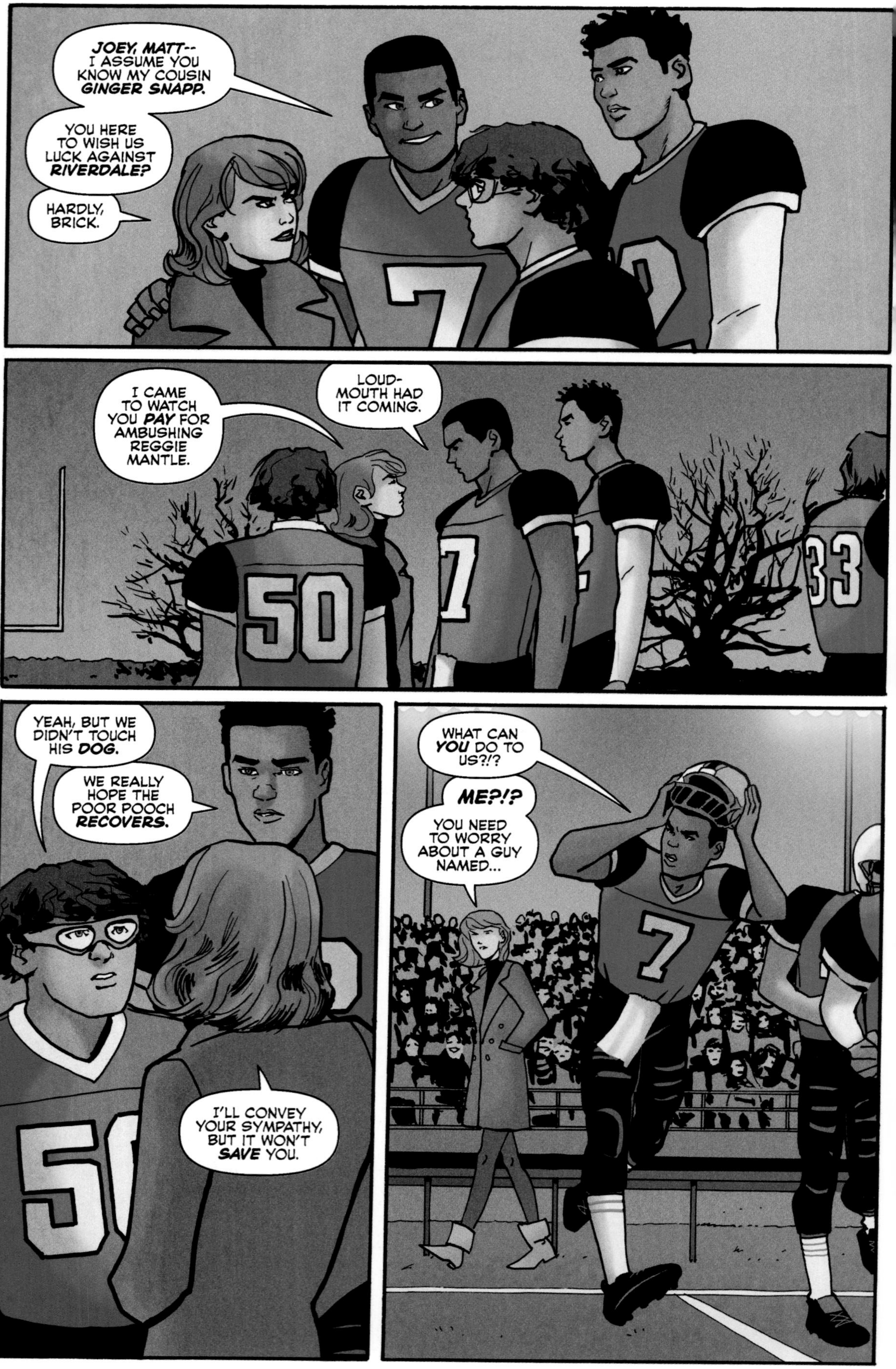
JOEY, MATT-- I ASSUME YOU KNOW MY COUSIN GINGER SNAPP.
YOU HERE TO WISH US LUCK AGAINST RIVERDALE?
HARDLY, BRICK.
I CAME TO WATCH YOU PAY FOR AMBUSHING REGGIE MANTLE.
LOUD-MOUTH HAD IT COMING.
50
7
33
YEAH, BUT WE DIDN'T TOUCH HIS DOG.
WE REALLY HOPE THE POOR POOCH RECOVERS.
I'LL CONVEY YOUR SYMPATHY, BUT IT WON'T SAVE YOU.
WHAT CAN YOU DO TO US?!?
ME?!?
YOU NEED TO WORRY ABOUT A GUY NAMED...
7

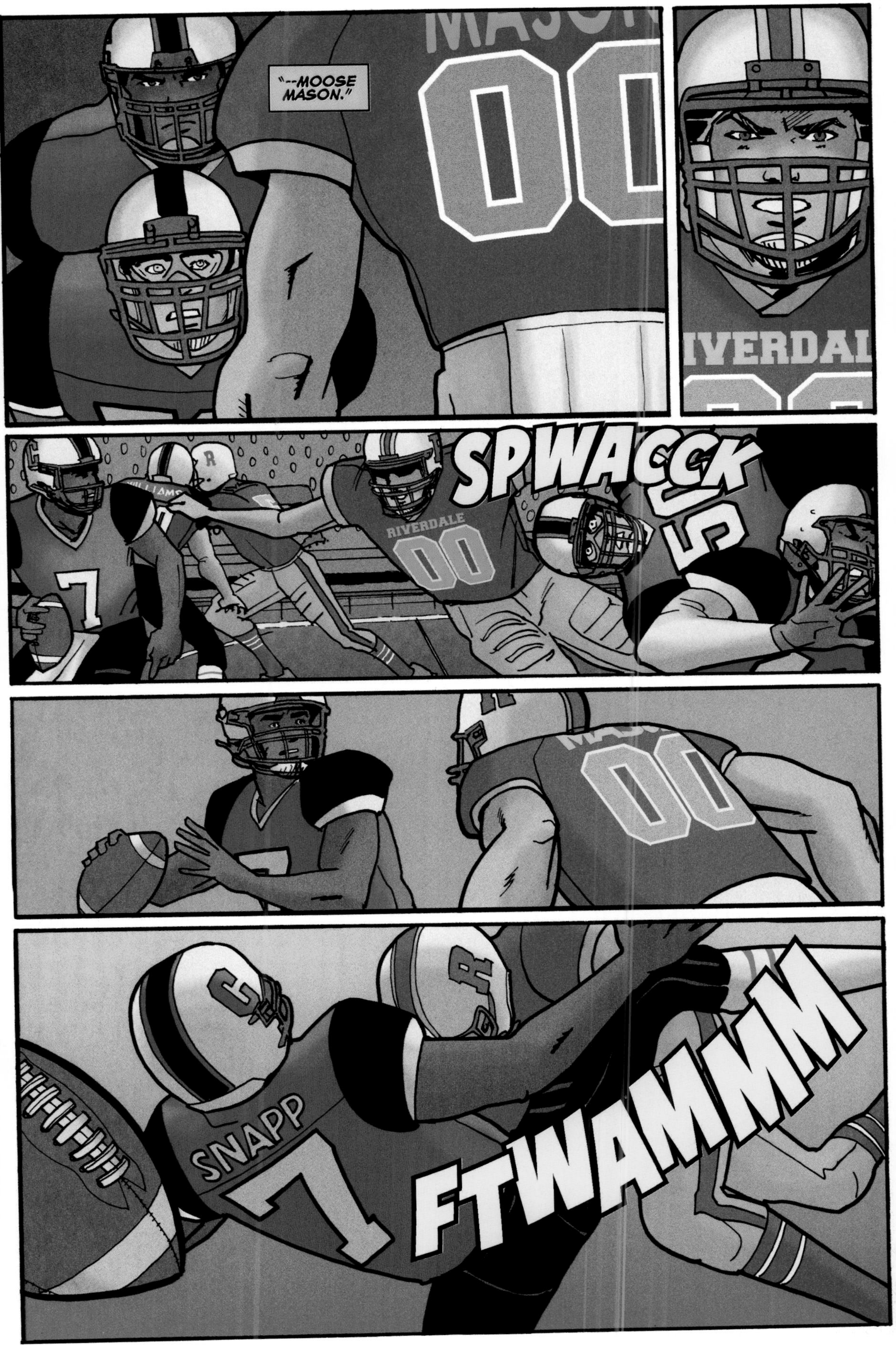
"--MOOSE MASON."
WILLIAMS
RIVERDALE
00
SPWACCK
SNAPP
7
FTWAMMM

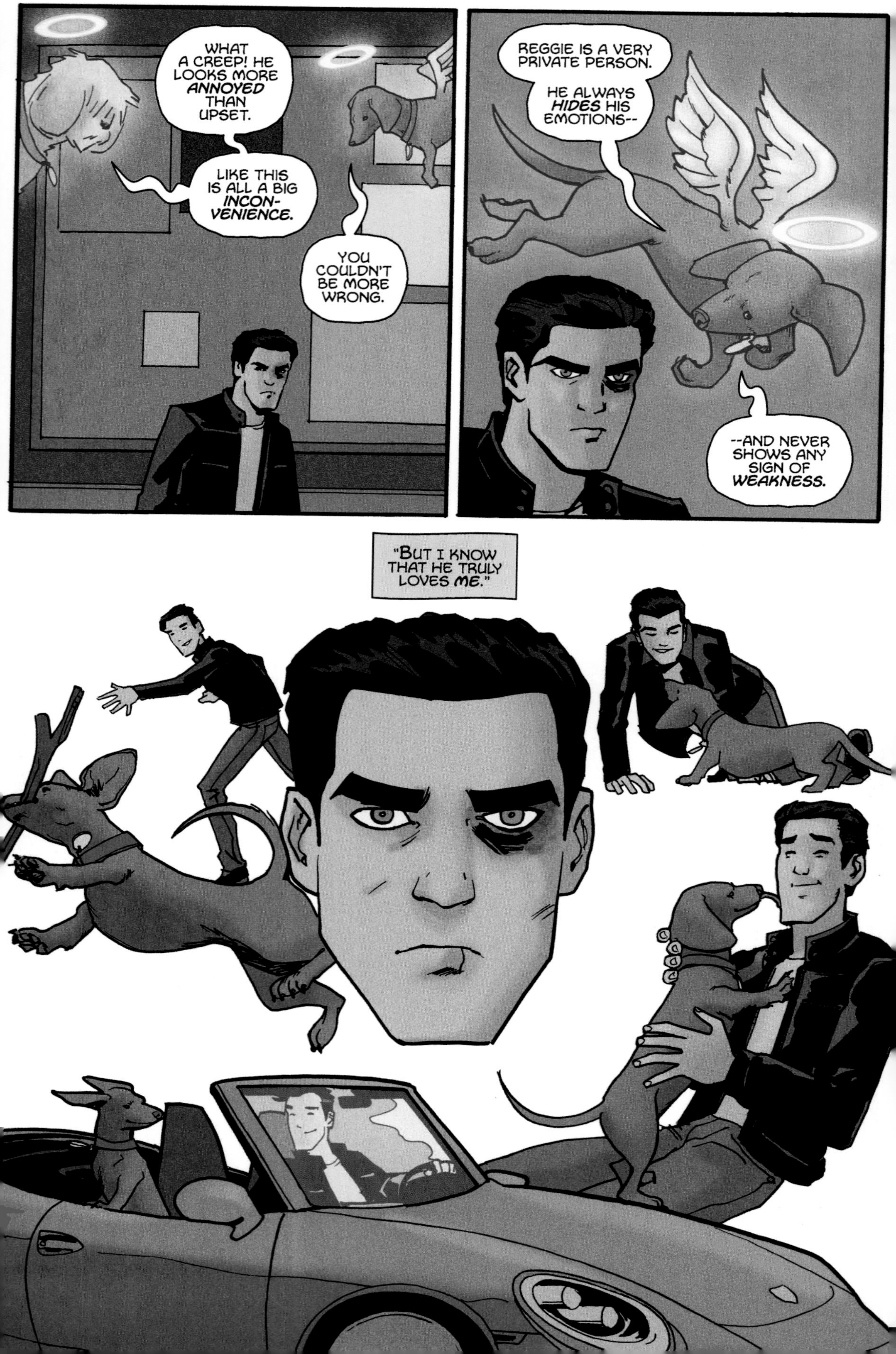
WHAT A CREEP! HE LOOKS MORE ANNOYED THAN UPSET.
LIKE THIS IS ALL A BIG INCON-VENIENCE.
YOU COULDN'T BE MORE WRONG.
REGGIE IS A VERY PRIVATE PERSON.
HE ALWAYS HIDES HIS EMOTIONS--
--AND NEVER SHOWS ANY SIGN OF WEAKNESS.
"BUT I KNOW THAT HE TRULY LOVES ME."

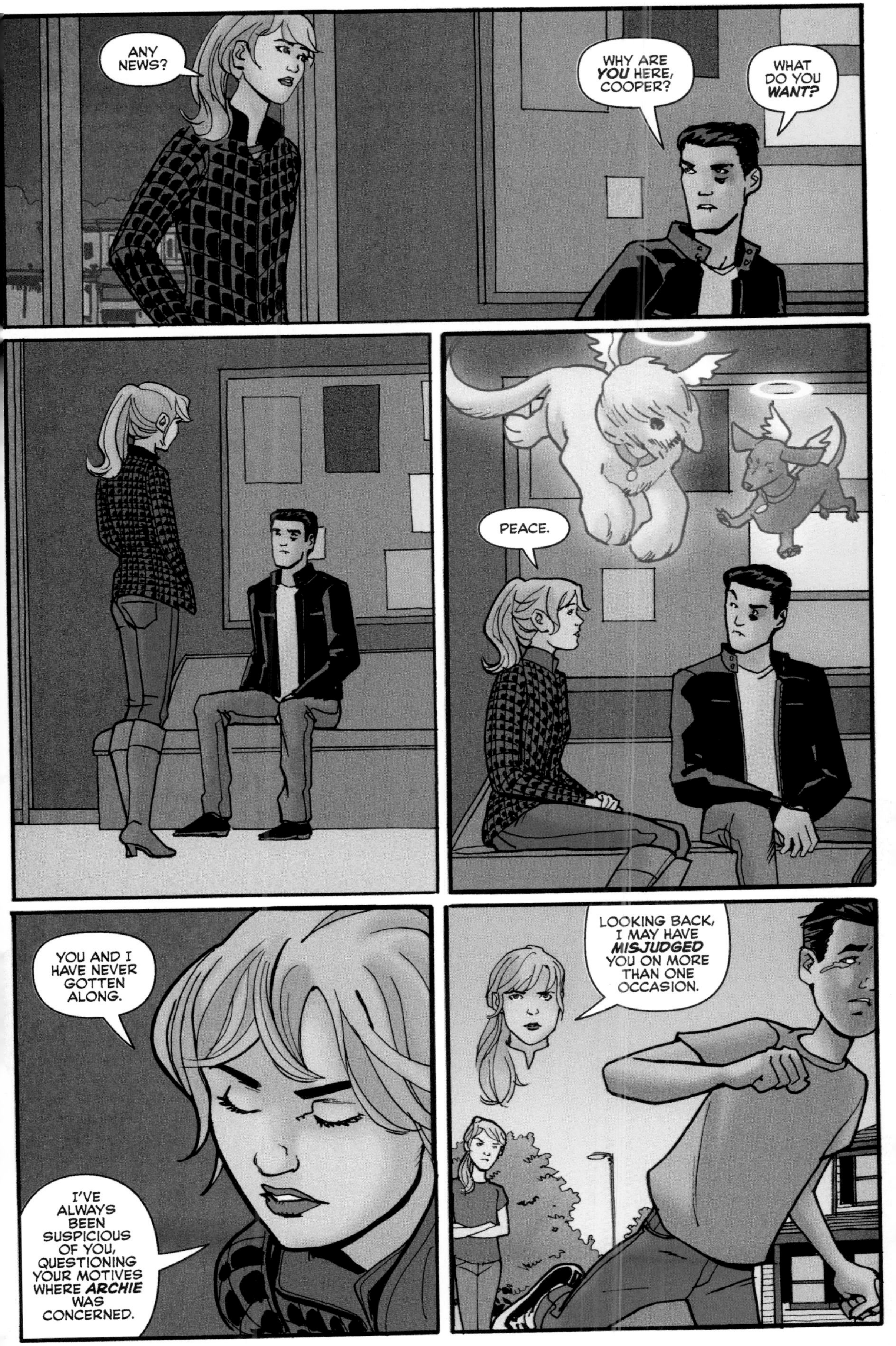
ANY NEWS?
WHY ARE YOU HERE, COOPER?
WHAT DO YOU WANT?
PEACE.
YOU AND I HAVE NEVER GOTTEN ALONG.
I'VE ALWAYS BEEN SUSPICIOUS OF YOU, QUESTIONING YOUR MOTIVES WHERE ARCHIE WAS CONCERNED.
LOOKING BACK, I MAY HAVE MISJUDGED YOU ON MORE THAN ONE OCCASION.

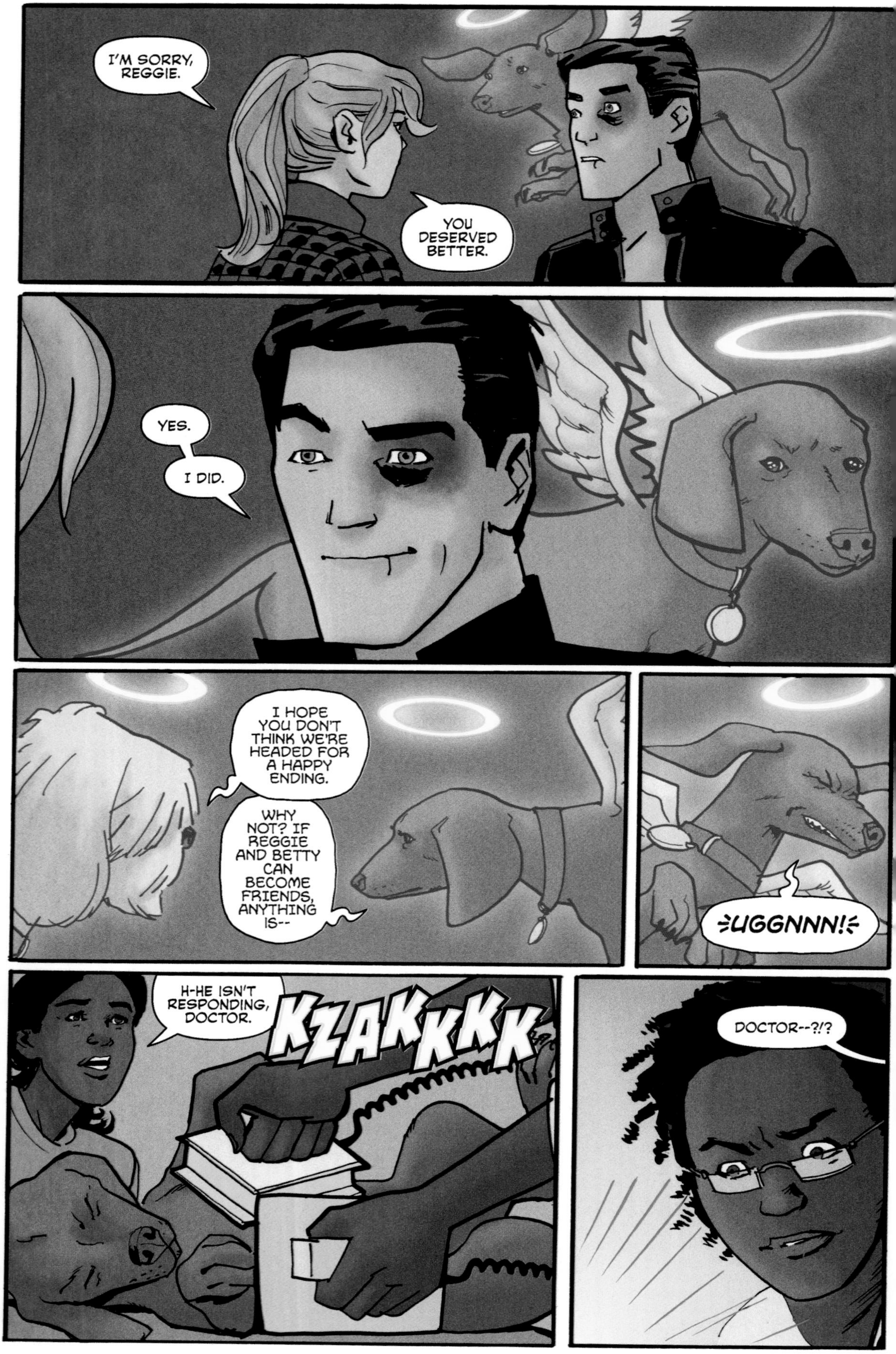
I'M SORRY, REGGIE.
YOU DESERVED BETTER.
YES.
I DID.
I HOPE YOU DON'T THINK WE'RE HEADED FOR A HAPPY ENDING.
WHY NOT? IF REGGIE AND BETTY CAN BECOME FRIENDS, ANYTHING IS--
UGGNNN!
H-HE ISN'T RESPONDING, DOCTOR.
KZAKKKK
DOCTOR--?!?

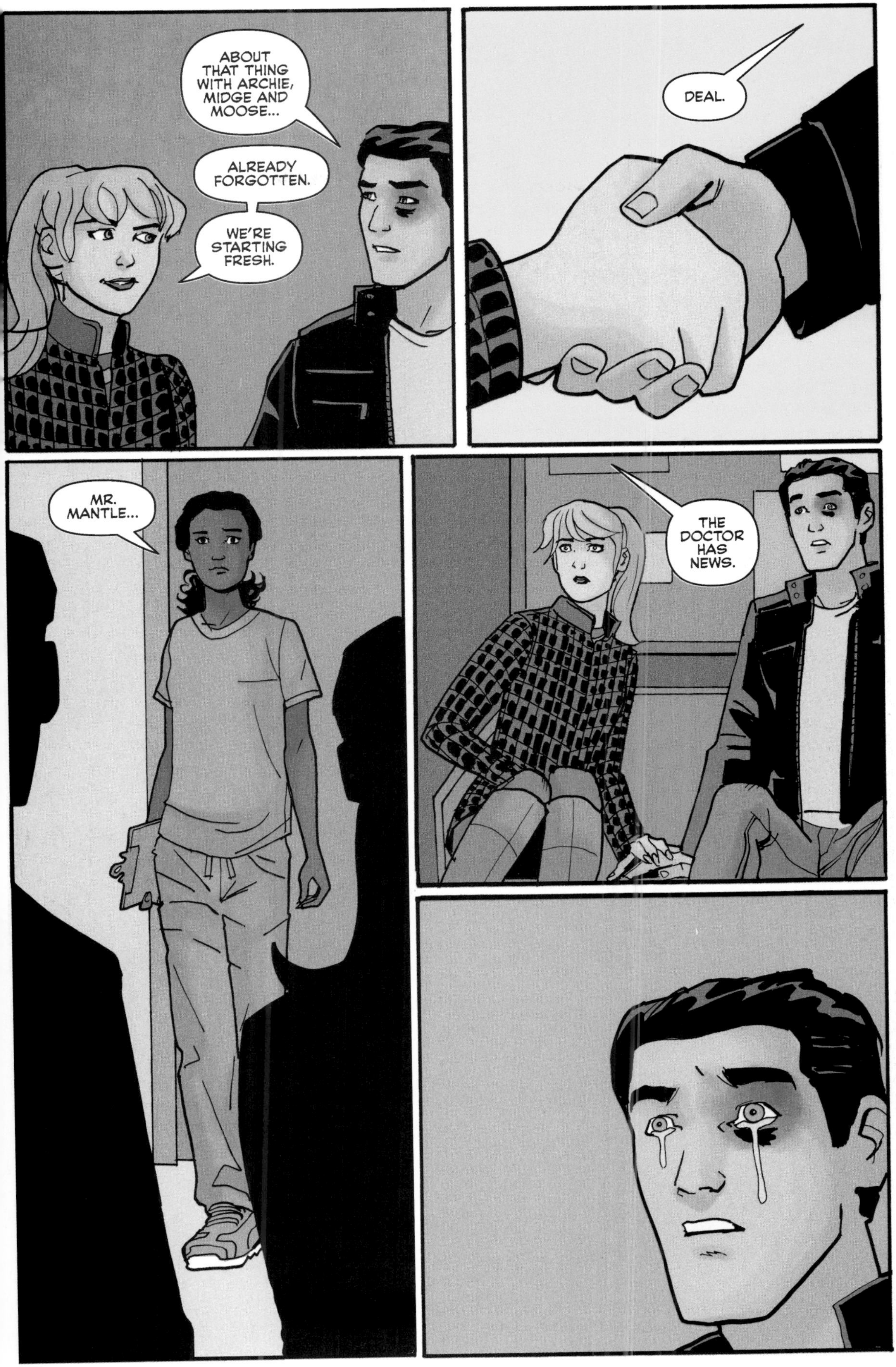
ABOUT THAT THING WITH ARCHIE, MIDGE AND MOOSE...
ALREADY FORGOTTEN.
WE'RE STARTING FRESH.
DEAL.
MR. MANTLE...
THE DOCTOR HAS NEWS.

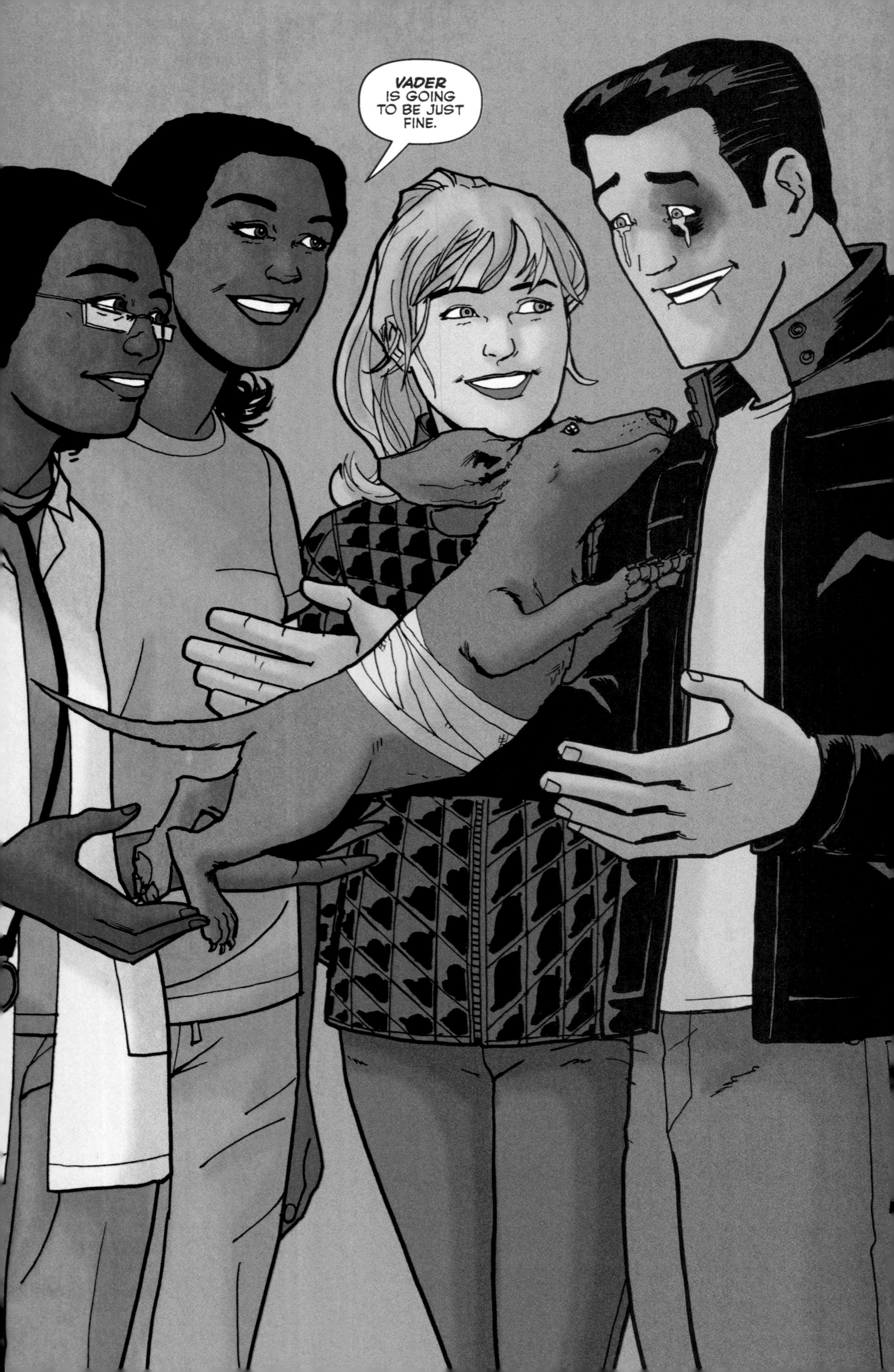
VADER IS GOING TO BE JUST FINE.

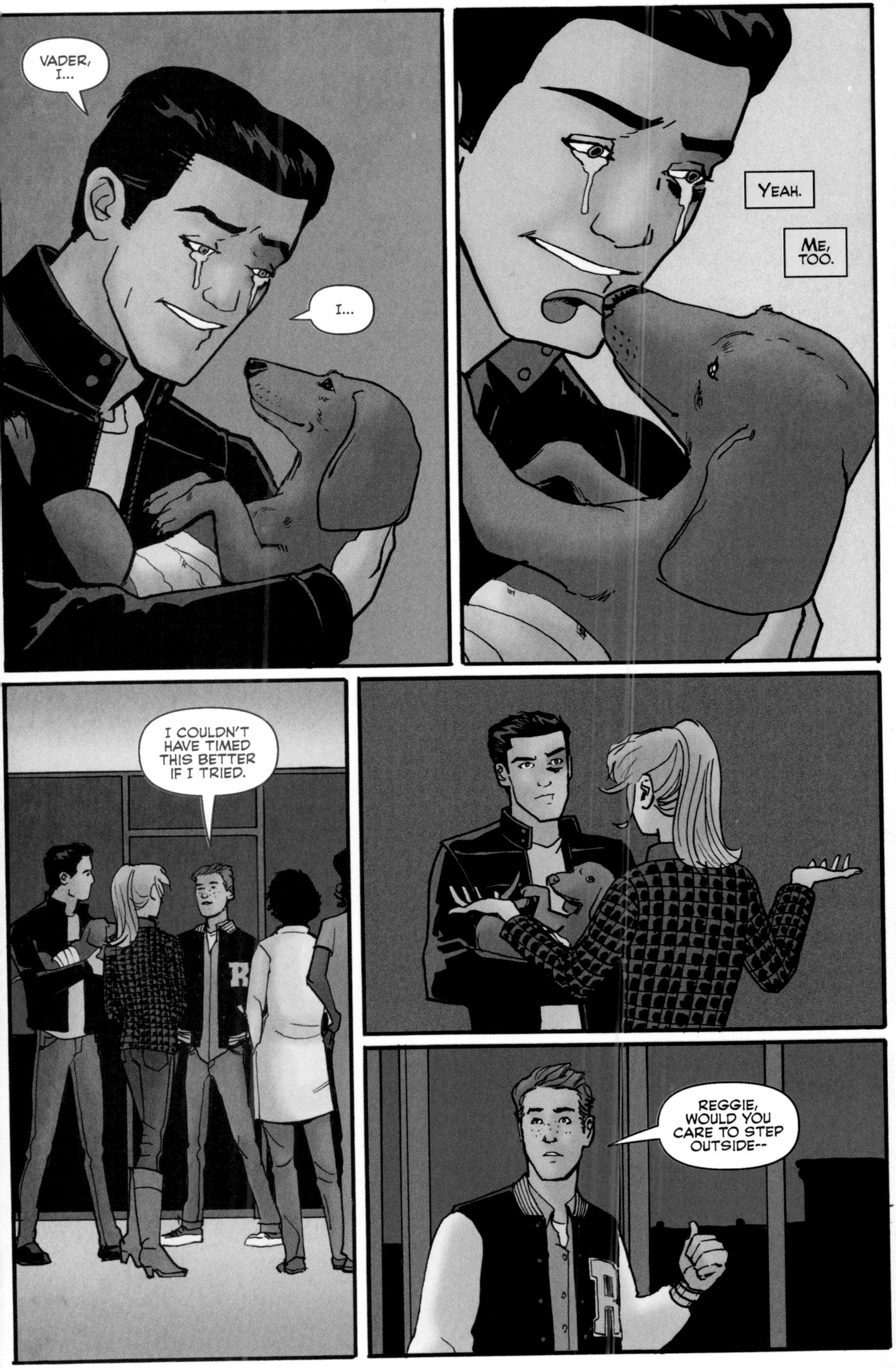
VADER, I...
I...
YEAH.
ME, TOO.
I COULDN'T HAVE TIMED THIS BETTER IF I TRIED.
REGGIE, WOULD YOU CARE TO STEP OUTSIDE--

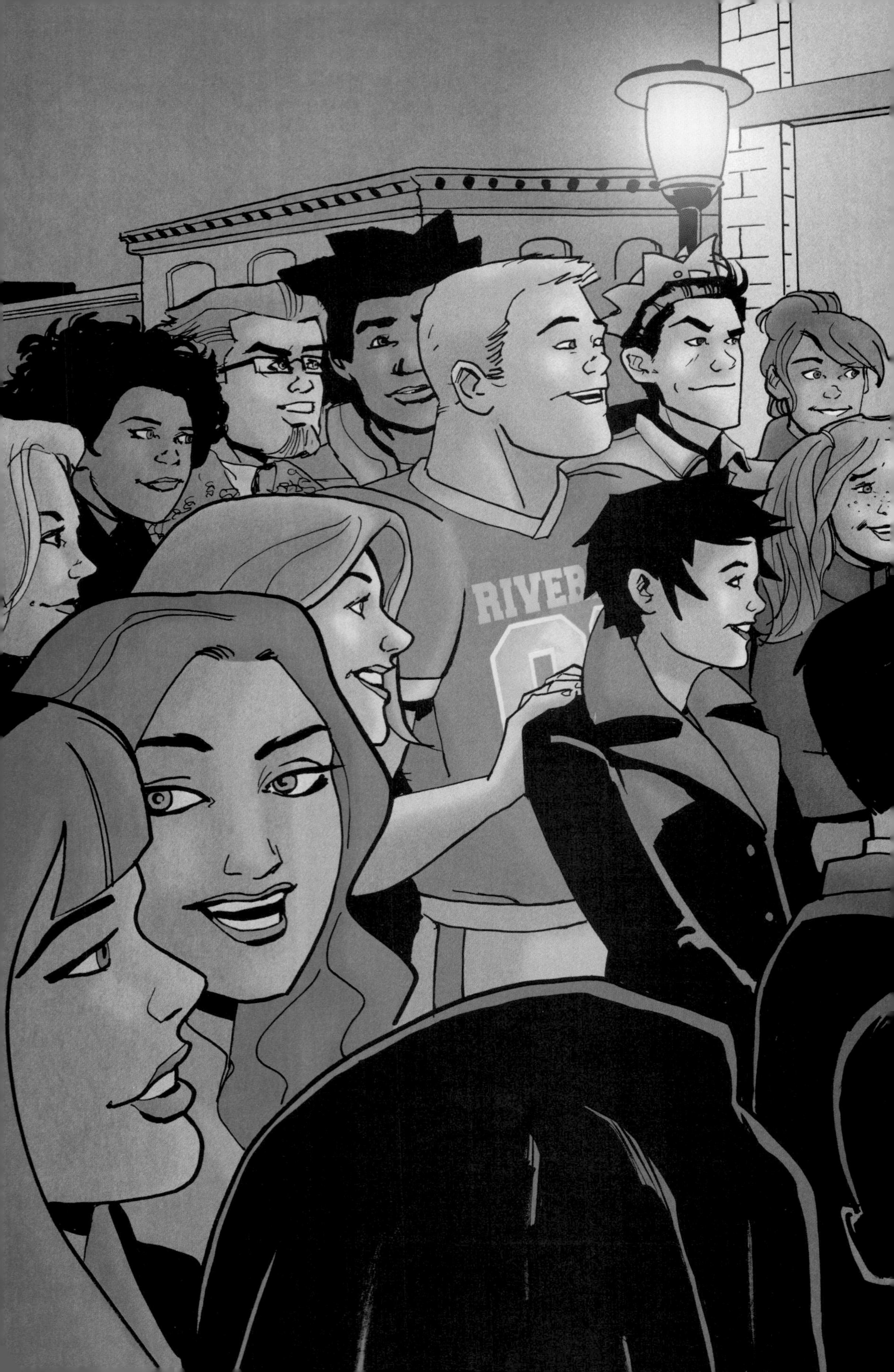
RIVER

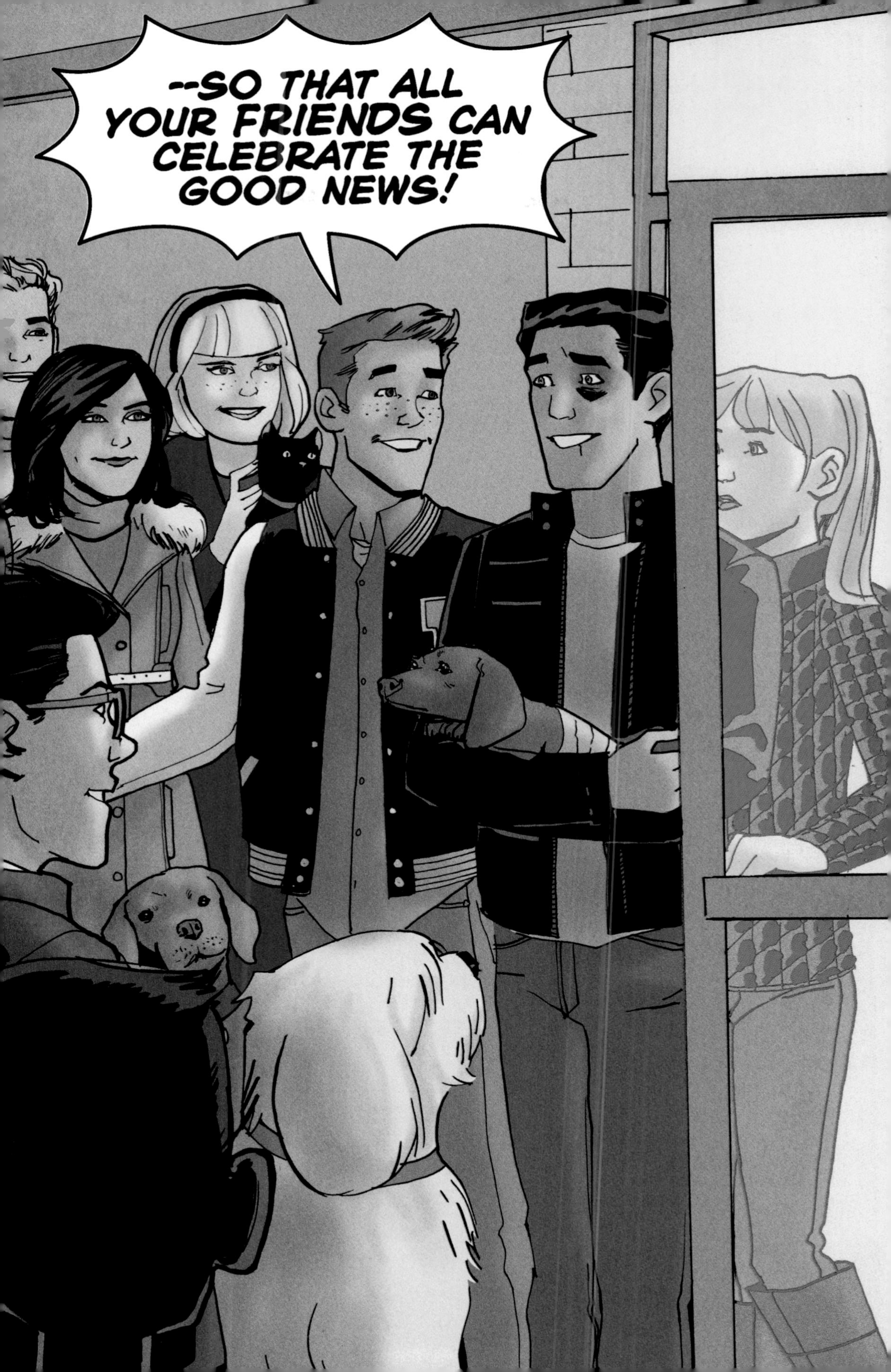
--SO THAT ALL YOUR FRIENDS CAN CELEBRATE THE GOOD NEWS!

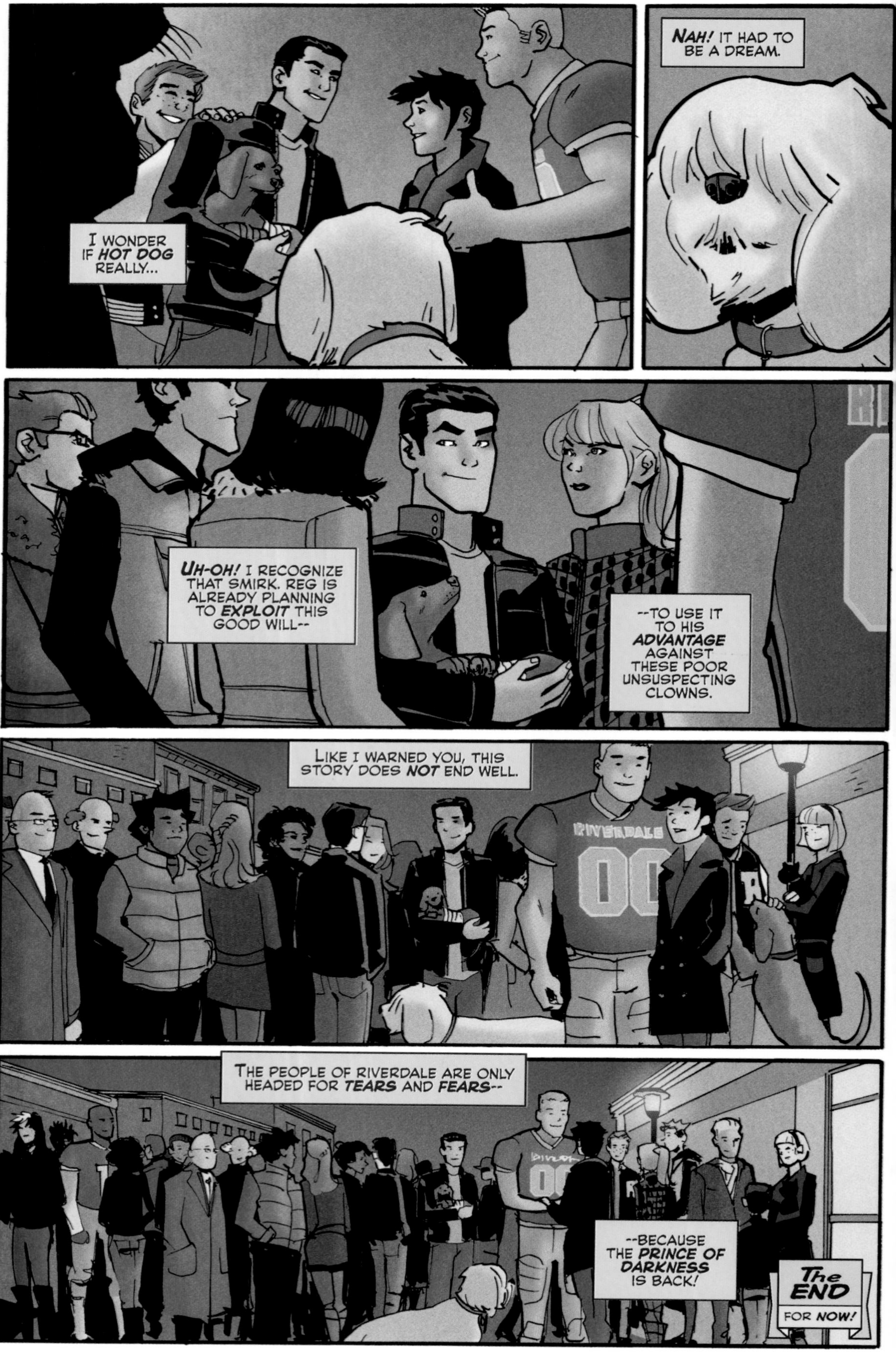

I WONDER IF HOT DOG REALLY...
NAH! IT HAD TO BE A DREAM.
UH-OH! I RECOGNIZE THAT SMIRK. REG IS ALREADY PLANNING TO EXPLOIT THIS GOOD WILL--
--TO USE IT TO HIS ADVANTAGE AGAINST THESE POOR UNSUSPECTING CLOWNS.
LIKE I WARNED YOU, THIS STORY DOES NOT END WELL.
RIVERDALE
00
THE PEOPLE OF RIVERDALE ARE ONLY HEADED FOR TEARS AND FEARS--
--BECAUSE THE PRINCE OF DARKNESS IS BACK!
The END
FOR NOW!

REGGIE AND ME

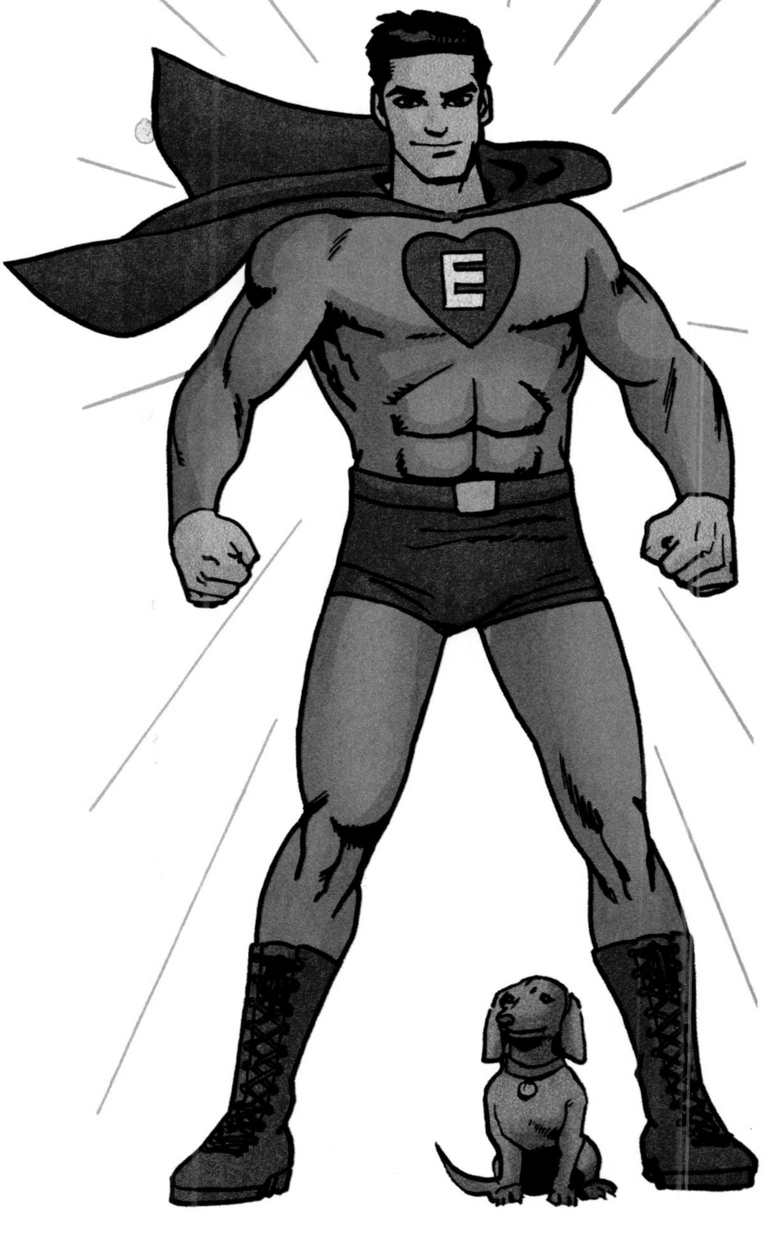

SPECIAL FEATURES

REGGIE AND ME

COVER GALLERY

In addition to the amazing main covers we have for each issue, we also receive gorgeous artwork from an array of talented artists for our direct market exclusive covers. Here are all of the main and variant covers for each of the five issues in *Reggie and Me*.

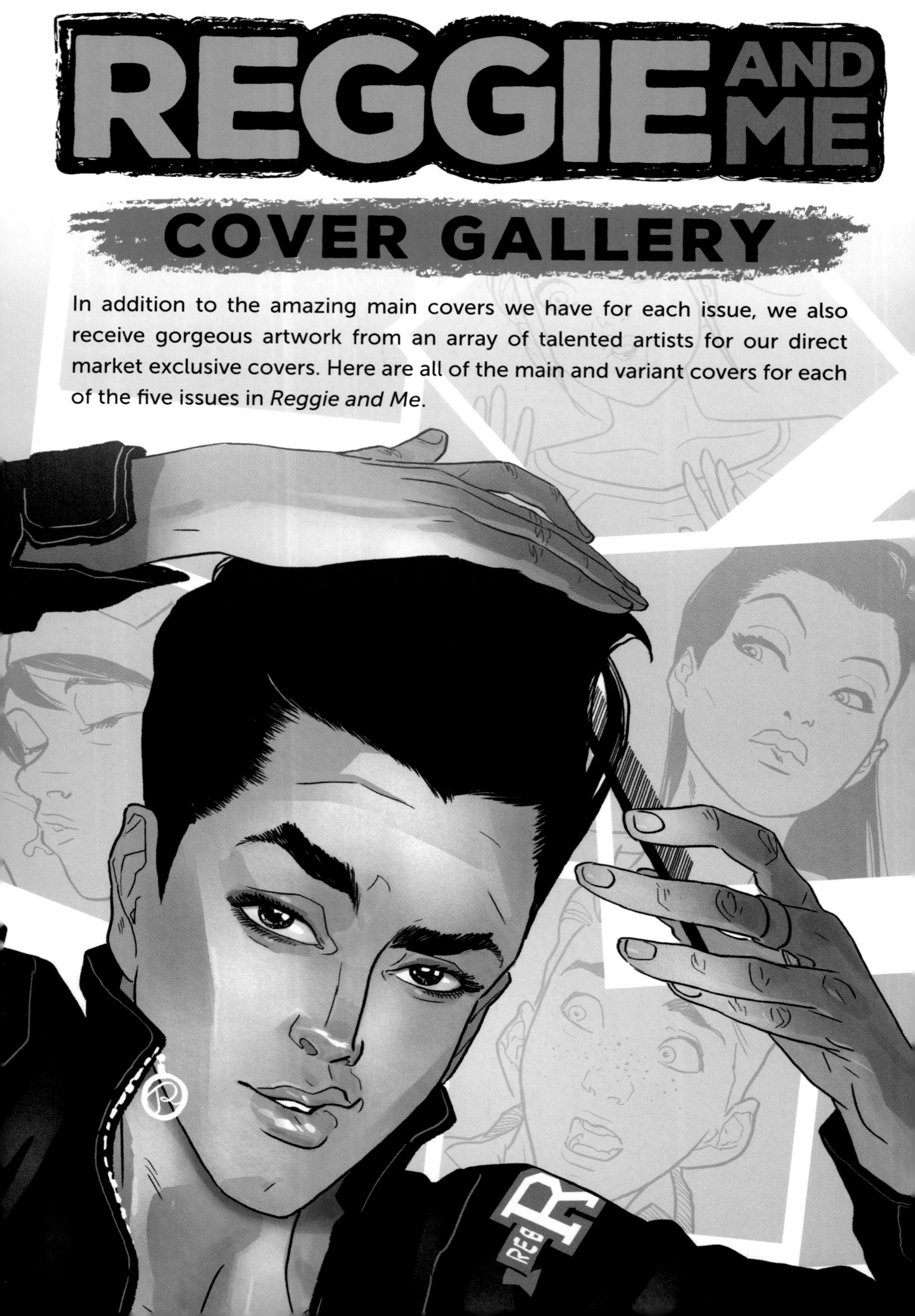

ISSUE ONE

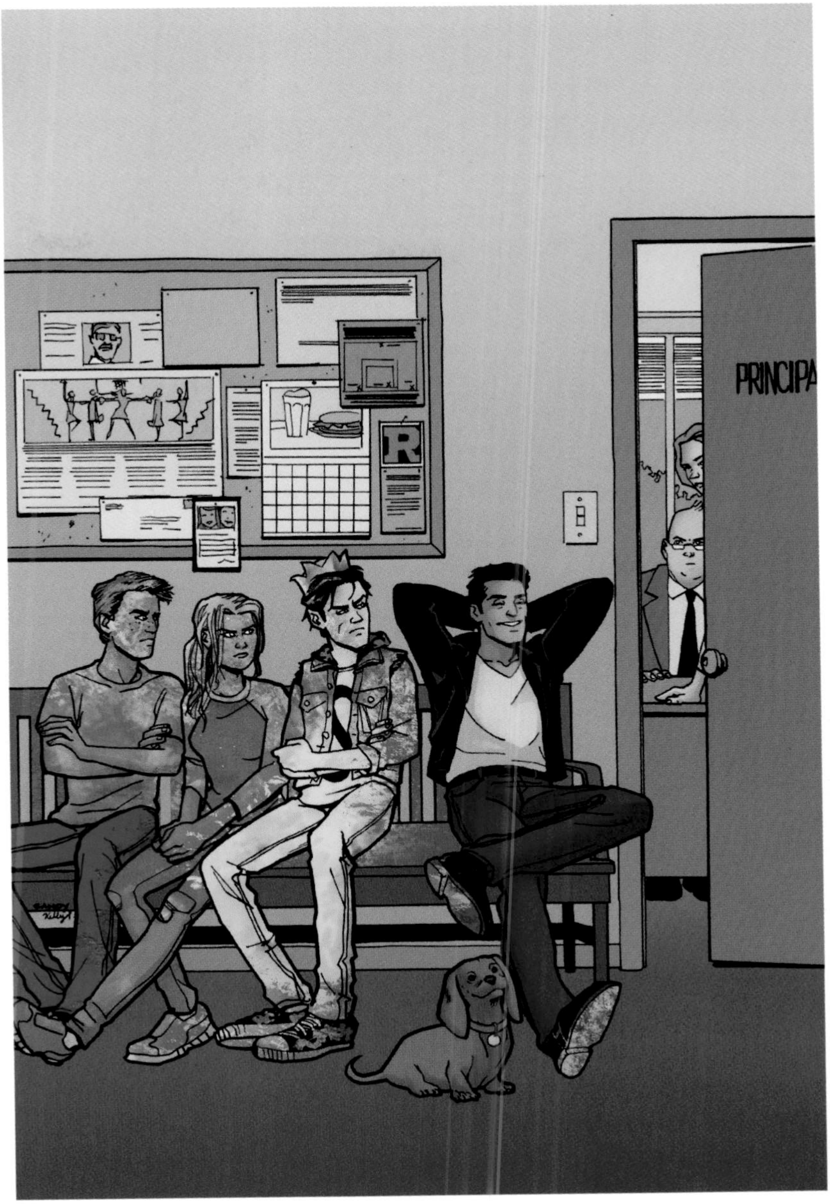
PRINCIPA

SANDY JARRELL

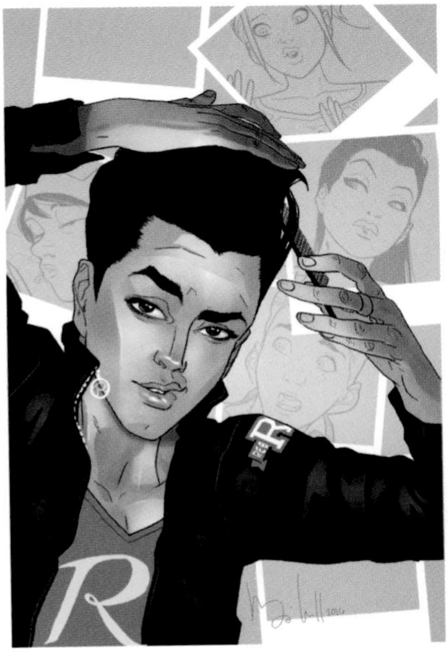

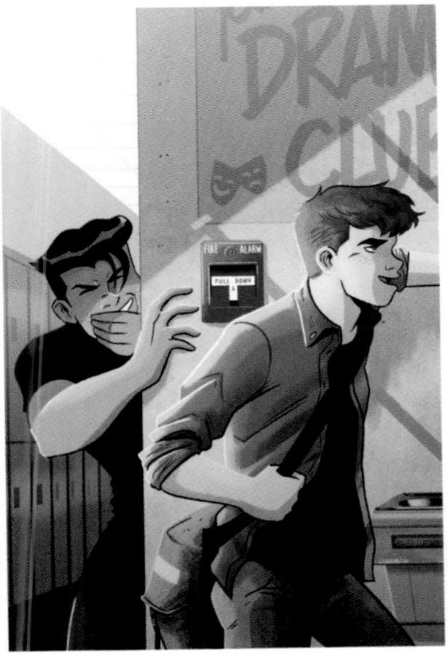
DRAM
CLU
FIRE ALARM
PULL DOWN

(L) BEN CALDWELL

(R) DEREK CHARM

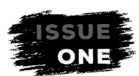

(L)
RON FRENZ

(R)
ROBERT HACK

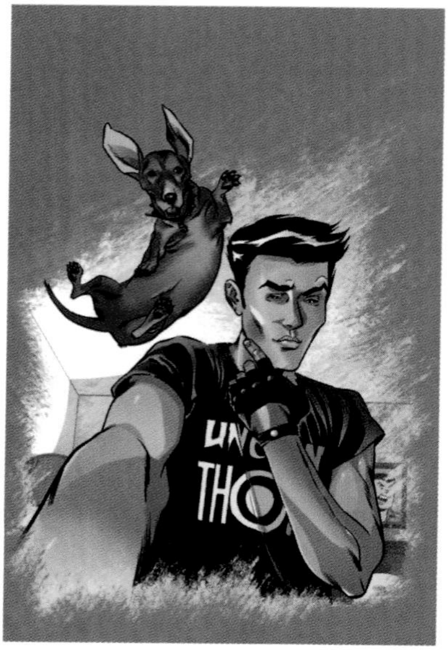

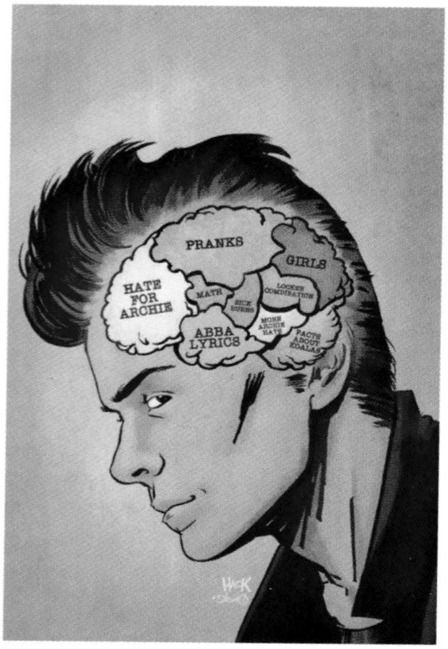
PRANKS
GIRLS
HATE FOR ARCHIE
MATH
LOCKER COMBINATION
ABBA LYRICS
FACTS ABOUT KOALAS
HACK

(L)
RYAN JAMPOLE

(R)
THOMAS PITILLI

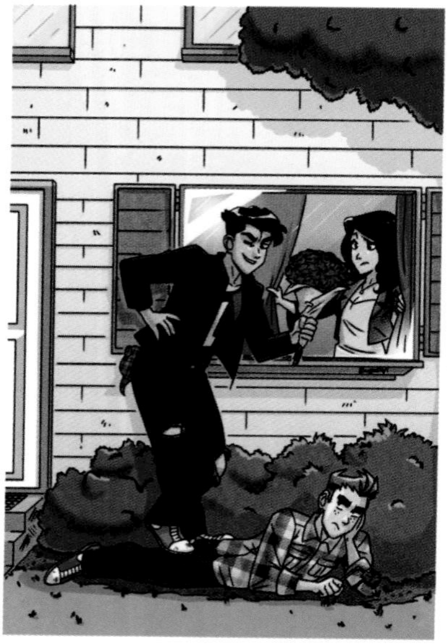

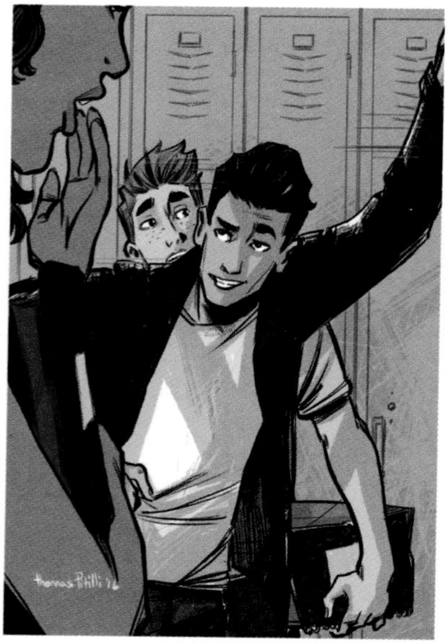

(L)
WILFREDO TORRES

(R)
MICHAEL WALSH

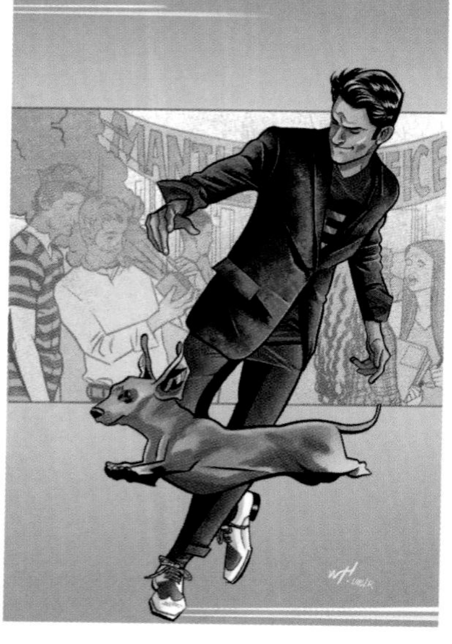

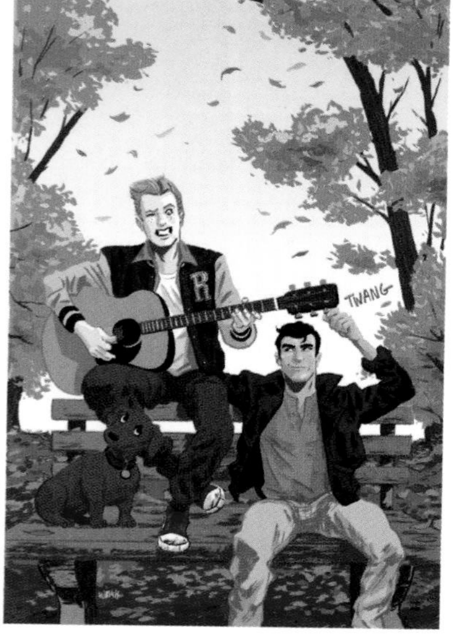
TWANG

ISSUE TWO

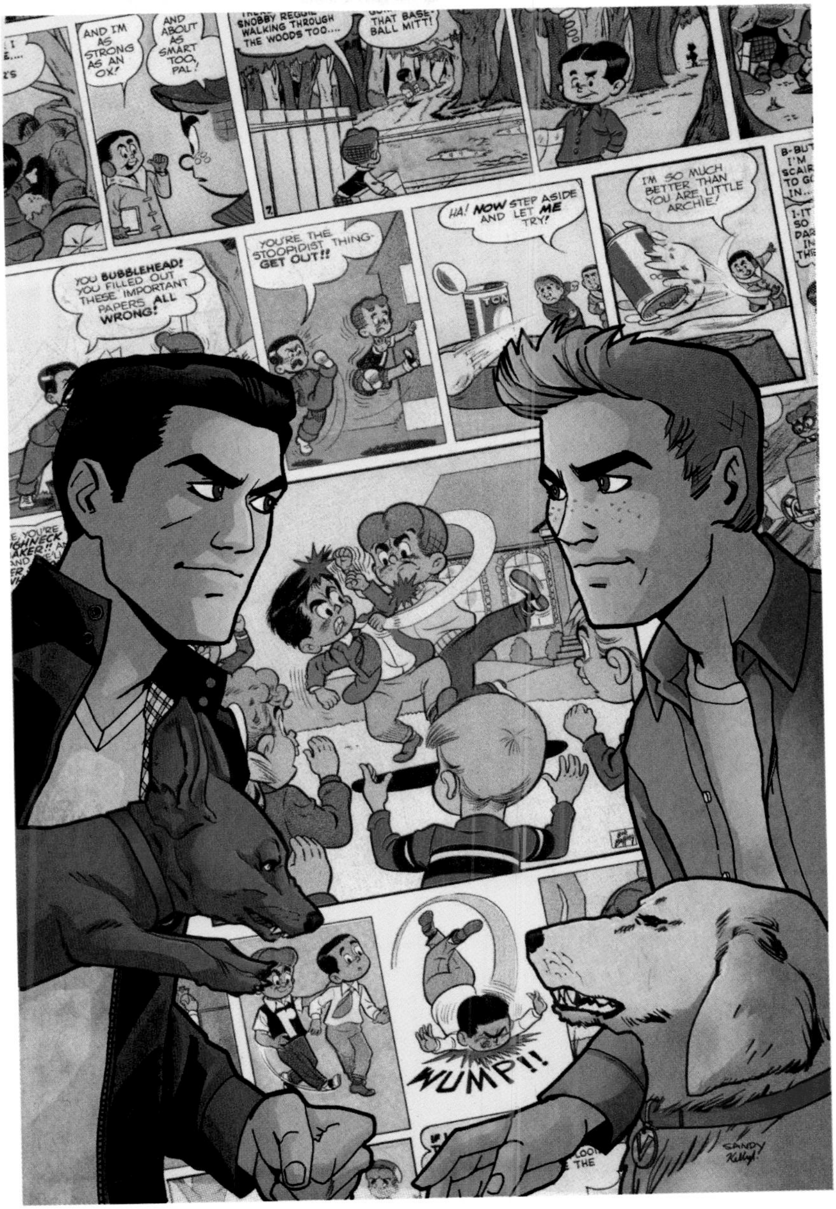
AND I'M AS STRONG AS AN OX!
AND ABOUT AS SMART TOO, PAL!
SNOBBY REGGIE WALKING THROUGH THE WOODS TOO....
B-BUT I'M SCARED TO GO IN...
I'M SO MUCH BETTER THAN YOU ARE, LITTLE ARCHIE!
HA! NOW STEP ASIDE AND LET ME TRY!
YOU'RE THE STOOPIDIST THING- GET OUT!!
YOU BUBBLEHEAD! YOU FILLED OUT THESE IMPORTANT PAPERS ALL WRONG!
WUMP!!

SANDY JARRELL
(with BOB BOLLING)

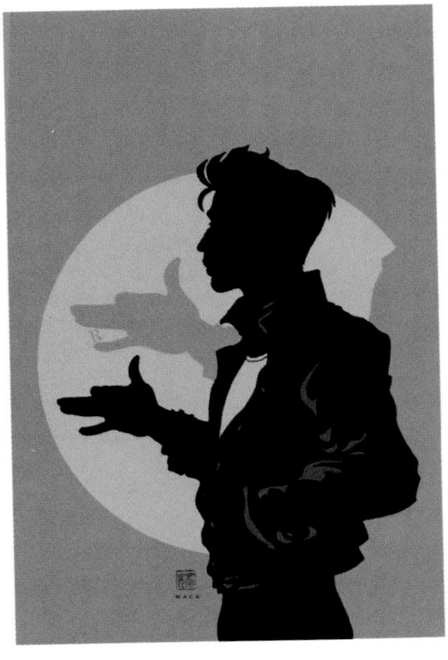

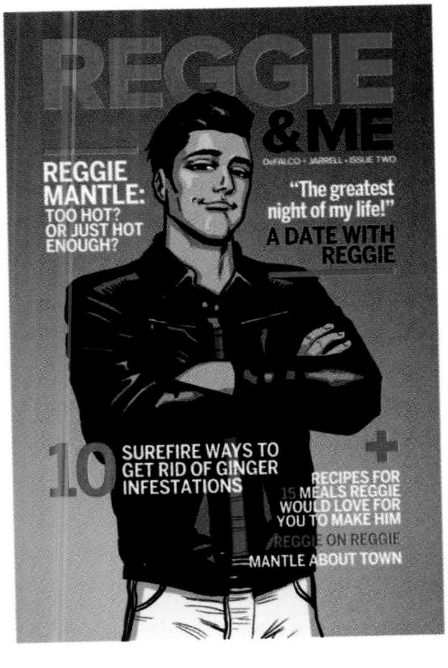
REGGIE
& ME
DeFALCO • JARRELL • ISSUE TWO
REGGIE MANTLE:
TOO HOT? OR JUST HOT ENOUGH?
"The greatest night of my life!"
A DATE WITH REGGIE
10 SUREFIRE WAYS TO GET RID OF GINGER INFESTATIONS
+ RECIPES FOR 15 MEALS REGGIE WOULD LOVE FOR YOU TO MAKE HIM
REGGIE ON REGGIE
MANTLE ABOUT TOWN

(L)
DAVID MACK

(R)
CHIP ZDARSKY

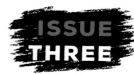

ISSUE THREE

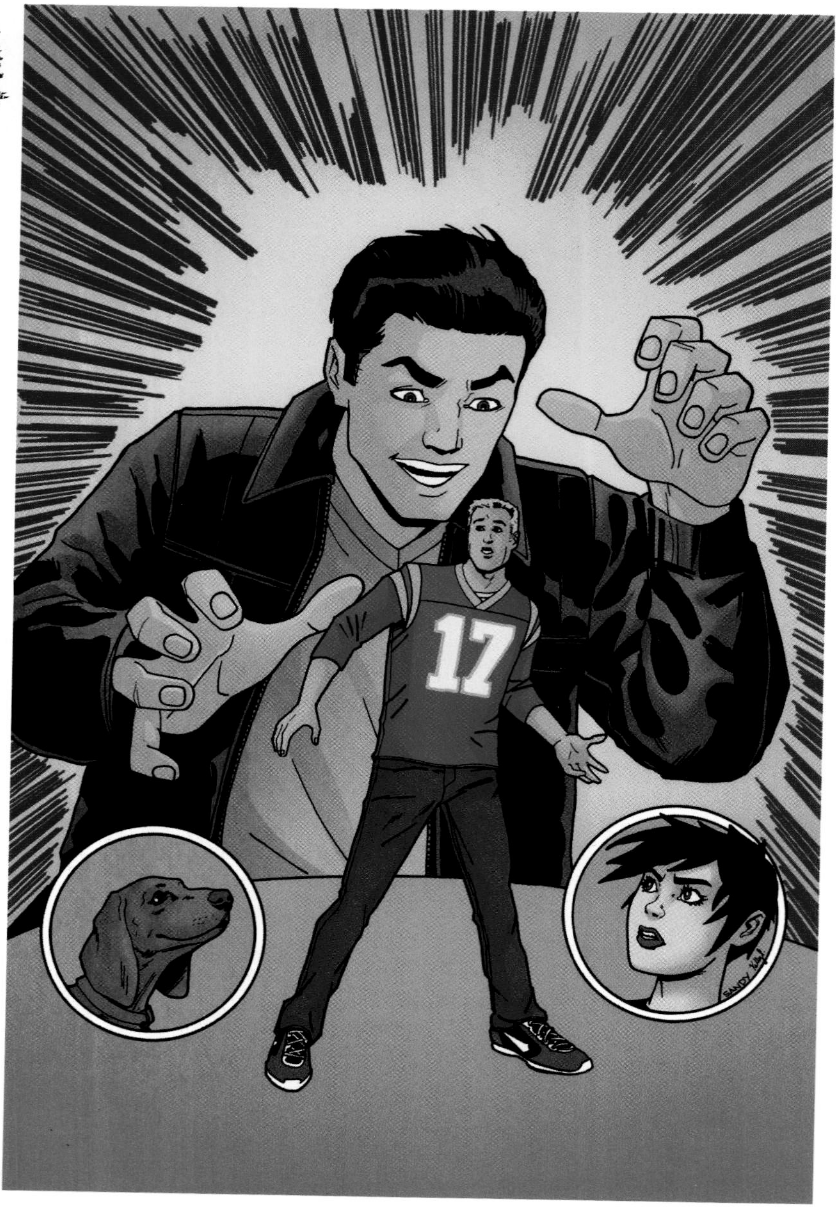
17

SANDY
JARRELL

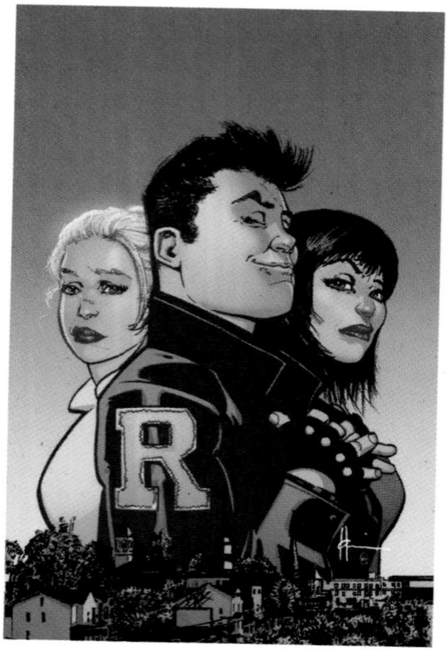
R

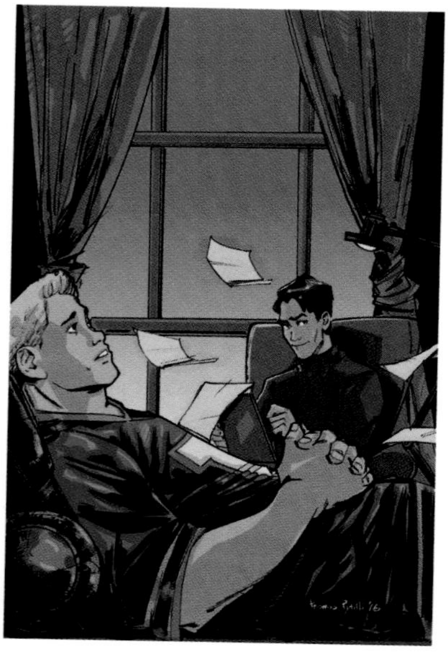

(L)
HOWARD
CHAYKIN

(R)
THOMAS
PITILLI

ISSUE FOUR

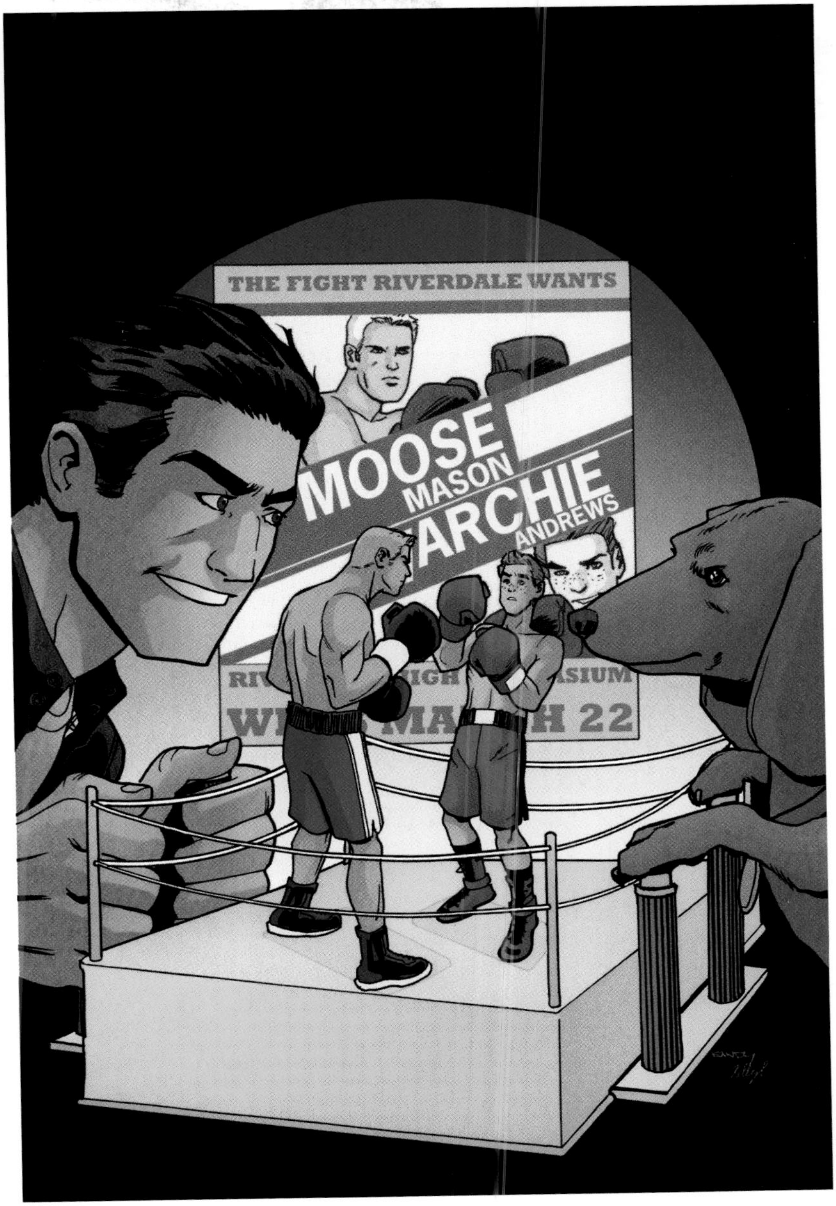
THE FIGHT RIVERDALE WANTS
MOOSE
MASON
ARCHIE
ANDREWS

SANDY JARRELL

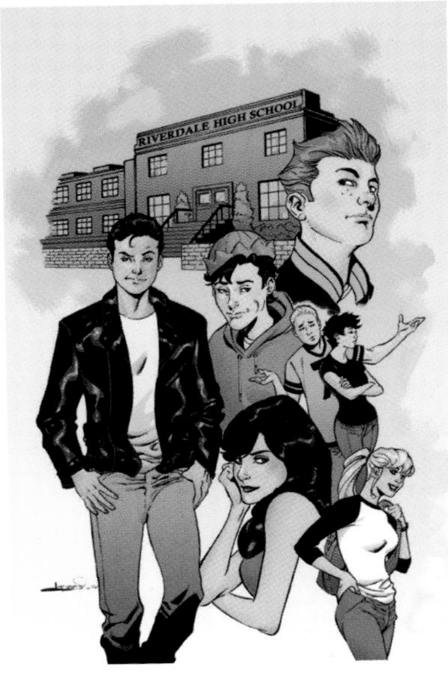
RIVERDALE HIGH SCHOOL

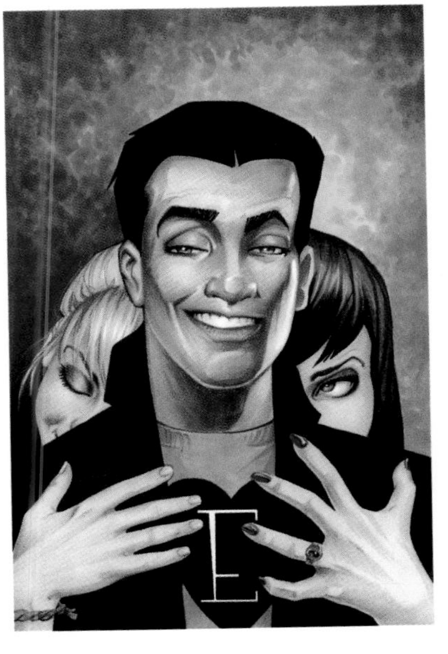

(L) AARON LOPRESTI

(R) ANDY PRICE

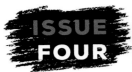

ISSUE FIVE

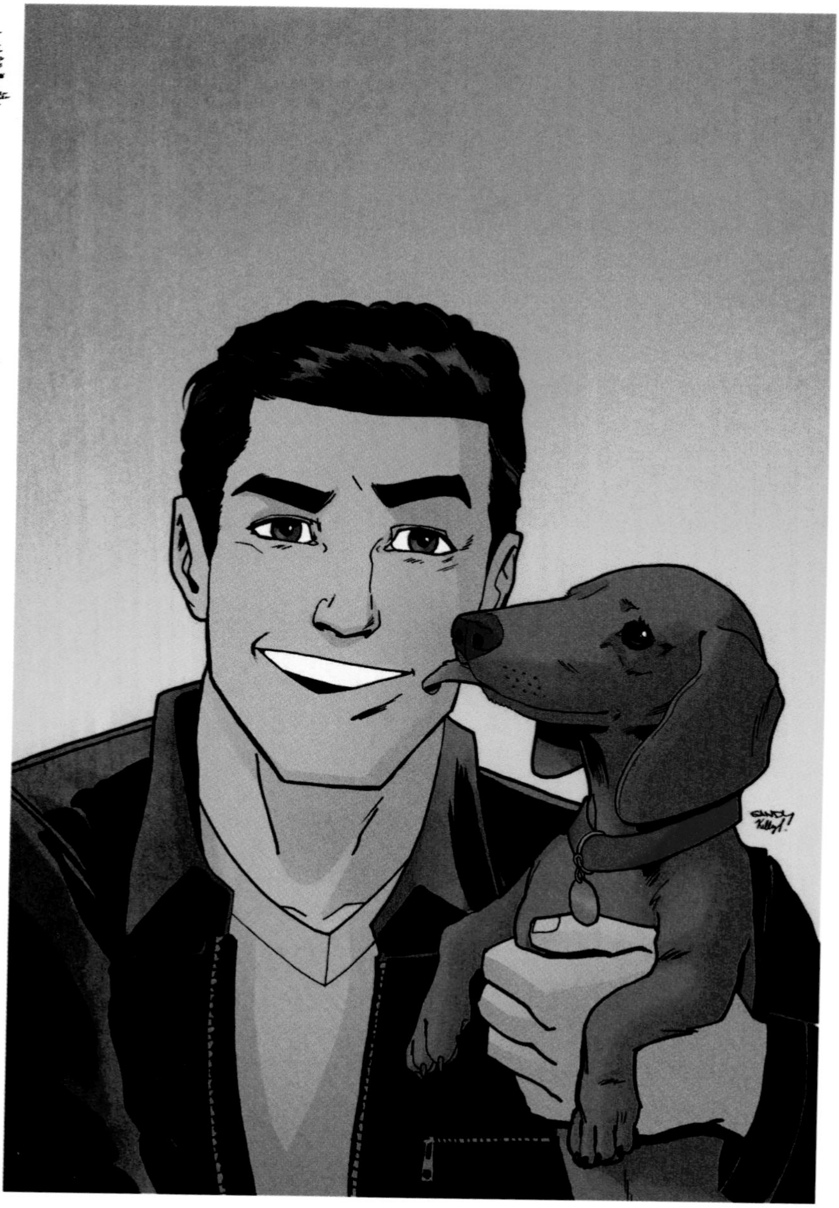

SANDY
JARRELL

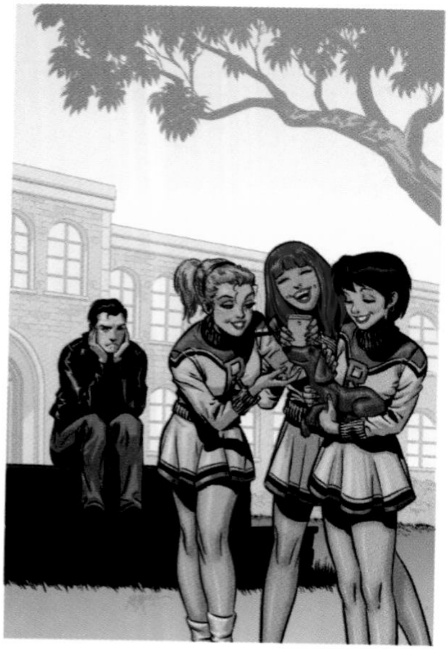

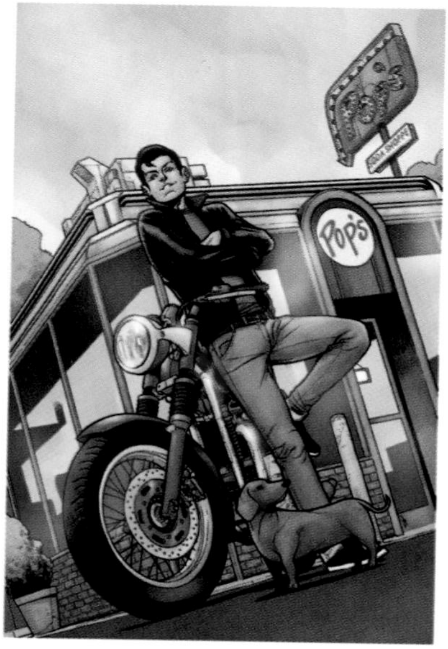
Pop's

(L)
SHAWN
McMANUS

(R)
JIM
TOWE

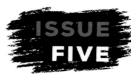

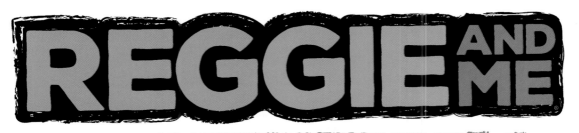

REGGIE AND ME

INITIAL SKETCHES

Here's a special peek at some of Sandy Jarrell's initial sketches for pages of issue one of *Reggie and Me* along with the final product.

PAGE ONE

SOME PEOPLE CALL HIM THE PRINCE OF DARKNESS.
THE WALKING DREAD.
THE CLOSEST THING RIVERDALE HAS TO A SUPER-VILLAIN.
THEY SAY HE'S A SELF-CENTERED, SCHEMING, ROTTEN JERK WHO ONLY LIVES TO PRANK PEOPLE.
I WISH I COULD DEFEND HIM.
IN ALL HONESTY, I CAN'T.
REGGIE MANTLE CAN BE A NASTY PIECE OF WORK.
A WORLD CLASS CREEP!
HE'S ALSO MY BEST FRIEND.
MY NAME IS VADER, AND I'M HERE TO TELL YOU ABOUT...

PAGE FOUR

NO MATTER WHAT ANYONE ELSE THINKS, REGGIE HAS ALWAYS BEEN A HERO TO ME--AS COURAGEOUS AND TRUE AS HE IS HANDSOME.
BUT, LIKE EVERY OTHER SUPER-DUDE, HE HAS ONE WEAKNESS.
MIDGE KLUMP.
I'VE NEVER UNDERSTOOD WHY HER WHEN HE CAN HAVE ANY GIRL HE WANTS.
(JUST ASK HIM.)
I JUST KNOW SHE DOMINATES HIS THOUGHTS... AND DREAMS.
MIDGE! OH, MIDGGGGGE...
UNFORTUNATELY, SHE COMES WITH A LOT OF BAGGAGE--
--TWO HUNDRED TWENTY POUNDS OF SOLID MUSCLE AND PURE SAVAGERY TO BE EXACT.

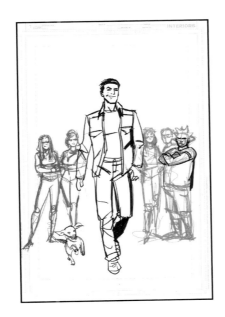

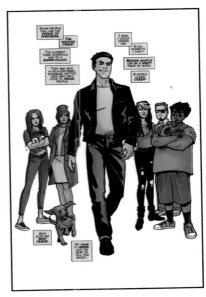

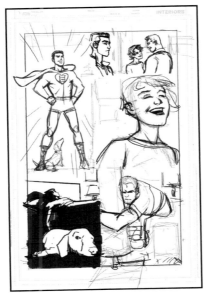

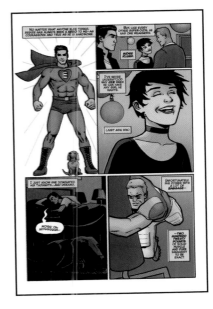

PAGE **TEN**

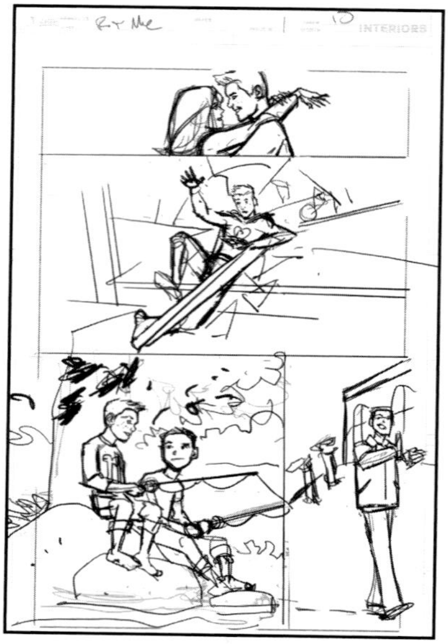
INTERIORS

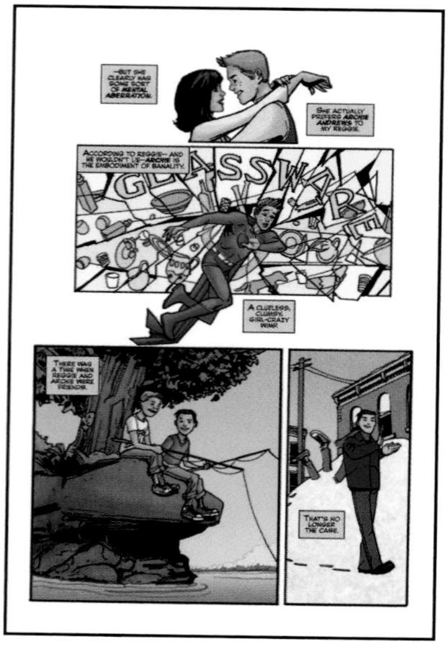
—BUT SHE CLEARLY HAS SOME SORT OF MENTAL ABERRATION.
SHE ACTUALLY PREFERS ARCHIE ANDREWS TO MY REGGIE.
ACCORDING TO REGGIE—AND HE WOULDN'T LIE—ARCHIE IS THE EMBODIMENT OF BANALITY.
GLASSWARE
A CLUELESS, CLUMSY, GIRL-CRAZY WIMP.
THERE WAS A TIME WHEN REGGIE AND ARCHIE WERE FRIENDS.
THAT'S NO LONGER THE CASE.

PAGE **THIRTEEN**

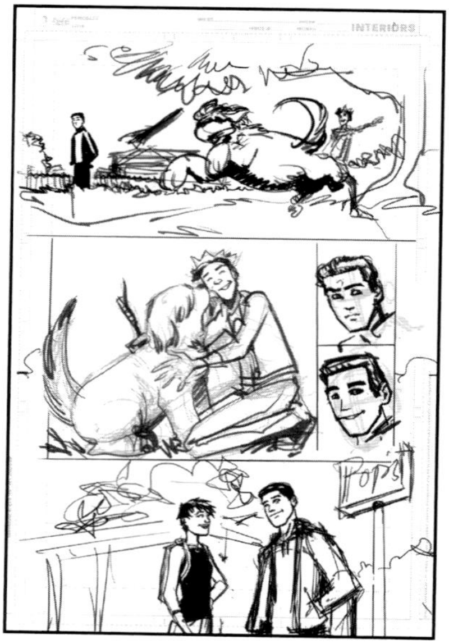
INTERIORS

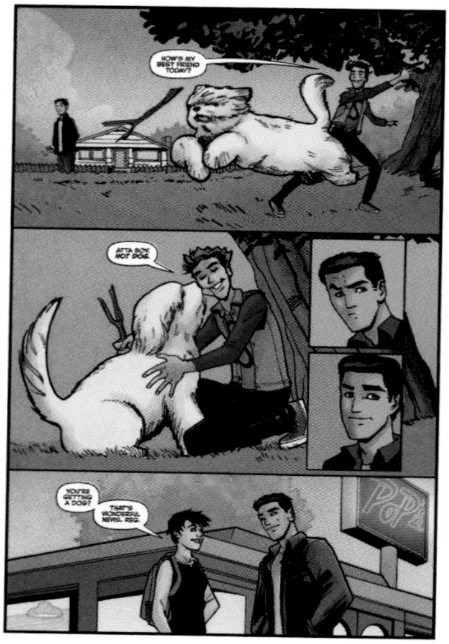
HOW'S MY BEST FRIEND TODAY?
ATTA BOY, HOT DOG.
YOU'RE GETTING A DOG?
THAT'S WONDERFUL NEWS, REG.
POP'S

PAGE **TWENTY**

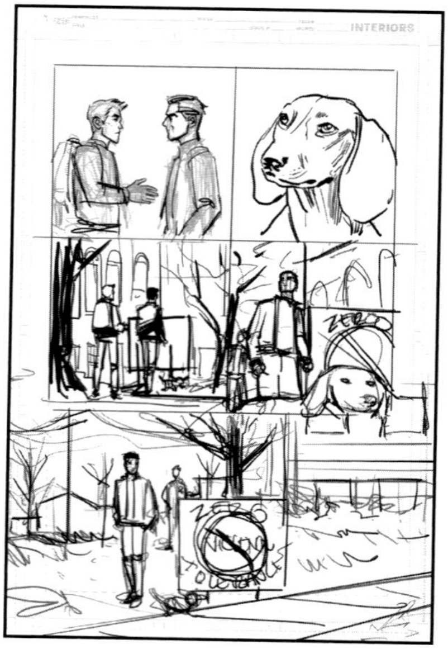
INTERIORS

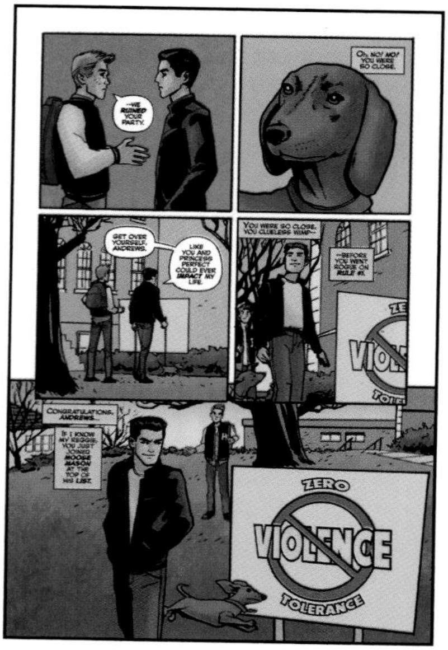
—WE RUINED YOUR PARTY.
OH, NO! NO! YOU WERE SO CLOSE.
GET OVER YOURSELF, ANDREWS.
LIKE YOU AND PRINCESS PERFECT COULD EVER IMPACT MY LIFE.
YOU WERE SO CLOSE, YOU CLUELESS WIMP—
—BEFORE YOU WENT ROGUE ON RULE #1.
CONGRATULATIONS, ANDREWS...
IF I KNOW MY REGGIE, YOU JUST JOINED MOOSE MASON AT THE TOP OF HIS LIST.
ZERO
VIOLENCE
TOLERANCE

SPECIAL PREVIEW

Your Pal Archie®

Classic-style Archie makes his return in this ALL-NEW, ALL-AGES comic featuring two stories from Eisner Award-winning writer TY TEMPLETON (Batman and Robin Adventures) and fan-favorite Archie Comics artist DAN PARENT (Life with Kevin)!

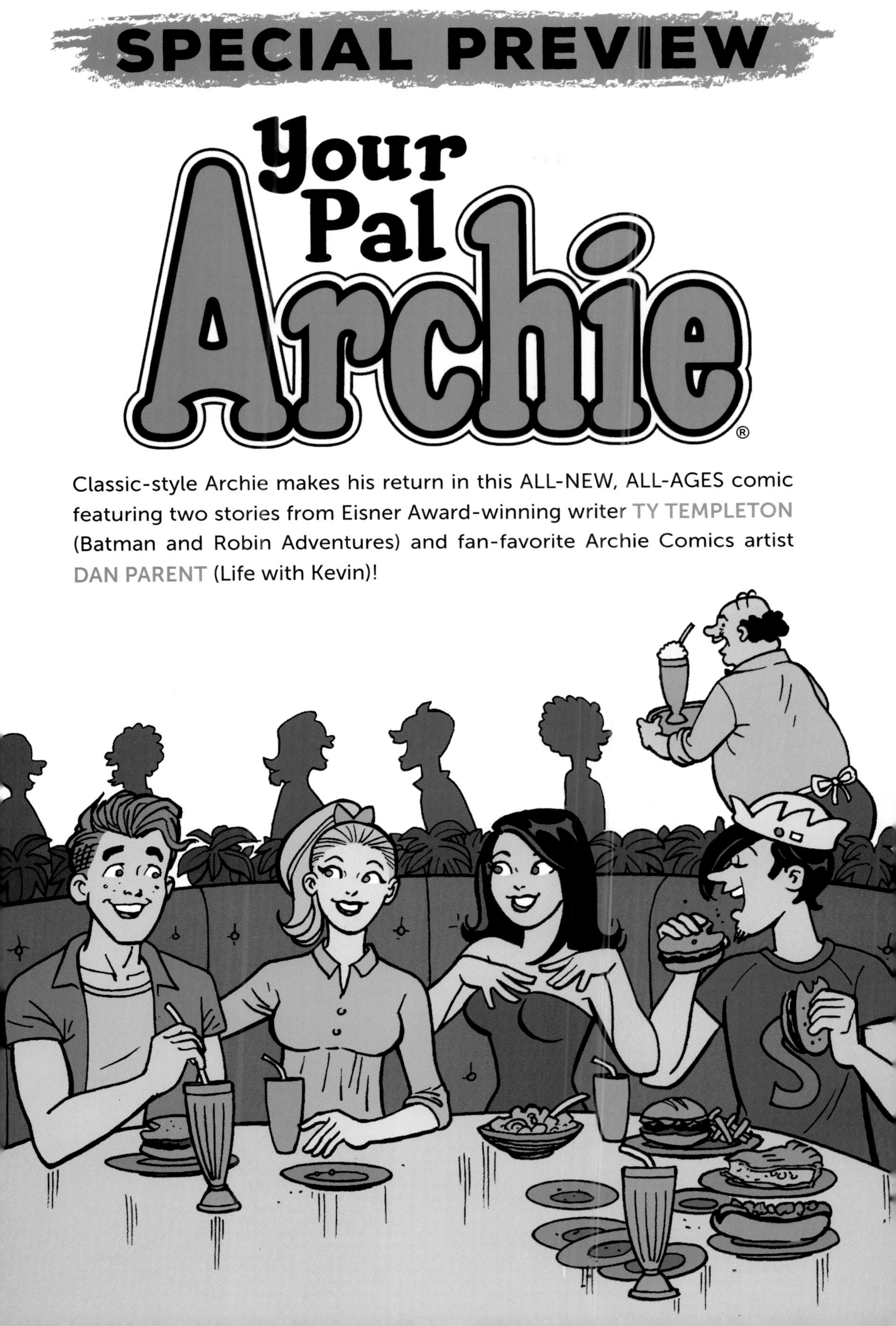

ISSUE ONE

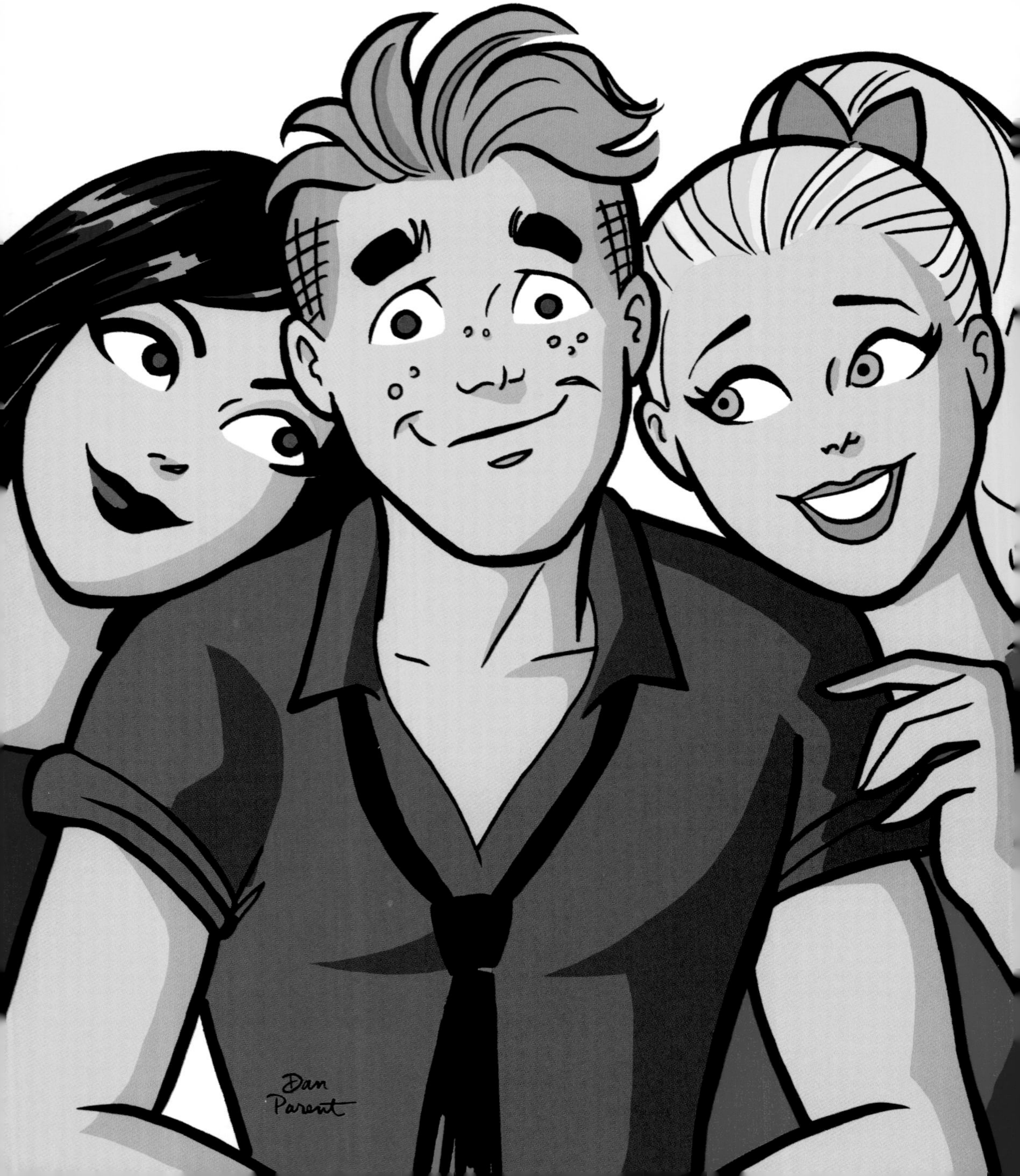
Dan Parent

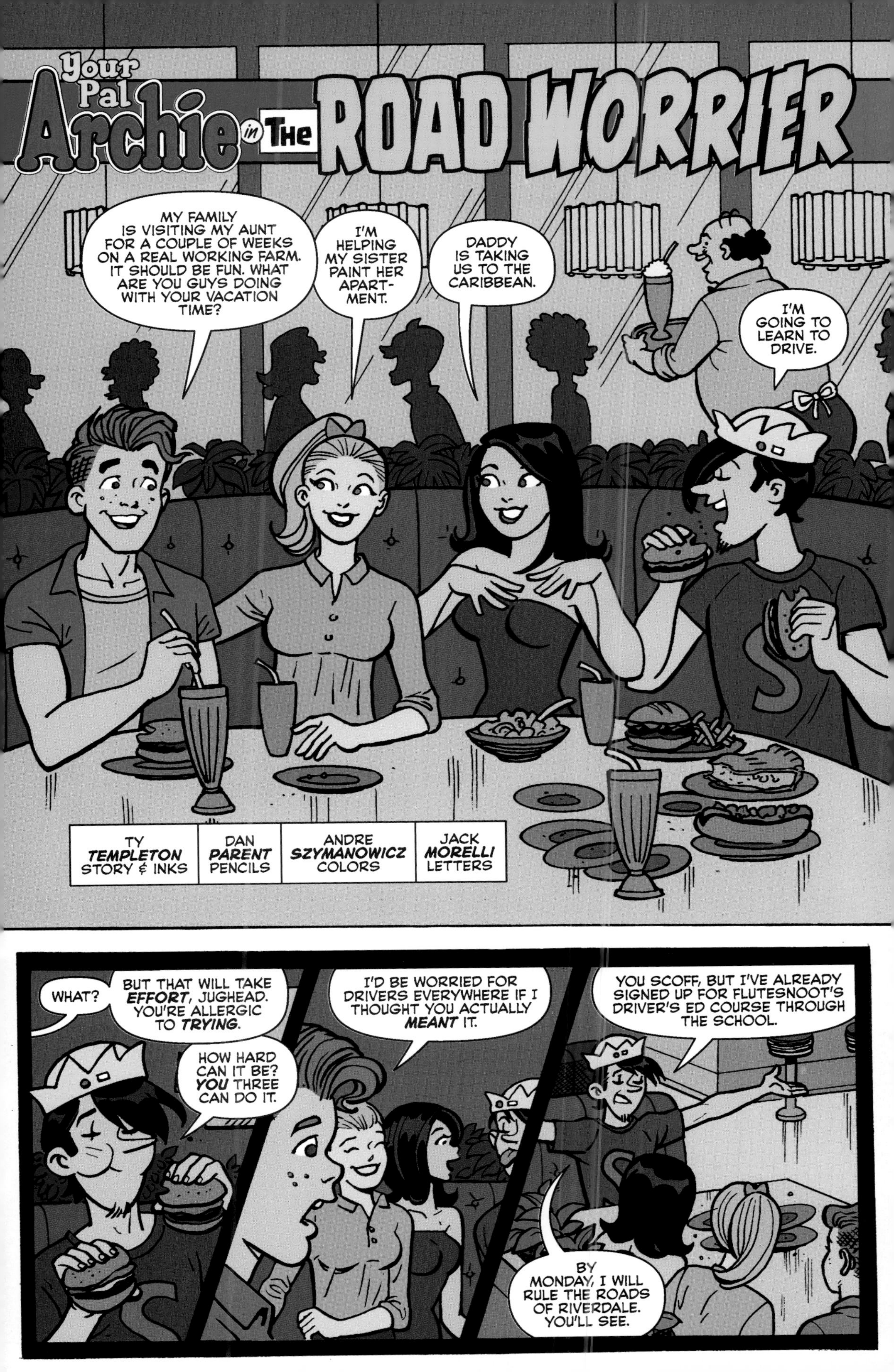
Your Pal Archie in THE ROAD WORRIER
MY FAMILY IS VISITING MY AUNT FOR A COUPLE OF WEEKS ON A REAL WORKING FARM. IT SHOULD BE FUN. WHAT ARE YOU GUYS DOING WITH YOUR VACATION TIME?
I'M HELPING MY SISTER PAINT HER APARTMENT.
DADDY IS TAKING US TO THE CARIBBEAN.
I'M GOING TO LEARN TO DRIVE.
TY TEMPLETON STORY & INKS
DAN PARENT PENCILS
ANDRE SZYMANOWICZ COLORS
JACK MORELLI LETTERS
WHAT?
BUT THAT WILL TAKE *EFFORT*, JUGHEAD. YOU'RE ALLERGIC TO *TRYING*.
HOW HARD CAN IT BE? *YOU* THREE CAN DO IT.
I'D BE WORRIED FOR DRIVERS EVERYWHERE IF I THOUGHT YOU ACTUALLY *MEANT* IT.
YOU SCOFF, BUT I'VE ALREADY SIGNED UP FOR FLUTESNOOT'S DRIVER'S ED COURSE THROUGH THE SCHOOL.
BY MONDAY, I WILL RULE THE ROADS OF RIVERDALE. YOU'LL SEE.

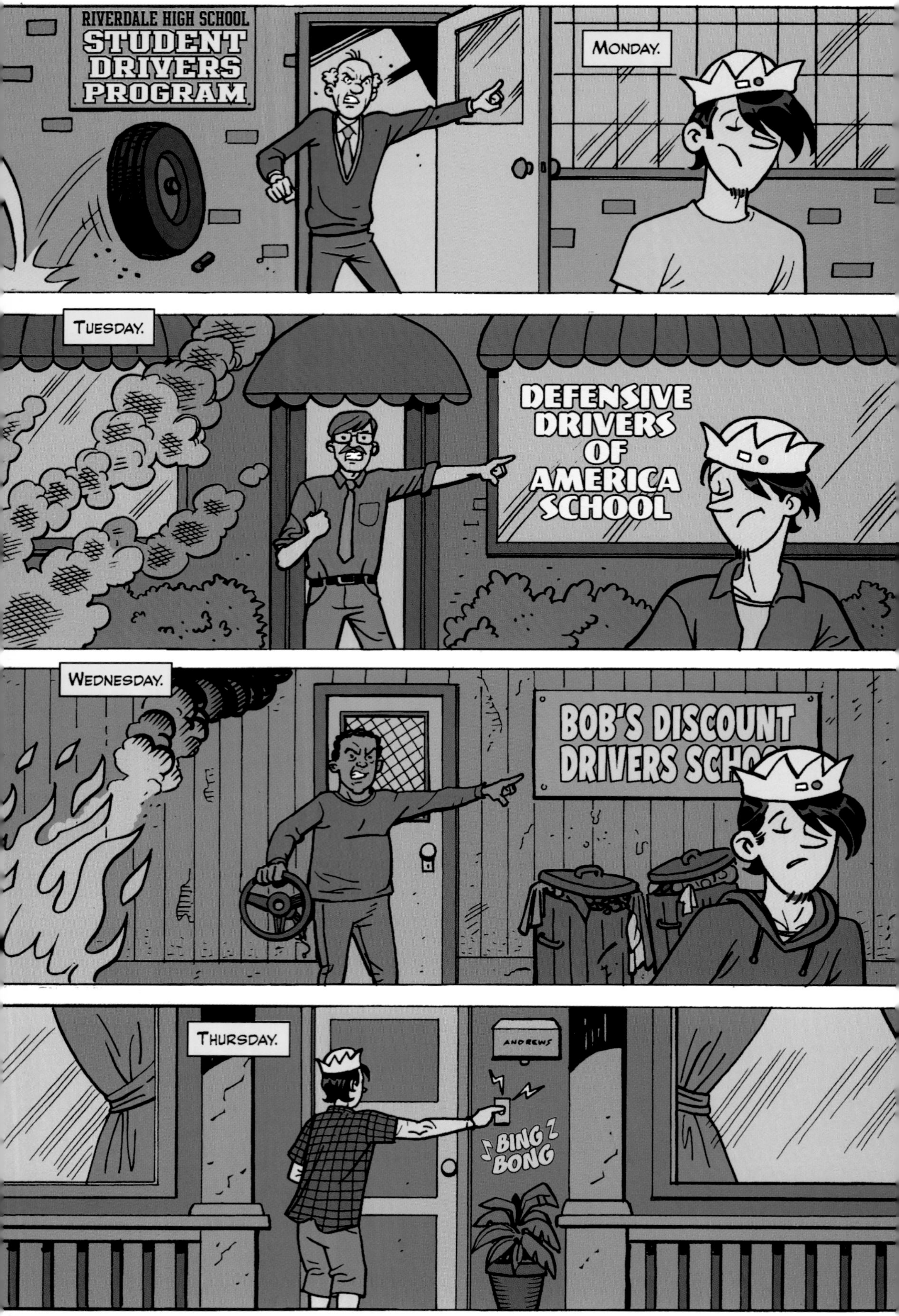
RIVERDALE HIGH SCHOOL
STUDENT DRIVERS PROGRAM
MONDAY.
TUESDAY.
DEFENSIVE DRIVERS OF AMERICA SCHOOL
WEDNESDAY.
BOB'S DISCOUNT DRIVERS SCHO
THURSDAY.
ANDREWS
BING BONG

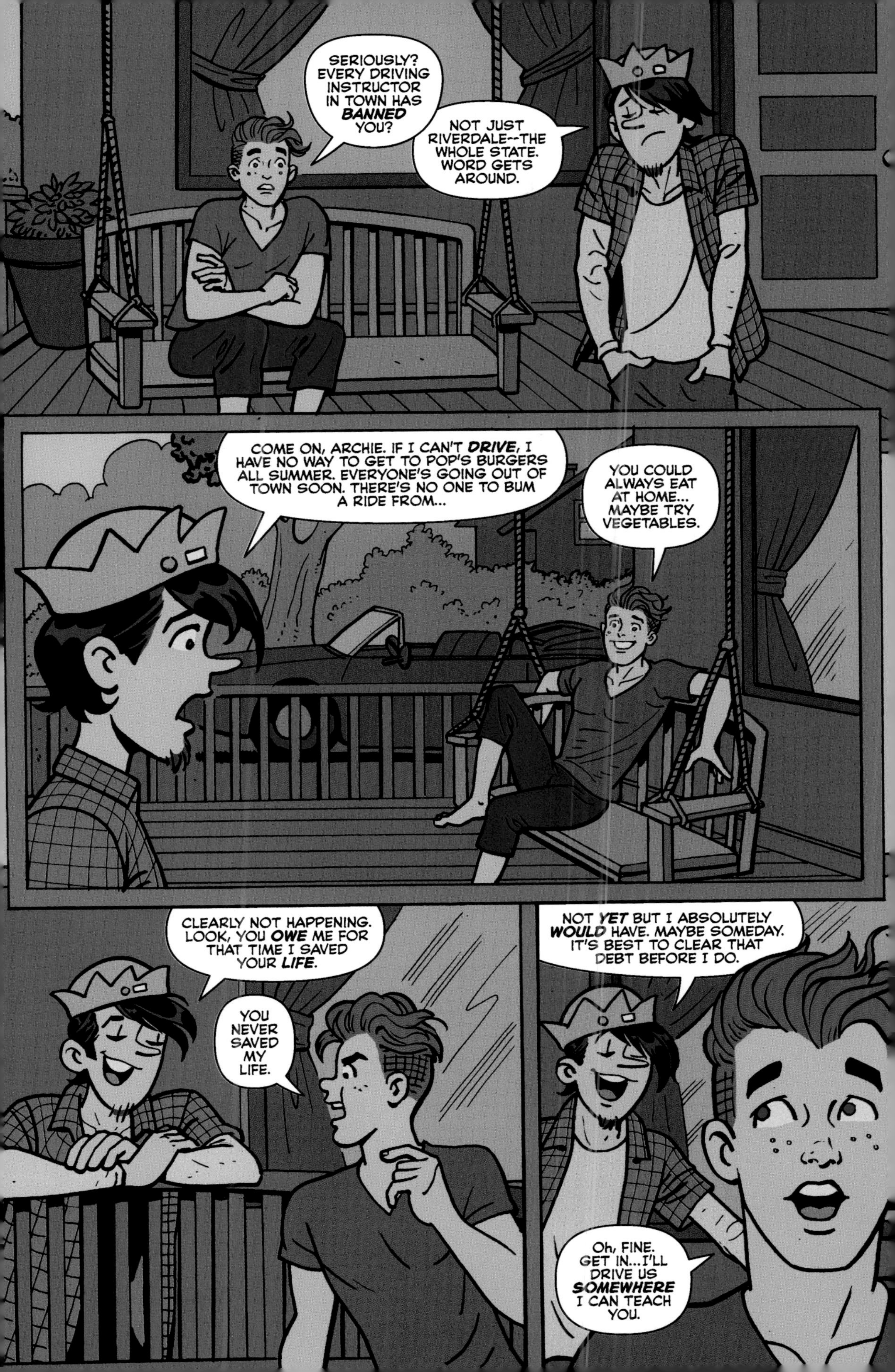
SERIOUSLY? EVERY DRIVING INSTRUCTOR IN TOWN HAS **BANNED** YOU?
NOT JUST RIVERDALE--THE WHOLE STATE. WORD GETS AROUND.
COME ON, ARCHIE. IF I CAN'T **DRIVE**, I HAVE NO WAY TO GET TO POP'S BURGERS ALL SUMMER. EVERYONE'S GOING OUT OF TOWN SOON. THERE'S NO ONE TO BUM A RIDE FROM...
YOU COULD ALWAYS EAT AT HOME... MAYBE TRY VEGETABLES.
CLEARLY NOT HAPPENING. LOOK, YOU **OWE** ME FOR THAT TIME I SAVED YOUR **LIFE**.
YOU NEVER SAVED MY LIFE.
NOT **YET** BUT I ABSOLUTELY **WOULD** HAVE. MAYBE SOMEDAY. IT'S BEST TO CLEAR THAT DEBT BEFORE I DO.
Oh, FINE. GET IN...I'LL DRIVE US **SOMEWHERE** I CAN TEACH YOU.

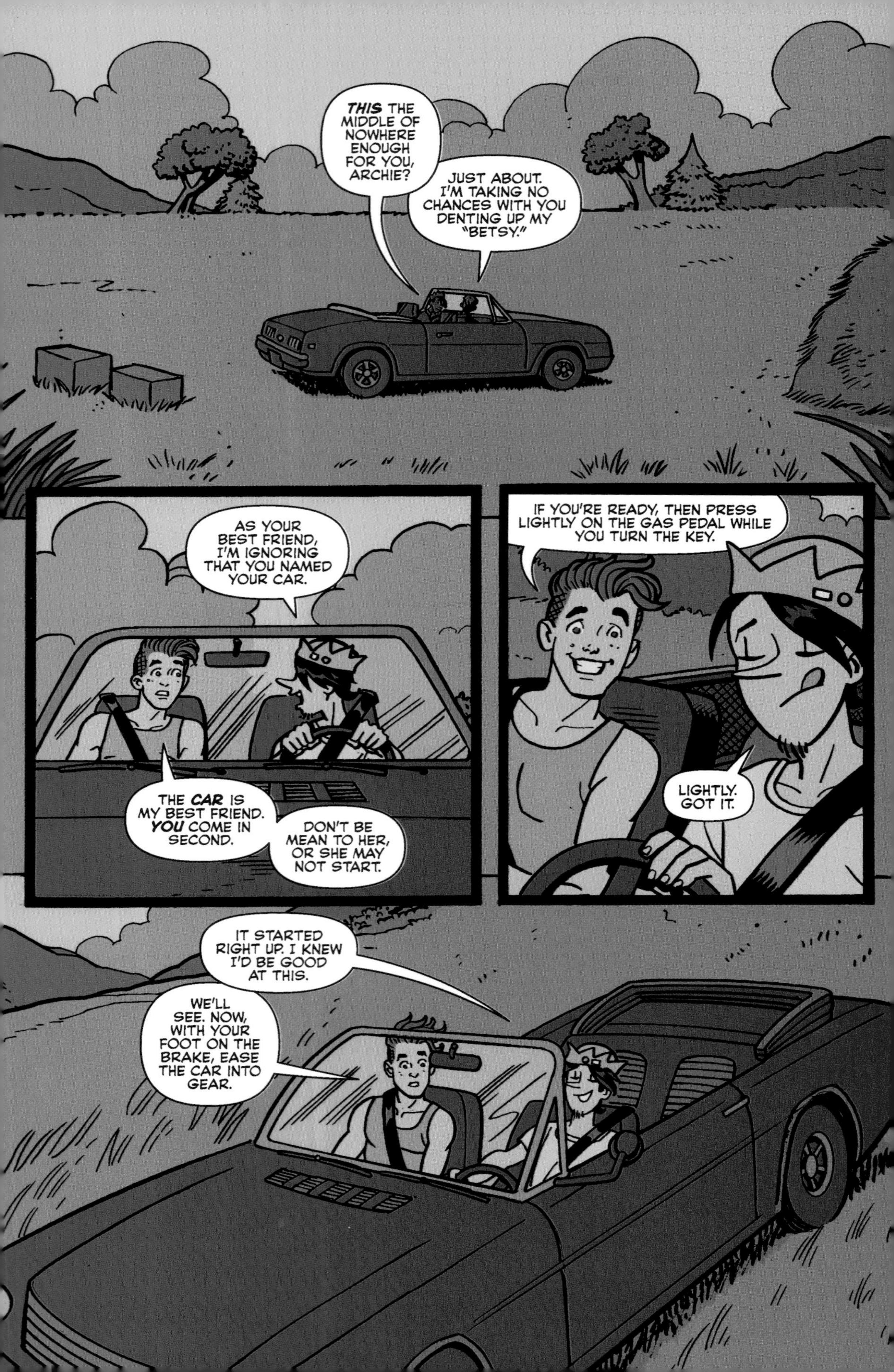
THIS THE MIDDLE OF NOWHERE ENOUGH FOR YOU, ARCHIE?
JUST ABOUT. I'M TAKING NO CHANCES WITH YOU DENTING UP MY "BETSY."
AS YOUR BEST FRIEND, I'M IGNORING THAT YOU NAMED YOUR CAR.
THE CAR IS MY BEST FRIEND. YOU COME IN SECOND.
DON'T BE MEAN TO HER, OR SHE MAY NOT START.
IF YOU'RE READY, THEN PRESS LIGHTLY ON THE GAS PEDAL WHILE YOU TURN THE KEY.
LIGHTLY. GOT IT.
IT STARTED RIGHT UP. I KNEW I'D BE GOOD AT THIS.
WE'LL SEE. NOW, WITH YOUR FOOT ON THE BRAKE, EASE THE CAR INTO GEAR.

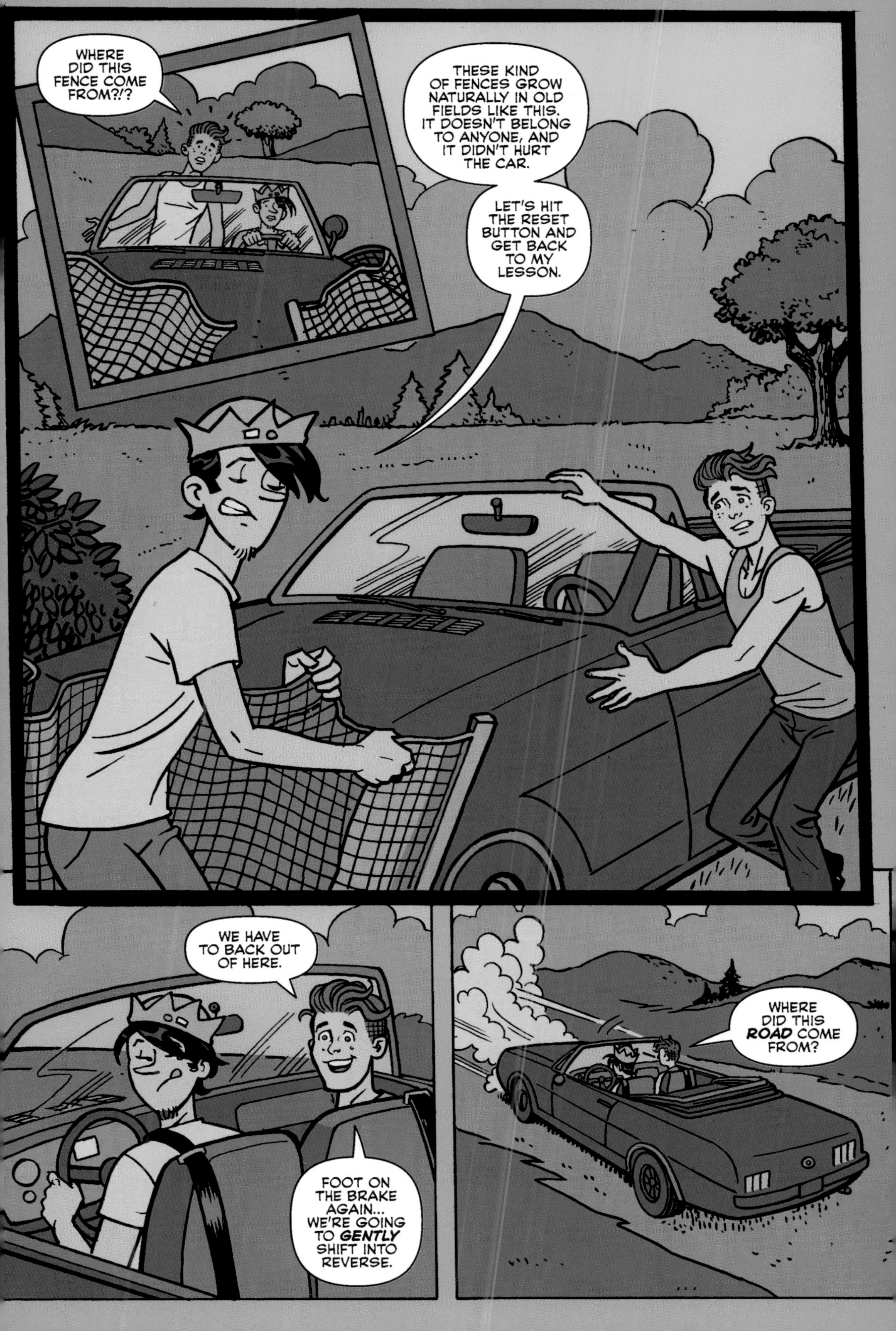

WHERE DID THIS FENCE COME FROM?!?
THESE KIND OF FENCES GROW NATURALLY IN OLD FIELDS LIKE THIS. IT DOESN'T BELONG TO ANYONE, AND IT DIDN'T HURT THE CAR.
LET'S HIT THE RESET BUTTON AND GET BACK TO MY LESSON.
WE HAVE TO BACK OUT OF HERE.
FOOT ON THE BRAKE AGAIN... WE'RE GOING TO GENTLY SHIFT INTO REVERSE.
WHERE DID THIS ROAD COME FROM?

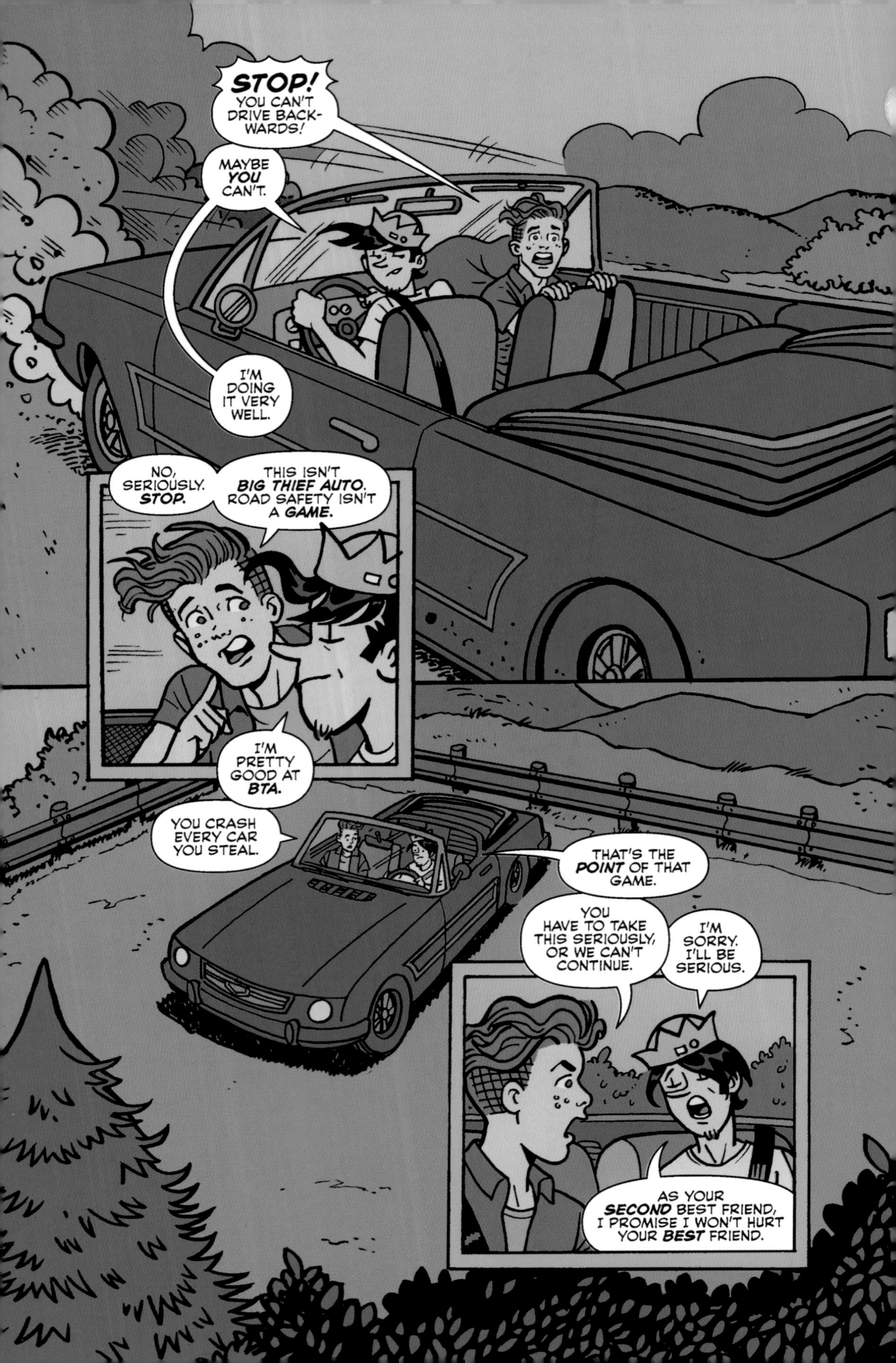
STOP! YOU CAN'T DRIVE BACK-WARDS!
MAYBE YOU CAN'T.
I'M DOING IT VERY WELL.
NO, SERIOUSLY. STOP.
THIS ISN'T BIG THIEF AUTO. ROAD SAFETY ISN'T A GAME.
I'M PRETTY GOOD AT BTA.
YOU CRASH EVERY CAR YOU STEAL.
THAT'S THE POINT OF THAT GAME.
YOU HAVE TO TAKE THIS SERIOUSLY, OR WE CAN'T CONTINUE.
I'M SORRY. I'LL BE SERIOUS.
AS YOUR SECOND BEST FRIEND, I PROMISE I WON'T HURT YOUR BEST FRIEND.

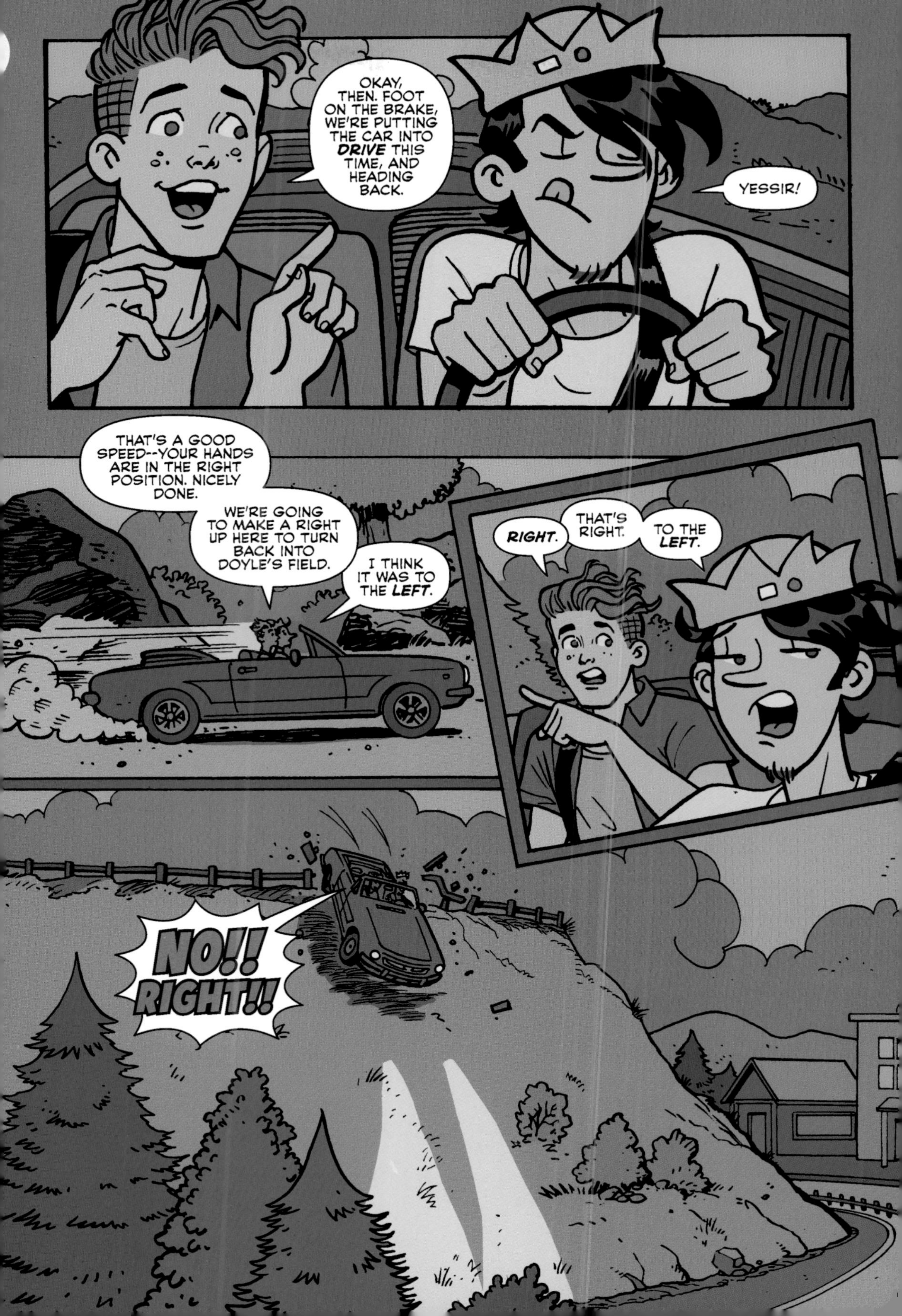
OKAY, THEN. FOOT ON THE BRAKE, WE'RE PUTTING THE CAR INTO **DRIVE** THIS TIME, AND HEADING BACK.
YESSIR!
THAT'S A GOOD SPEED--YOUR HANDS ARE IN THE RIGHT POSITION. NICELY DONE.
WE'RE GOING TO MAKE A RIGHT UP HERE TO TURN BACK INTO DOYLE'S FIELD.
I THINK IT WAS TO THE **LEFT**.
RIGHT.
THAT'S RIGHT.
TO THE **LEFT**.
NO!! RIGHT!!

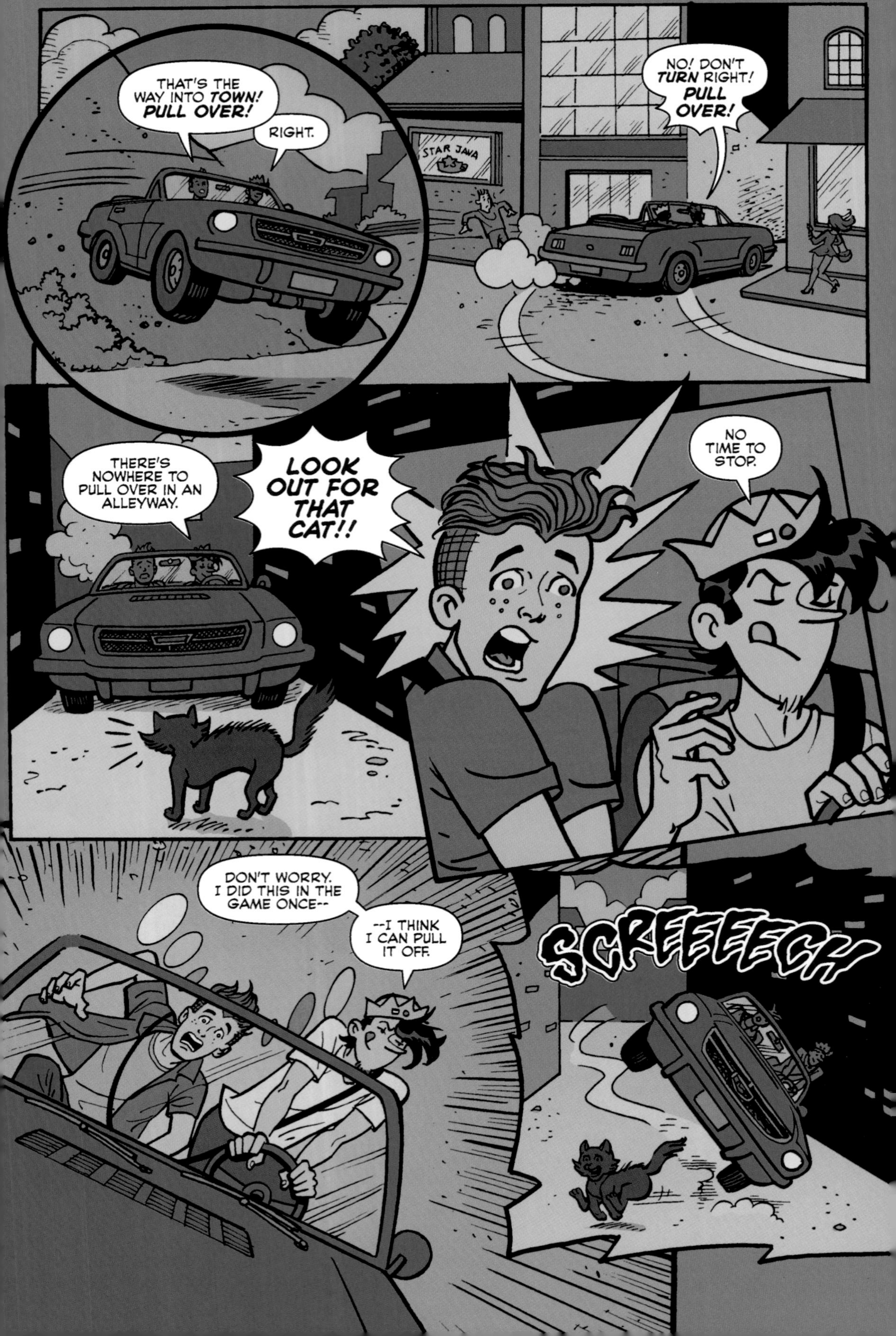
THAT'S THE WAY INTO TOWN! PULL OVER!
RIGHT.
STAR JAVA
NO! DON'T TURN RIGHT! PULL OVER!
THERE'S NOWHERE TO PULL OVER IN AN ALLEYWAY.
LOOK OUT FOR THAT CAT!!
NO TIME TO STOP.
DON'T WORRY. I DID THIS IN THE GAME ONCE--
--I THINK I CAN PULL IT OFF.
SCREEEECH

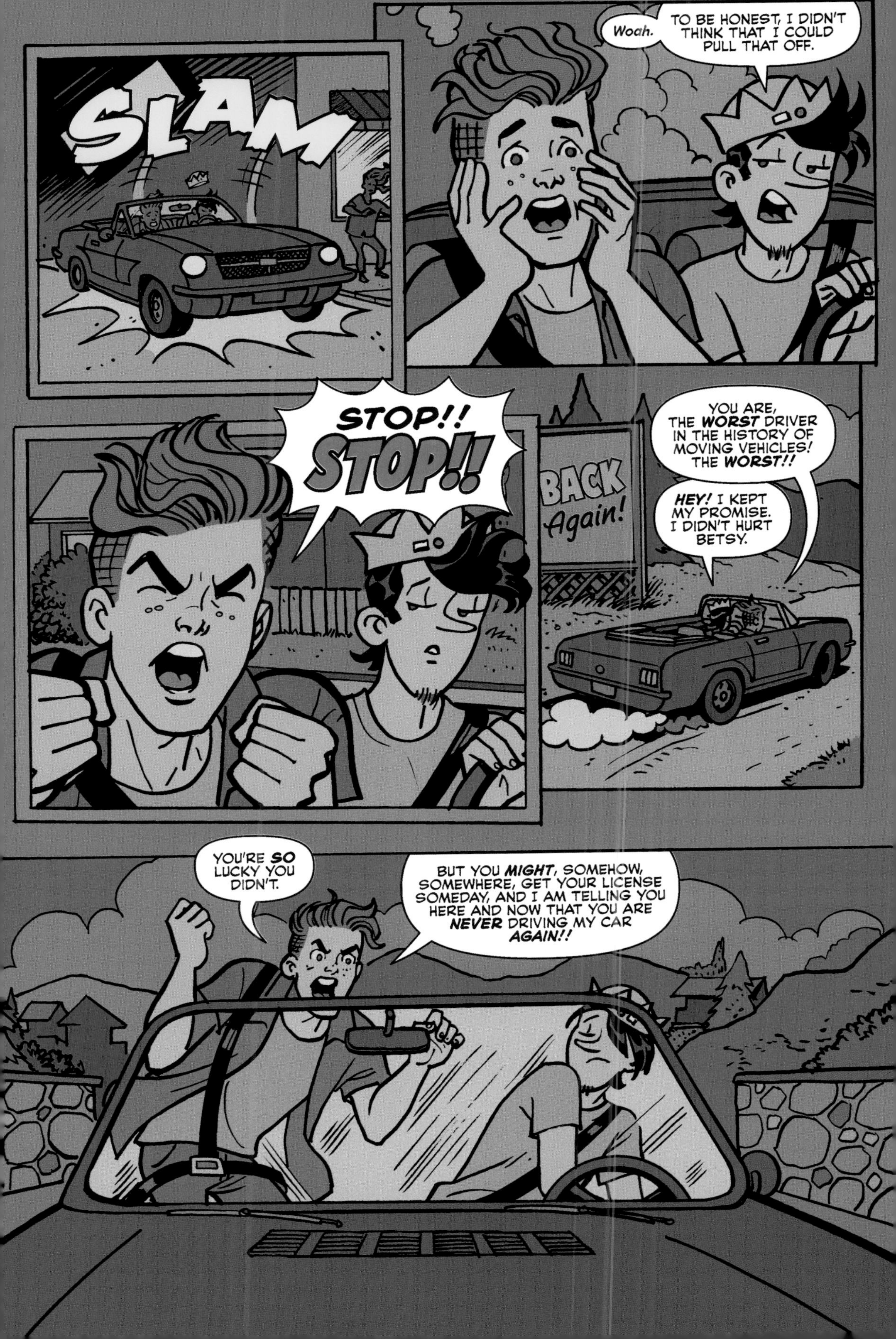

SLAM
Woah.
TO BE HONEST, I DIDN'T THINK THAT I COULD PULL THAT OFF.
STOP!! STOP!!
BACK Again!
YOU ARE, THE **WORST** DRIVER IN THE HISTORY OF MOVING VEHICLES! THE **WORST!!**
HEY! I KEPT MY PROMISE. I DIDN'T HURT BETSY.
YOU'RE **SO** LUCKY YOU DIDN'T.
BUT YOU **MIGHT**, SOMEHOW, SOMEWHERE, GET YOUR LICENSE SOMEDAY, AND I AM TELLING YOU HERE AND NOW THAT YOU ARE **NEVER** DRIVING MY CAR **AGAIN!!**

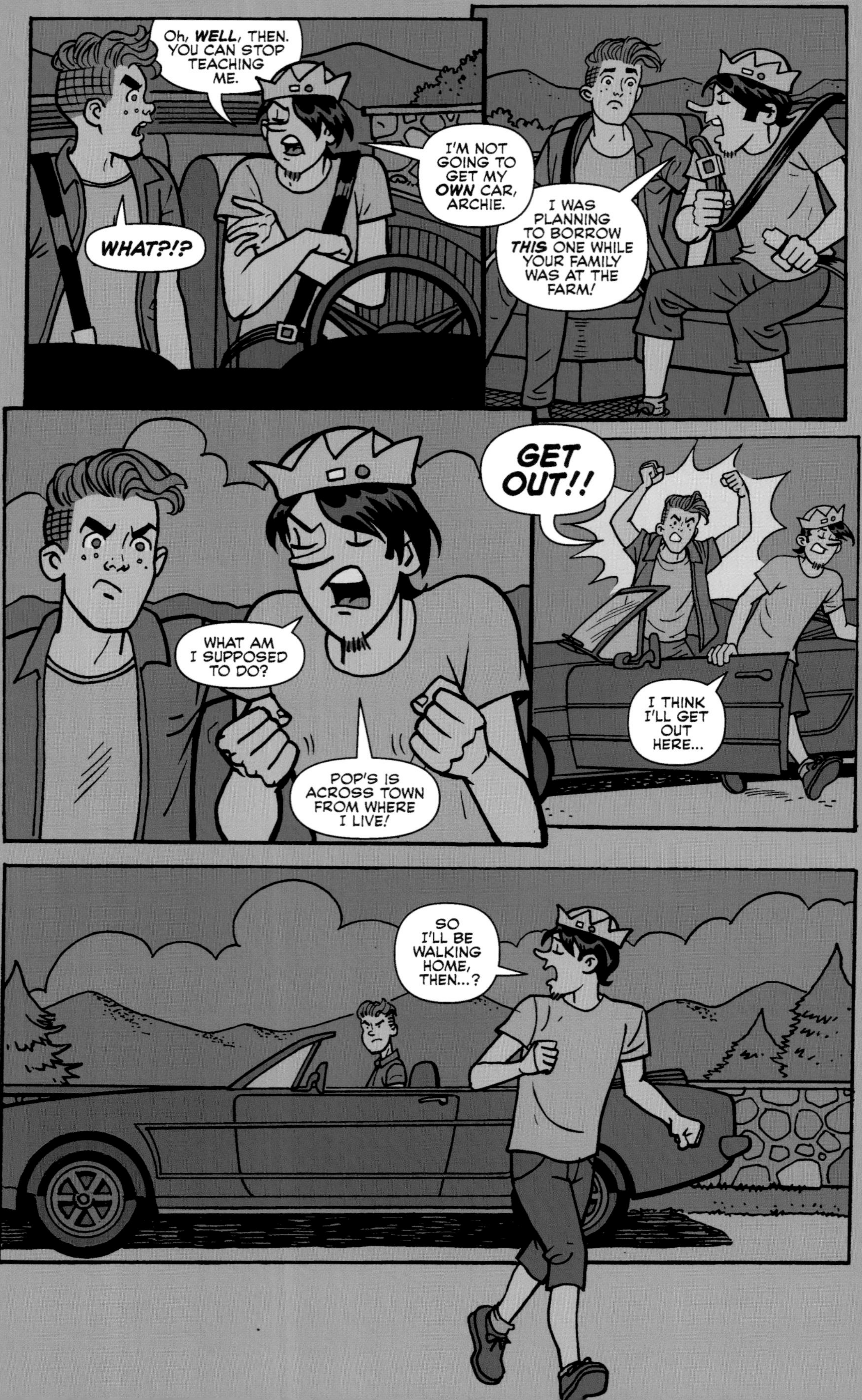
Oh, WELL, THEN. YOU CAN STOP TEACHING ME.
WHAT?!?
I'M NOT GOING TO GET MY OWN CAR, ARCHIE.
I WAS PLANNING TO BORROW THIS ONE WHILE YOUR FAMILY WAS AT THE FARM!
WHAT AM I SUPPOSED TO DO?
POP'S IS ACROSS TOWN FROM WHERE I LIVE!
GET OUT!!
I THINK I'LL GET OUT HERE...
SO I'LL BE WALKING HOME, THEN...?

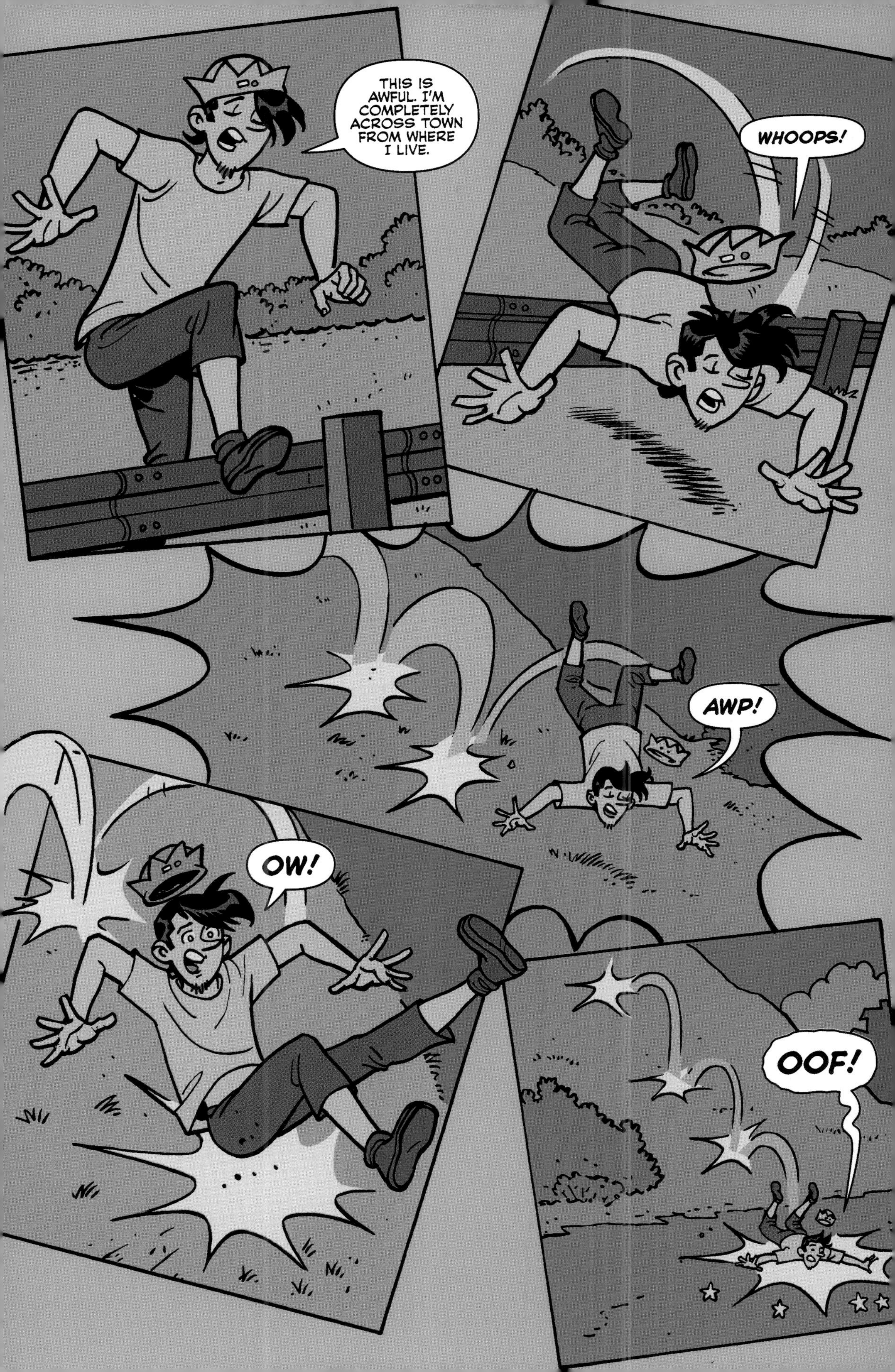
THIS IS AWFUL. I'M COMPLETELY ACROSS TOWN FROM WHERE I LIVE.
WHOOPS!
AWP!
OW!
OOF!

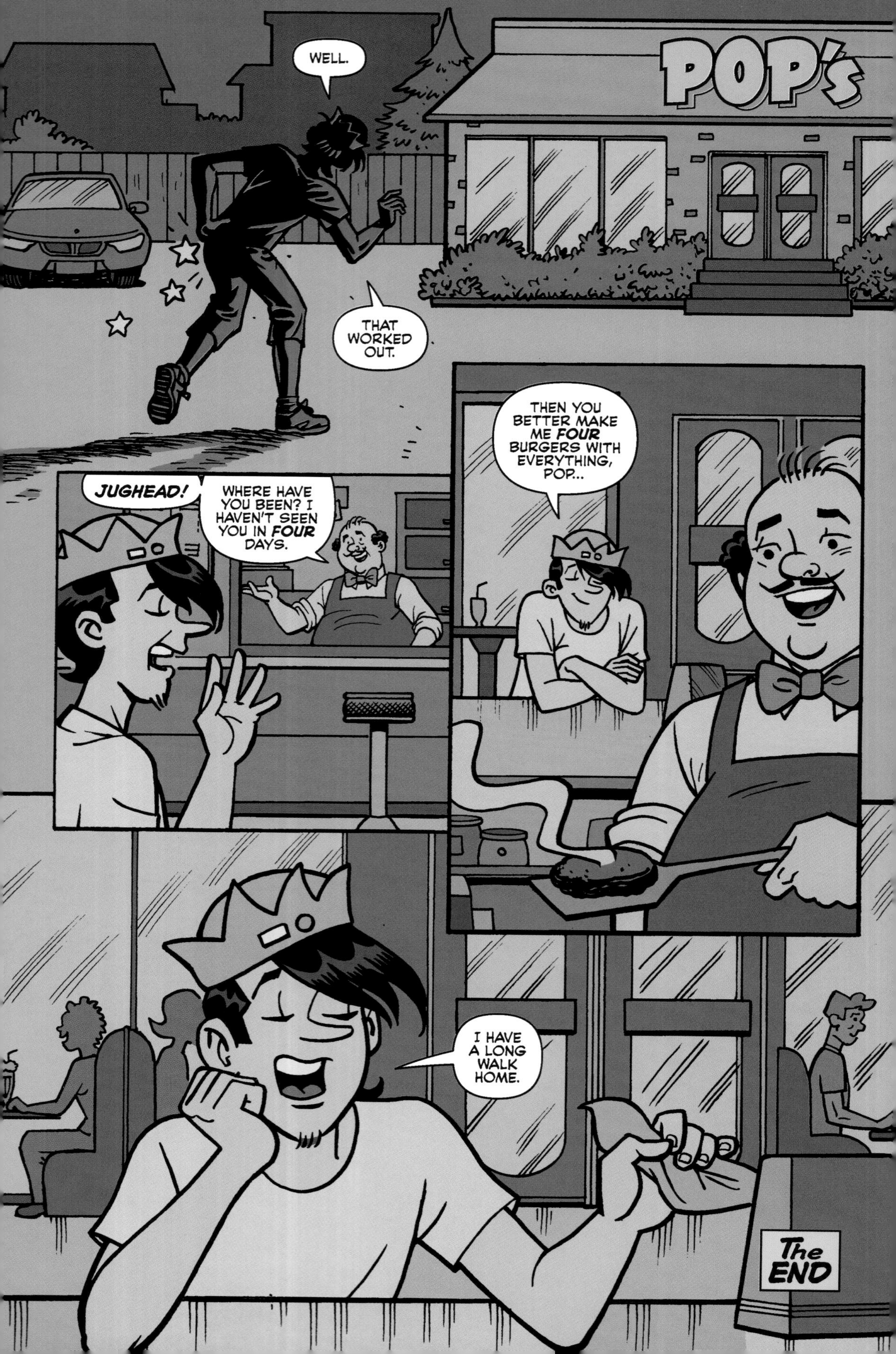
POP's
WELL.
THAT WORKED OUT.
JUGHEAD!
WHERE HAVE YOU BEEN? I HAVEN'T SEEN YOU IN FOUR DAYS.
THEN YOU BETTER MAKE ME FOUR BURGERS WITH EVERYTHING, POP...
I HAVE A LONG WALK HOME.
The END

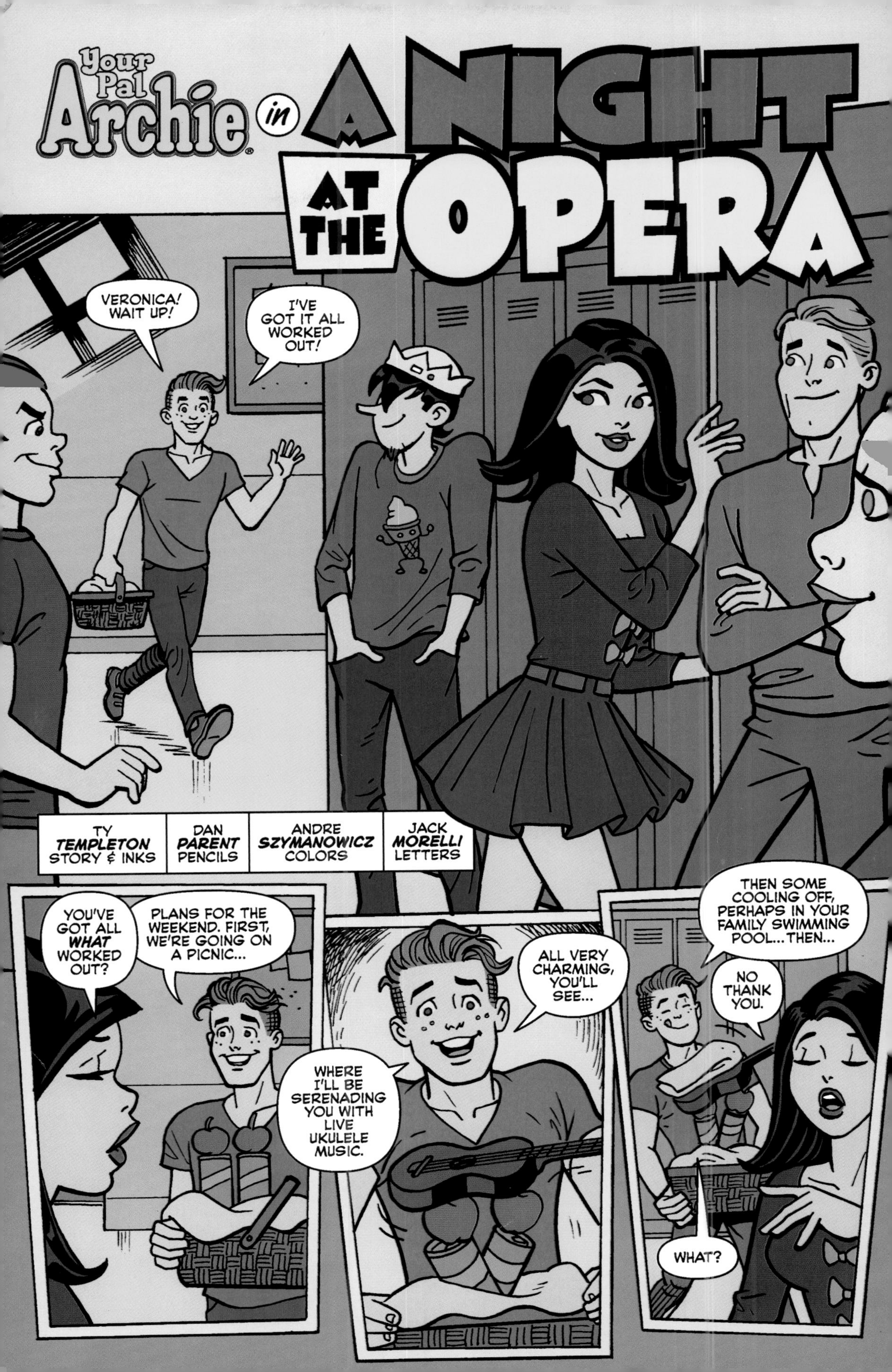
Your Pal Archie in
A NIGHT AT THE OPERA
VERONICA! WAIT UP!
I'VE GOT IT ALL WORKED OUT!
TY TEMPLETON STORY & INKS
DAN PARENT PENCILS
ANDRE SZYMANOWICZ COLORS
JACK MORELLI LETTERS
YOU'VE GOT ALL WHAT WORKED OUT?
PLANS FOR THE WEEKEND. FIRST, WE'RE GOING ON A PICNIC...
ALL VERY CHARMING, YOU'LL SEE...
WHERE I'LL BE SERENADING YOU WITH LIVE UKULELE MUSIC.
THEN SOME COOLING OFF, PERHAPS IN YOUR FAMILY SWIMMING POOL...THEN...
NO THANK YOU.
WHAT?

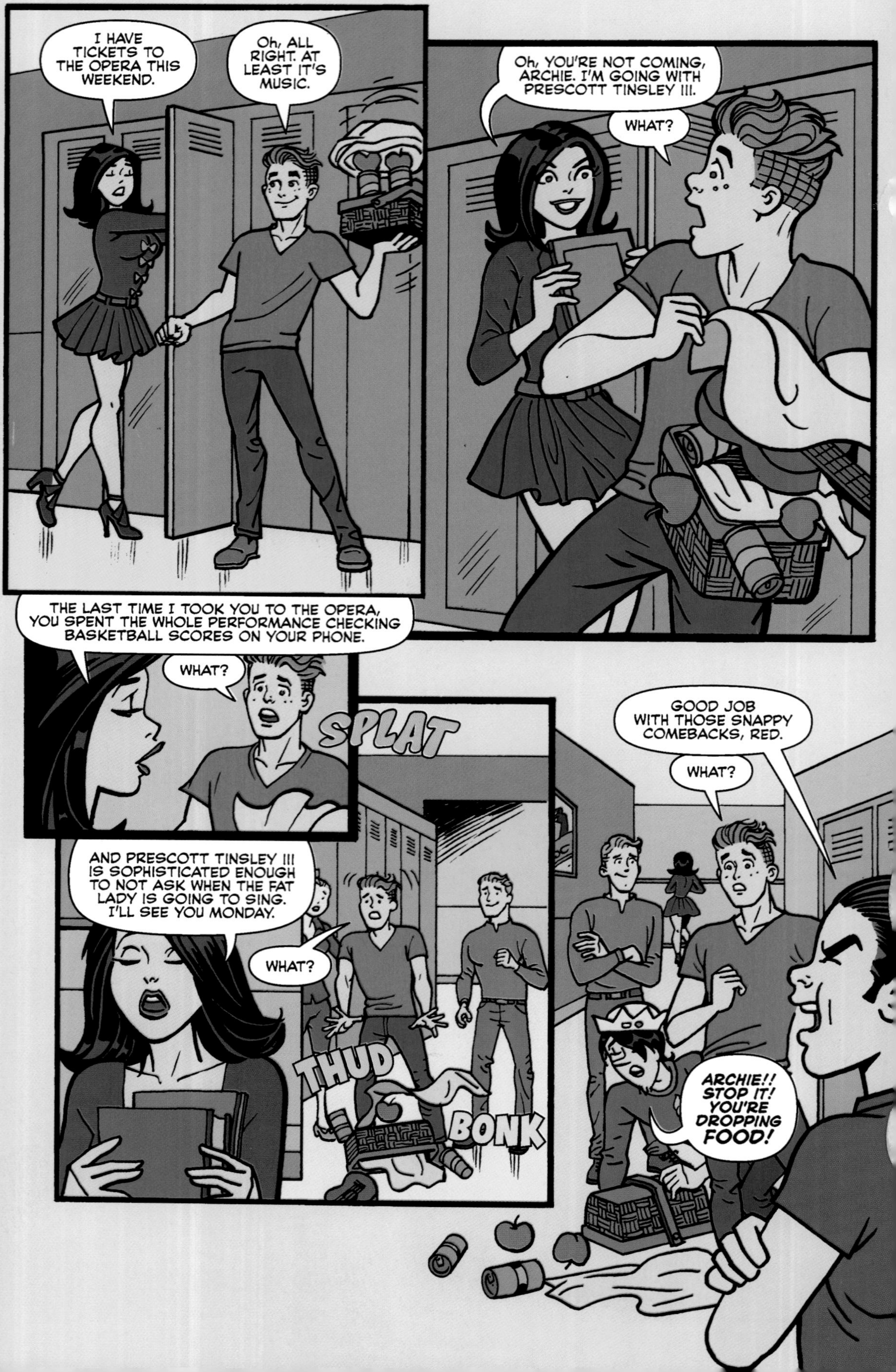
I HAVE TICKETS TO THE OPERA THIS WEEKEND.
Oh, ALL RIGHT. AT LEAST IT'S MUSIC.
Oh, YOU'RE NOT COMING, ARCHIE. I'M GOING WITH PRESCOTT TINSLEY III.
WHAT?
THE LAST TIME I TOOK YOU TO THE OPERA, YOU SPENT THE WHOLE PERFORMANCE CHECKING BASKETBALL SCORES ON YOUR PHONE.
WHAT?
SPLAT
AND PRESCOTT TINSLEY III IS SOPHISTICATED ENOUGH TO NOT ASK WHEN THE FAT LADY IS GOING TO SING. I'LL SEE YOU MONDAY.
WHAT?
THUD
BONK
GOOD JOB WITH THOSE SNAPPY COMEBACKS, RED.
WHAT?
ARCHIE!! STOP IT! YOU'RE DROPPING FOOD!

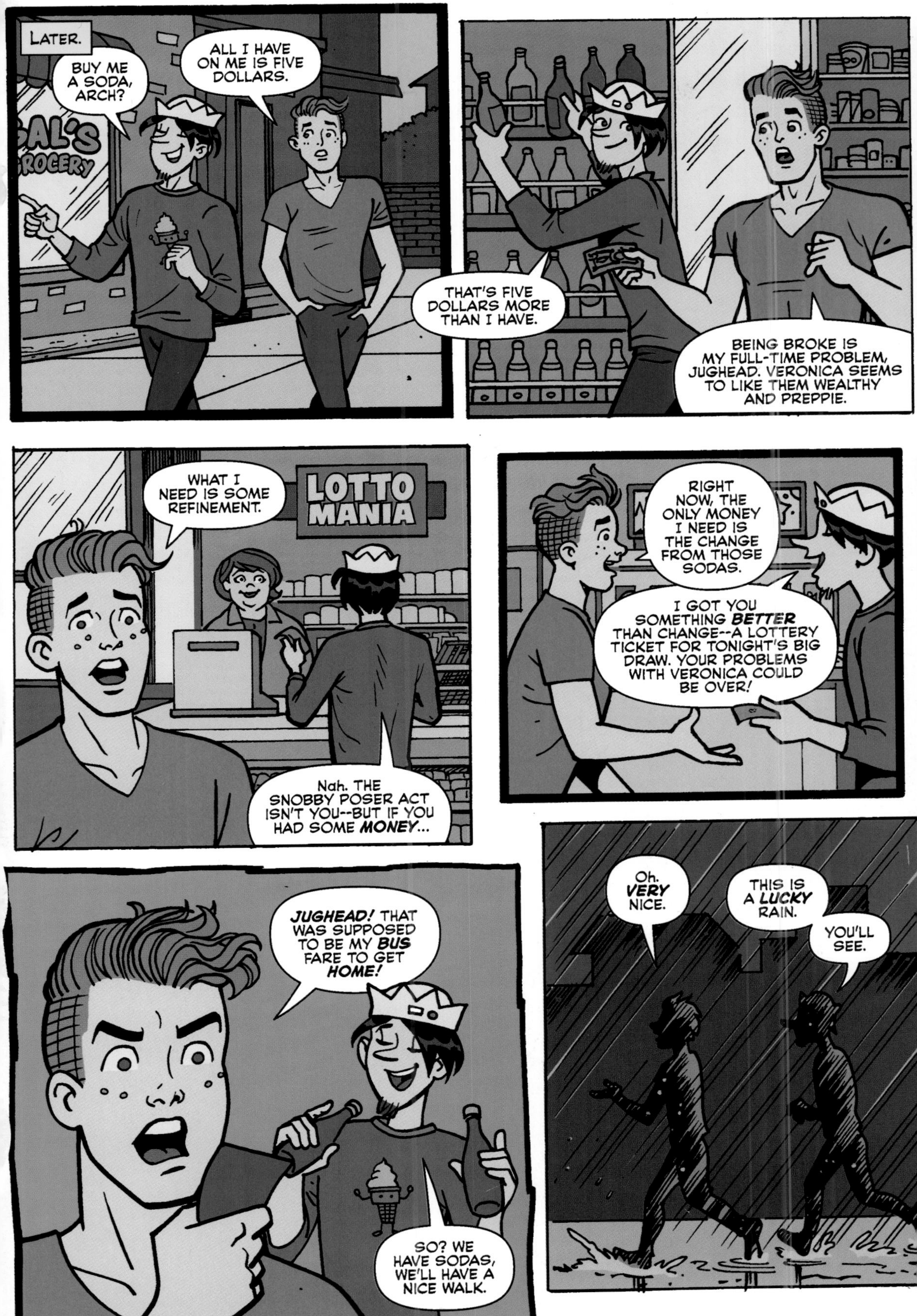
LATER.
BUY ME A SODA, ARCH?
ALL I HAVE ON ME IS FIVE DOLLARS.
SAL'S GROCERY
THAT'S FIVE DOLLARS MORE THAN I HAVE.
BEING BROKE IS MY FULL-TIME PROBLEM, JUGHEAD. VERONICA SEEMS TO LIKE THEM WEALTHY AND PREPPIE.
WHAT I NEED IS SOME REFINEMENT.
LOTTO MANIA
Nah. THE SNOBBY POSER ACT ISN'T YOU--BUT IF YOU HAD SOME MONEY...
RIGHT NOW, THE ONLY MONEY I NEED IS THE CHANGE FROM THOSE SODAS.
I GOT YOU SOMETHING BETTER THAN CHANGE--A LOTTERY TICKET FOR TONIGHT'S BIG DRAW. YOUR PROBLEMS WITH VERONICA COULD BE OVER!
JUGHEAD! THAT WAS SUPPOSED TO BE MY BUS FARE TO GET HOME!
SO? WE HAVE SODAS, WE'LL HAVE A NICE WALK.
Oh. VERY NICE.
THIS IS A LUCKY RAIN.
YOU'LL SEE.

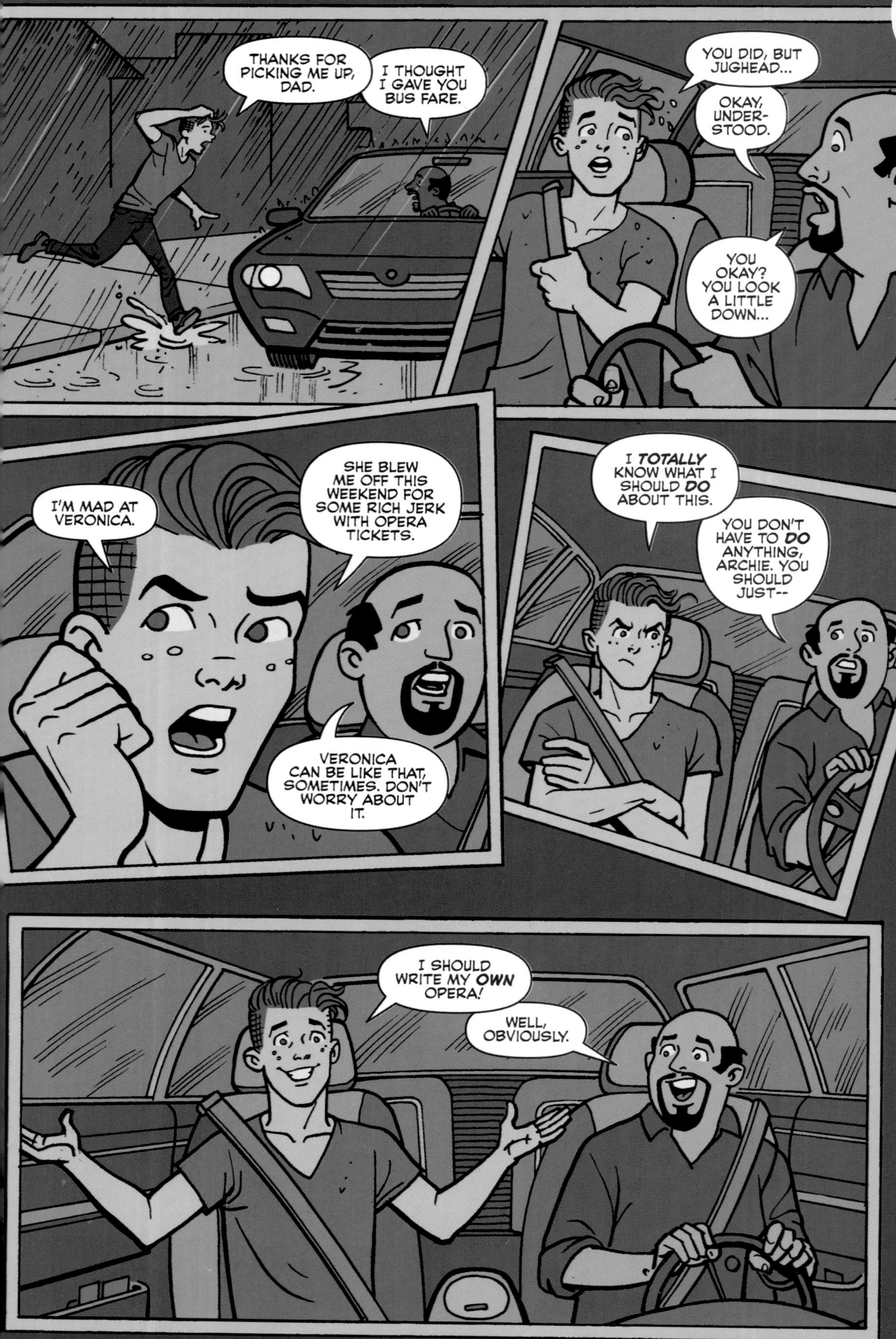
THANKS FOR PICKING ME UP, DAD.
I THOUGHT I GAVE YOU BUS FARE.
YOU DID, BUT JUGHEAD...
OKAY, UNDER-STOOD.
YOU OKAY? YOU LOOK A LITTLE DOWN...
I'M MAD AT VERONICA.
SHE BLEW ME OFF THIS WEEKEND FOR SOME RICH JERK WITH OPERA TICKETS.
VERONICA CAN BE LIKE THAT, SOMETIMES. DON'T WORRY ABOUT IT.
I *TOTALLY* KNOW WHAT I SHOULD *DO* ABOUT THIS.
YOU DON'T HAVE TO *DO* ANYTHING, ARCHIE. YOU SHOULD JUST--
I SHOULD WRITE MY *OWN* OPERA!
WELL, OBVIOUSLY.

I FOUND SOME OF MY FAVORITE OPERAS ON CD. WILL THESE HELP?

Um. NOT REALLY.

THIS ONE IS SELECTIONS FROM "THE BARBER OF SEVILLE."

BUT I DON'T HAVE A CD PLAYER IN MY ROOM...

The Barber of Seville

I GUESS THESE CASSETTES AREN'T MUCH HELP, THEN...

NEVER FEAR. FRED ANDREWS IS HERE...

Magic Flute

I HAVE QUITE A NUMBER OF OPERA ALBUMS IN MY COLLECTION.

OLD VINYL! COOL! THANKS, DAD!

Le nozze di Figaro

The Ring of the Nibelung

BUT YOU CAN'T PLAY THOSE, EITHER, ARCHIE. YOU DON'T HAVE A TURNTABLE.

DON'T NEED ONE. THESE VINYL RECORDS ARE BIG ENOUGH TO READ THE OPERA PLOTS PRINTED ON THE BACK.

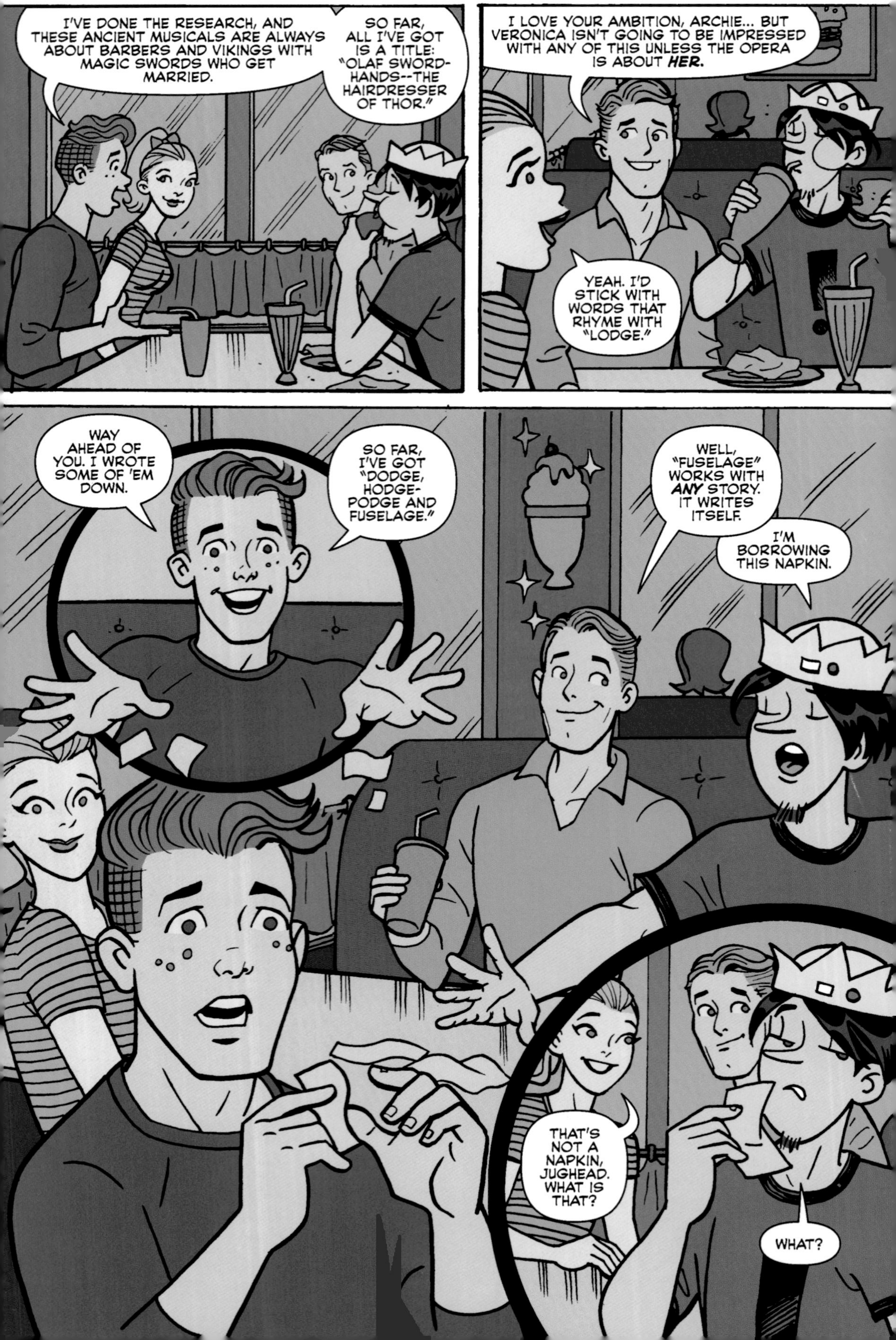
I'VE DONE THE RESEARCH, AND THESE ANCIENT MUSICALS ARE ALWAYS ABOUT BARBERS AND VIKINGS WITH MAGIC SWORDS WHO GET MARRIED.
SO FAR, ALL I'VE GOT IS A TITLE: "OLAF SWORD-HANDS--THE HAIRDRESSER OF THOR."
I LOVE YOUR AMBITION, ARCHIE... BUT VERONICA ISN'T GOING TO BE IMPRESSED WITH ANY OF THIS UNLESS THE OPERA IS ABOUT *HER.*
YEAH. I'D STICK WITH WORDS THAT RHYME WITH "LODGE."
WAY AHEAD OF YOU. I WROTE SOME OF 'EM DOWN.
SO FAR, I'VE GOT "DODGE, HODGE-PODGE AND FUSELAGE."
WELL, "FUSELAGE" WORKS WITH *ANY* STORY. IT WRITES ITSELF.
I'M BORROWING THIS NAPKIN.
THAT'S NOT A NAPKIN, JUGHEAD. WHAT IS THAT?
WHAT?

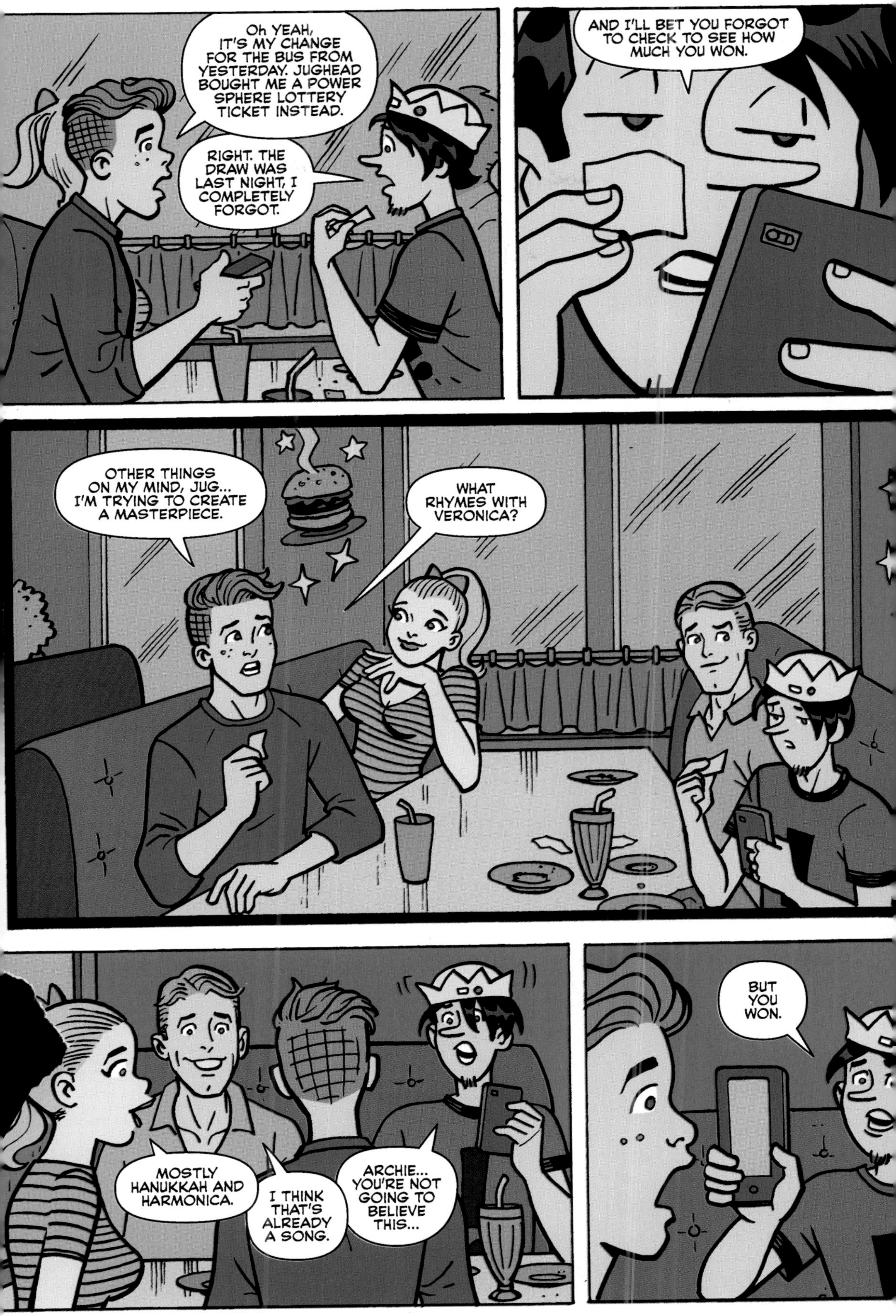

Oh YEAH, IT'S MY CHANGE FOR THE BUS FROM YESTERDAY. JUGHEAD BOUGHT ME A POWER SPHERE LOTTERY TICKET INSTEAD.
RIGHT. THE DRAW WAS LAST NIGHT, I COMPLETELY FORGOT.
AND I'LL BET YOU FORGOT TO CHECK TO SEE HOW MUCH YOU WON.
OTHER THINGS ON MY MIND, JUG... I'M TRYING TO CREATE A MASTERPIECE.
WHAT RHYMES WITH VERONICA?
MOSTLY HANUKKAH AND HARMONICA.
I THINK THAT'S ALREADY A SONG.
ARCHIE... YOU'RE NOT GOING TO BELIEVE THIS...
BUT YOU WON.

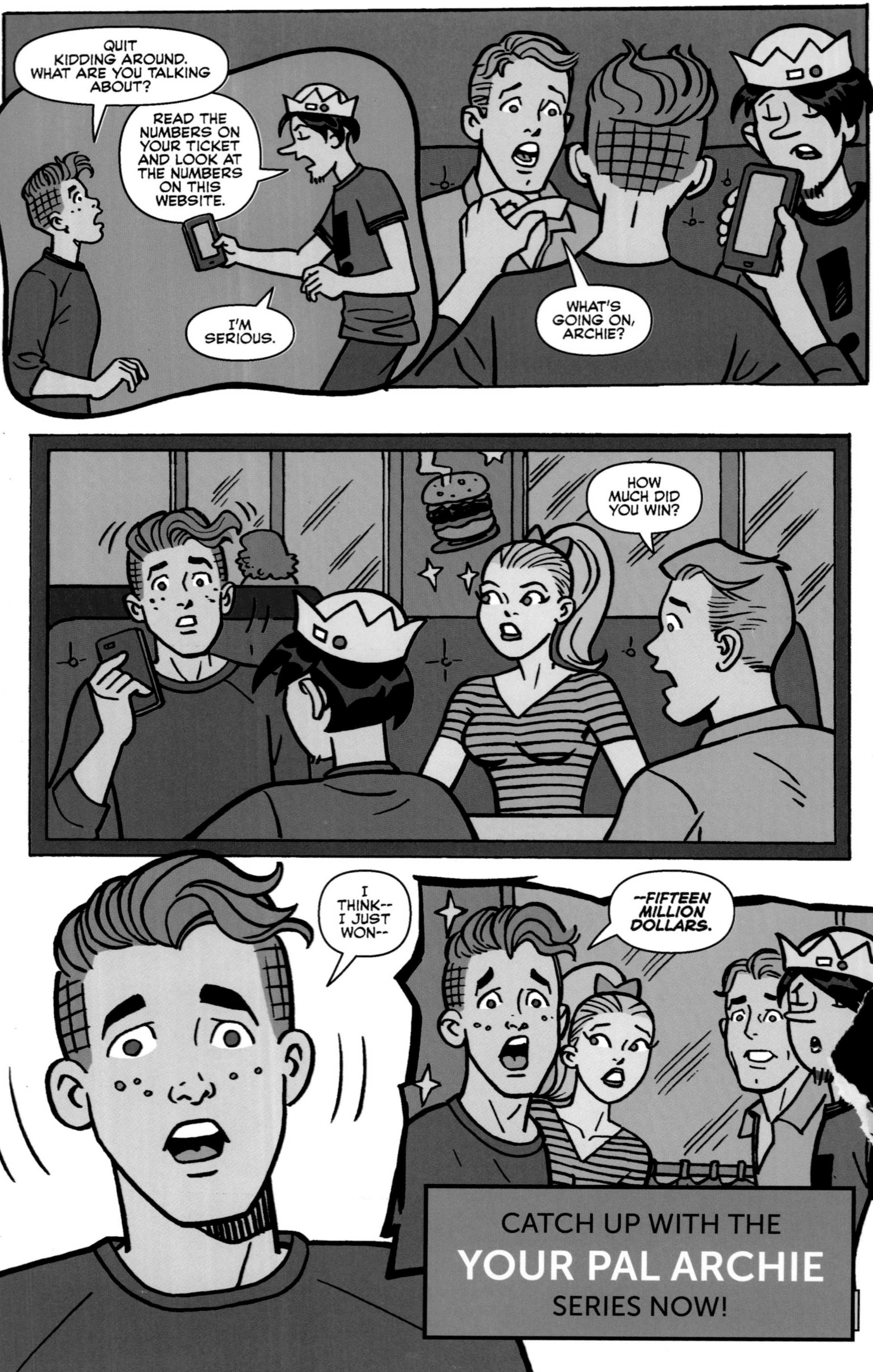
QUIT KIDDING AROUND. WHAT ARE YOU TALKING ABOUT?
READ THE NUMBERS ON YOUR TICKET AND LOOK AT THE NUMBERS ON THIS WEBSITE.
I'M SERIOUS.
WHAT'S GOING ON, ARCHIE?
HOW MUCH DID YOU WIN?
I THINK-- I JUST WON--
--FIFTEEN MILLION DOLLARS.
CATCH UP WITH THE
YOUR PAL ARCHIE
SERIES NOW!